Bargaining in the UN Security Council

Bargaining in the UN Security Council

Setting the Global Agenda

SUSAN HANNAH ALLEN
AMY YUEN

OXFORD
UNIVERSITY PRESS

OXFORD
UNIVERSITY PRESS

Great Clarendon Street, Oxford, OX2 6DP,
United Kingdom

Oxford University Press is a department of the University of Oxford.
It furthers the University's objective of excellence in research, scholarship,
and education by publishing worldwide. Oxford is a registered trade mark of
Oxford University Press in the UK and in certain other countries

Published in the United States of America by Oxford University Press
198 Madison Avenue, New York, NY 10016, United States of America

British Library Cataloguing in Publication Data
Data available

Library of Congress Control Number: 2021944611

ISBN 978–0–19–284975–5

DOI: 10.1093/oso/9780192849755.001.0001

Printed and bound by
CPI Group (UK) Ltd, Croydon, CR0 4YY

Cover image: U.S. Department of State photo by Ron Przysucha/Public Domain.

Preface

We stumbled onto this book by accident, and by that we mean, we were often tripped up by a gap in the study of security institutions and the Security Council in particular. We published an article in International Studies Quarterly about peacekeeping mandates and how tightly the Security Council monitors the missions and the Department of Peacekeeping Operations (DPKO) (Allen and Yuen, 2014). Along the way, we had numerous debates about how the Council produces resolutions and why they look the way they do, but we struggled to find systematic analyses about the bargaining process that happens before a resolution is ever put to a vote. There are wonderful histories describing the creation of the UN. There are detailed narratives about how the Council has handled particular issues. There are oodles of studies about peacekeeping and sanctions, with detailed data to match. There are dozens of proposals to reform the Council, but almost all studies of how the Council decides anything start and end with the resolution vote. What was going on behind the scenes?

We immediately ran into challenges. Neither of us had a clear sense of the institution's rules, so we spent lots of time reading the UN Charter, the provisional rules of the Security Council, and numerous presidential statements trying to figure out how the rules had changed over time. It turns out, they haven't changed very much at all, but anyone looking at the record of resolutions and the meeting calendar can tell there have been big swings in activity over time. The most obvious change was the end of the Cold War. That shift precedes a shift in the frequency of meetings and resolutions, so a natural conclusion is that the US and Russia were no longer diametrically opposed to each other on every issue. Very soon after, though, we noticed a form of meeting that had always been available becoming much more frequent—the informal consultations of the whole, the private meetings. We can't fully disentangle the changing preferences from the effects private negotiations had, but we think they are both important, and perhaps they reinforce each other. We suspected that the process of deciding what to do about pressing issues was subject to the same constraints and influences that any other institution has. So, we started looking closely at the older, legislative bargaining literature in American and comparative politics. Our second challenge was that the only systematic data that exists about Council's action is the record of the resolution votes. Even worse, we had the same problem that stymies legislative scholarship; how do you measure the content of policies, laws, or resolutions that makes them comparable across issues? There was very little systematic data available to say anything about the Council's actions.

We developed a sequential, spatial model to help us untangle the process and find entry points for different players to influences bargaining over resolutions. We also began a data collection process that took us to New York City, visiting the UN repository at New York University, and doing interviews with experts outside (right outside—just down the street, actually) and bureaucrats inside the UN. We learned about transparency efforts and how the Council sets its agenda (with lots of input from the bureaucrats, of course). We spent years collecting and refining the data. At several points, we had so many ideas that we weren't always sure exactly what the book was about. After culling the data and sharpening our arguments, we finally produced this book. It has been a labor of love and frustration, but it is also the seed for a thousand other ideas that remain unexplored. This book, for us, represents a beginning.

Acknowledgements

This project has been a long and winding journey, and we never would have made it to completion without a lot of help. Collectively, we are very grateful to numerous discussants and conference participants who read pieces of this along the way and encouraged us to keep going. Eliane Helitzer provided great research assistance during her time at Middlebury College. We really appreciate Paul Poast and Austin Carson for inviting us to present our work at their outstanding conference on "Compliance in International Security Institutions." There, we received terrific feedback from Alex Thompson among many others. The University of Mississippi's Coalition of the Willing reading group has offered feedback on more parts of this manuscript than they probably care to remember. Special thanks to Ben Jones, Yael Zeira, and Greg Love on that front. Thanks also to the Faculty Research Group at Middlebury College for early feedback, as well as Cliff Morgan, Bill Reed, and Scott Wolford who commented on the formal and empirical modeling. Dan Reiter and Terry Chapman both graciously agreed to read full drafts of the manuscript, a herculean task that they took on voluntarily, and this book has been greatly improved by their feedback.

We owe a debt of gratitude to Marc Lerner and Nina Rifkind for loaning us their New York apartment—which was walking distance to UN headquarters—during our research in the city. We also appreciate the time that Shamala Kandiah from The Security Council Report spent with us, discussing the ins and outs of Council working procedures. Movses Abelian, Director of Security Council Affairs in DPA of the UN, also gave us an afternoon to talk about the functioning of the Council in practice.

Susan would like to thank everyone at the Quaker United Nations Office, an affiliate of American Friends Service Committee. That experience greatly expanded my knowledge and inspired continuing interest in the Security Council when I interned there before graduate school. So much of this book and my entire research agenda has been informed by lessons learned at Quaker United Nations Office (QUNO). A special thanks to Dan and Mary Allen for encouraging me to dream big, to seek the answers to any and all of the questions that the world throws at me, and to work diligently for peace.

Thanks to my in-laws (Tom and Amy Feitel) who let my husband and four-year-old Daniel come raise havoc at their house so we could finish a revised version of the manuscript during COVID. Thanks to Daniel for bring smiles and laughs during the stressful moments. Most importantly, thanks to Don for copy-editing, listening, and tolerating the ups and downs of the research process.

Amy would like to thank Sarah Stroup for local moral support and book manuscript preparation expertise and advice. Very special thanks to Janet and Francis Yuen for cheerleading the work and teaching me perseverance, and to Rebecca Lee for the humor and perspective. I could not have finished this work without the support of my husband, Brett, who patiently endured years of my babble about models, data, and what the Security Council was up to next and who provided technical assistance at critical junctures.Thanks finally to Connor and Charlotte for reminding me every day how exciting and rewarding it is trying to understand humans.

Contents

1
Introduction

The United Nations Security Council is an enduring feature of the post-World War II international system. It has survived an intense rivalry between two permanent members almost immediately after its creation, made wobbly adjustments and weathered pointed criticism as its activities shifted focus to internal conflicts, and began a program of shaping and promoting new international norms on critical issues like human rights and nuclear proliferation. New challenges continue to appear as commitments to international institutions, broadly speaking, shift and the postures of the permanent members take on new configurations.[1]

Yet, the Council, in these tense years, has continued to meet and discuss pressing issues, even as they threaten to divide the Council members and risk the mission of maintaining international peace and security. Between 2017 and 2019, the Council held an average of 281 public meetings and 131 closed-door consultations and passed an average of 56 resolutions.[2] The members of the Council interact very frequently in both formal and informal settings, and have continued to do so despite the perception of increasing tensions within.

What are they discussing? The focus on maintaining international peace and security encompasses a diverse set of global and regional threats. Recent topics have included South Sudan, Cyprus, Somalia, Libya, and Palestine. Many meetings concern ongoing peacekeeping missions, and others take on thematic issues such as women's issues, peace and security, non-proliferation, and protection of civilians in armed conflict. What is equally interesting, however, is what the Council does not discuss. Why does the Security Council take up some issues for discussion and not others? What factors shape the Council's actions, if they take any action at all? The most common answer to these questions has been that the powerful states (those with veto power) drive the discussion and the actions taken. The vote that allows a veto to be cast, however,

[1] Remarkably, the Council even found ways to continue to meet under the challenge of a global pandemic in 2020.

[2] These figures average out to 2.5 meetings per working day. Meeting and resolution counts are reported in the Annual Highlights of the Security Council, https://www.un.org/securitycouncil/content/annual-highlight.

Bargaining in the UN Security Council. Susan Hannah Allen and Amy Yuen, Oxford University Press.
 DOI: 10.1093/oso/9780192849755.003.0001

is the last step in a long process of bargaining within the institution. Too often, the focus has been on vetoes cast, resolutions passed and the peacekeeping missions created in the Council. We argue that the bargaining process, shaped by the rules of the institution well before the final vote, can materially affect the scope of actions the Council takes and whether the Council acts at all.

The Council follows specific rules in setting its agenda and conducting its discussions, much like any national or subnational legislature or even a local council. Rules that are like those used in legislatures, like particular members setting the agenda and whether meetings are public or private, will have similar effects on Security Council resolutions as they might on a piece of legislation. The Council is not a legislature, but it shares some of the same institutional features, so we look to insights from the literature on legislative bargaining to explain why the Council discusses some issues and not others. The delegation sitting in the Council presidency determines the agenda. Because the presidency rotates monthly, most of the time the agenda setter is not a permanent member. The Council president also decides whether issues are discussed in *consultations of the whole*, which are closed-door meetings with no record, or public meetings with an official record. Public meetings reveal the verbatim discussions among the Council members to domestic and international audiences. These revelations may motivate delegations to choose different negotiating tactics in public than they would in private. We show, then, that the selection of the type of meeting itself is strategic, intended to influence the terms of the resolution. Finally, our analysis suggests an additional puzzle. Agenda-setting means Council presidents can avoid bringing up issues that they know cannot pass the full Council. Because of the informal interactions among the delegations at the United Nations (UN), a veto is almost never a surprise.[3] Since Council presidents generally know a veto is coming, why would they ever expend precious meeting time on a resolution that is doomed to fail? We argue that the veto is usually an instance of grandstanding, using the moment to make a public case for or against the position of the other delegations. What is less appreciated about these events but is crucial to their occurrence is the willingness of the Council president to allow the vote to proceed. Thus, while the veto is still very important for defining the bounds of what a resolution text can include, other actors, specifically the Council president and the domestic and international audiences, influence what the Council members

[3] One notable exception is the Chinese veto of the renewal of the United Nations Preventive Deployment Force (UNPREDEP) in February of 1999.

might be able to agree on, and thus whether the Council will act or even take up an issue for discussion.

1.1 Security Institutions in International Relations

Our understanding of security institutions suffers under a patchwork of common misconceptions and distortions about how they function and why they do what they do. Institutions scholars have already convincingly pushed back against some of these for economic institutions, but they are persistent problems for security institutions, and especially the Security Council. These misconceptions narrow the scope, implying that the Council is best understood by following the interest of the powerful states and forbidding any comparison between economic and security institutions, even if they share similar rules.

We know that powerful states influence the Security Council; in fact, it has rules that tilt the institution in their favor because the five most powerful states have permanent seats on the Council and veto power on resolutions. While many believe the Council serves the permanent members and is incapable of doing anything else, these conclusions stem from several misconceptions about security institutions that have persisted in international relations for decades.

1.1.1 The Security Council and Powerful States

Most students of international relations hear a common refrain—institutions are effective when they do what the powerful states would have done anyway. A related claim is that powerful states can circumvent the Council if they can't get what they want on the inside. The upshot of these claims is that institutions are unnecessary or ineffective, because they cannot enforce or restrain powerful states. If true, these claims are quite damning, but a closer look at what happens inside the Security Council shows that these claims selectively highlight some behaviors while ignoring other important ones.

The first claim suggests that institutions just do whatever the powerful states tell them to or else resign themselves to irrelevancy. Of course, if this is true, it begs the question of why there are institutions at all and further why powerful states would ever use them. The established institutions literature answers this question well—institutions can help share the costs of any action that a powerful state might have taken on its own. In sharing that cost, the other members of the institution gain some leverage over what that policy will be. This means resolutions passed in the UN Security Council usually are not what the most powerful states would have done on their own. For example, to deal with North Korean nuclear proliferation, the US wanted a set of robust, painful sanctions on the regime to halt proliferation in its tracks. Negotiations inside the Security Council, however, produced an incremental, cautious program of sanctions that reacted to North Korea's behavior, ratcheting up pressure each time North Korea violated the Nuclear Non-proliferation Treaty (NPT) and previous resolutions. The US might have pursued unilateral sanctions, but they would have imposed very little cost on North Korea since the US barely aided them at all. The institution made the desired policy more effective but it came with concessions on the US position on North Korea.

The second claim, that powerful states can circumvent the Council and therefore that the Council must follow the whim of powerful states, ignores the other important parts of the equation. Any action a powerful state may take incurs some costs, whether they be direct costs, like casualties and money, or indirect costs, like devoting resources elsewhere (opportunity costs) or jeopardizing future cooperation. So while it is certainly *possible* for powerful states to circumvent an institution there are many incentives that motivate states to work through institutions (Axelrod, 1984; Keohane, 1984, 1998; Krasner, 1982, 1983). There are a few bits of evidence to suggest powerful states do and will continue to use security institutions. They devote significant financial and diplomatic resources to them. For example, the United States Ambassador to the United Nations has traditionally been a post given to highly skilled and experienced diplomats in the US government. Further, the Council is very active. Meeting records and calendars reflect a constant flurry of activity and interaction. There are also relatively few instances where powerful states have circumvented the institution, including, for example, the Iraq War in 2003 and the Russian annexation of Crimea in 2014. While a few high-profile cases undermine the impression that states use the Council frequently, the reality is that it remains a center of diplomatic activity around issues of international peace and security.

1.1.2 The Security Council Is Ineffective

Another common critique of the Security Council is that it is ineffective. Naturally, we might ask, "(in)effective at what?" There are two strains to this critique: (1) that the policies are too watered down to address the issue at hand or (2) that deadlock inside the institution forces states to act outside of it, rendering the institution impotent.

The first critique is really an assessment of the policies themselves. Numerous studies try to figure out whether peacekeeping really keeps peace, whether sanctions really change state behavior and whether attempts to address social issues, like child soldiers or human rights, ever change the human condition. A requirement of each of these studies is to determine a benchmark against which the effect of the Council's (in)action can be compared. These are compelling questions akin to asking whether a healthcare policy or subsidy program is having the intended effect in a domestic government, but this type of analysis frequently starts with the intention, the benchmark, and examines whether intervention policies meet that benchmark. The explanation for success or failure may touch upon the political wrangling that created the action, but these assessments most often serve as a motivation for advocating reform or to support a different policy choice that was not selected. We argue that if you want to understand why the policy looks the way it does, we should examine how the institution shapes that policy based on institutional rules.[4]

The second critique is more concerning because deadlock can be a big problem for any institution. But that's just it, *any* institution can suffer deadlock, so if we are comfortable thinking domestic institutions matter even if they deadlock sometimes, then we need to consider whether the occurrence of deadlock is sufficient to dismiss security institutions. What happens when domestic institutions deadlock? Often, the relevant actors seek relief in other venues. In the United States, they might find alternatives through litigation or at the subnational level through state governments. Another option is to do nothing. When the US Congress cannot find enough common ground to pass a statute, they do not declare Congress null and void.[5] Instead, Congress passes what they can pass, and the rest is left to other solutions. A similar process plays out at the international level.[6]

The threat that deadlock presents to any institution is when it becomes so frequent that no one consults the institution anymore. In a domestic setting,

[4] It's worth noting that there is a vocal segment of the policy world calling for reform in the Security Council, mostly by advocating for expanding the veto power to more states or removing the permanent seats on the Council. Each change would shift what resolutions look like and whether they would pass, but before we can determine just what would change, we need to understand how it works in its current form. Each change potentially brings unintended consequences that a formal analysis of the bargaining process would help us anticipate. See, for example, O'eill (1996).

[5] As much as the cynical citizen might want to.

[6] In fact, some of the other critiques are predicated on venue-shopping behavior, even though it is a very common occurrence in domestic politics.

this often means a group fundamentally seeks to change the governmental structure (we generally recognize this as regime change, whether it takes a violent or non-violent path). In the international system, we might experience a violent change, as that which followed the League of Nations, or we might experience the waning influence of an institution such that nations continually reduce their investments in the institution or withdraw completely. For now, the evidence suggests that the Security Council does still matter given the activity and investment member nations put toward the institution.

1.1.3 Security Institutions Are Different

Challenging the entrenched belief that institutions don't matter, international institutions scholars have proclaimed the ascendance of global governance. Randall Stone begins his book *Controlling Institutions* with this statement, "Government is gradually replacing anarchy in the international system, and international governance is largely accomplished by means of international organizations" (Stone, 2011, p. 1). Yet, most scholarly studies of international institutions like Stone (2011) focus primarily on efforts to manage economic, or at least non-security-related, interactions. They offer sophisticated analyses of how these institutions do and do not affect international economic relationships differently than we might expect. Institutions scholars have tread carefully around security institutions to the point that there exists a virtual blind spot in scholarly attention to the workings of security institutions.[7] This gap is even more puzzling when we consider that every introductory international relations student is taught that anarchy is the cause of war. If international institutions are muffling the effects of anarchy, why don't we give more credence and focus to how security institutions function and persist? Some students of international relations may accept that institutions matter for economic issues or endeavors that seem to be more cooperative in nature but continue to reject the relevance of security institutions because they deal with issues that highlight the conflicting interests and are easier to imagine carrying existential implications for states.

[7] There are a few prominent exceptions that consider the strategic use and influence of the Security Council, including Chapman (2009, 2011); Fang (2008); Thompson (2009); Voeten (2001, 2005), but none of these studies look very far into the Council's rules. Voeten (2001) is the closest, considering the Council veto member preferences in a policy space, but so much of the Council's deliberating process shapes what the members are voting on. Our study is the next logical step forward in opening the black box of the Council.

The (artificial) divide between economic and security institutions is a holdover from the dominant paradigms of neorealism and neoliberalism. The neorealist paradigm that dominated international relations for decades argued that in matters of security, true cooperation was risky, and nations that participated in security institutions only did so as long is it served their interests, concluding that security institutions could have no real independent effect. They pointed to the failure of many past security institutions, like the Concert of Europe and the League of Nations, as evidence that institutions were meaningless for security issues, and argued that any state could and would circumvent a security institution if it could not get what it wanted. Neoliberalism challenged this perspective and argued that cooperation was possible and institutions were meaningful across a range of issues that stand to benefit from cooperation, like international trade pointing to the developing European Union, the growing World Trade Organization (WTO) and other financial institutions that, though suffering some criticism, seemed more robust. They ceded ground on claims about the effects institutions had on influencing state behavior in matters of security because threats to security were often seen in the extreme as threats to existence (Axelrod and Keohane, 1985; Lipson, 1984; Mearsheimer, 1995).

Our approach to the Security Council challenges the broad claims that security issues and economic ones are fundamentally different and therefore the institutions built for them cannot be understood in the same way. Economic institutions also face the possibility that states dissatisfied with the institution find ways to circumvent it or act unilaterally. Indeed, the literature on regional trade illustrates the other avenues around the WTO and further, the WTO has been unable to resolve critical issues like domestic farm subsidies and intellectual property, leading states to set their policies unilaterally. Security and economic institutions present similar choices for member nations regarding whether to work inside or outside the institution on a given issue.

Perhaps more controversial is our analysis through the lens of legislative bargaining.[8] Institutions scholars, however, precede us and apply insights from

[8] International relations scholars that subscribe to the dominant paradigms have traditionally treated the hierarchy of domestic government and the anarchy of the international system as fundamentally different ways to organize systems. They argue that domestic governments can enforce but international institutions cannot. Wagner (2007) argues that this is a fundamental misunderstanding of domestic governments. He points out that governments can enforce against *individuals*, but as individuals organize and get larger vis-a-vis the government, the ability to enforce decreases as the relative power of the organized group increases. Domestic governments, he argues, should be understood as "bargains" among organized groups that set rules as to how a state will operate. If organized groups can be large enough to be whole states themselves, then international institutions are also "bargains" about how the system will operate. Further, organized groups within states also have outside options if they

legislative bargaining to international institutions that have agenda-setting rules, requirements around reporting information and voting rules (see for example, Tsebelis (2002) in which he examines the power of the veto on the European Union and Voeten (2001), who examines the veto in the Security Council).[9] Others consider the role of bureaucrats in the bargaining process (Fang and Stone, 2012; Johns, 2007). Institutions scholars have likewise conducted extensive analysis of the effects international courts have on international cooperation, state behavior and enforcement (e.g., Carrubba, Gabel and Hankla, 2008; Ritter and Wolford, 2012). If international economic institutions and international security institutions have rules that are similar to rules within legislatures, and those rules are followed, then we can legitimately apply some of the insights of legislative bargaining to the Security Council.

In domestic politics, institutions matter. In fact, they are crucial to understanding why policies look the way they do, primarily by figuring out who has the most influence over a policy at a given point in the legislative process. The concepts of veto players, agenda-setting, and public information all originated in studies about legislatures (Groseclose and McCarty, 2001; Shepsle, 1979; Shepsle and Weingast, 1987). Rules that grant these same powers to members of international institutions arguably have a similar effect on the final policy. Domestic institutions continue to matter despite a wide array of alternatives citizens may use to get the policy they want. This study extends those insights to the Security Council, which is much less complex, but similarly situated to domestic institutions as one option among many to address security issues in the international system.

1.2 Argument of the Book

This book is about how and why the UN Security Council addresses some issues and not others. Members of the Council are comparing the options available to them inside and outside the institution. Prior analyses have considered important aspects of outside options, but they have not lifted the veil on

can't get what they want through their bargain. In the domestic context, this most often looks like no action taken by the government on a particular policy. In the international context, a state circumventing an institution may also simply look like the institution takes no action. National governments and international institutions share the status of "bargain," which implies all participants agree to follow the rules laid out in the bargain, and just as international institutions can come apart, so too can domestic governments, as the extensive civil war literature shows.

[9] European integration is probably the clearest example of the connections and similarities between domestic and international politics. The literature is enormous but very much focused on the development and effects of legislative rules that migrate from domestic to international bodies.

what bargaining and compromise look like inside the Council that generates the "internal" option (Thompson, 2009; Voeten, 2001). This analysis explores the primary factors that influence the internal option, the potential compromise that makes action through the Council attractive. Three primary factors are paramount: the preferences of the permanent members, the preferences of the delegation setting the agenda and the public accountability costs that accompany various actions in the Council. We argue that these factors matter because of the structure of the Council's process. The Council has two features that shape how these factors matter: a formal agenda-setting procedure and the option to meet publicly or privately.

In Chapter 3, we develop a formal model to show how these features interact with preferences and costs to create a possible range of outcomes. We show a simple diagram of how the process flows (Figure 1.1). An issue is brought to the attention of the Council through various forms (e.g., a formal letter addressed to the Security Council) and exists on a list of potential issues for discussion.[10] In the first step, the Council president considers whether to discuss an issue or ignore it, and decides whether the discussion takes place in a public meeting or a closed-door consultation. Next, a "penholder" delegation writes the resolution text, and finally a vote takes place.

We argue that the agenda is set strategically. The time available to discuss issues is scarce. Even more precious is the opportunity to set the agenda while serving as Council president, which rotates alphabetically each month. We assume that the Council president wants to maximize the number of successes, that is, agreements that come out of its stint in the presidency. Thus, delegations in the presidency will only choose issues in which the preferences of the permanent members overlap enough to avoid a veto and that they care about themselves. The implication is that the resolutions we observe are a selected set of cases, and that the interests of the permanent members matter, but so does the preference of the Council president.

Council presidents can also influence possible resolutions through the deliberative process. Because the Council president can choose whether a meeting is public or private, we consider how revealing true positions can generate different forms of public accountability costs for Council delegations. These costs affect what bargains are acceptable to delegations, independent of their preferences, which has important effects on what resolutions are possible in a private context versus a public one. We show that the Council president can leverage

[10] In our empirical chapters, we rely on the Council's Summary Statements as the selection list for data availability.

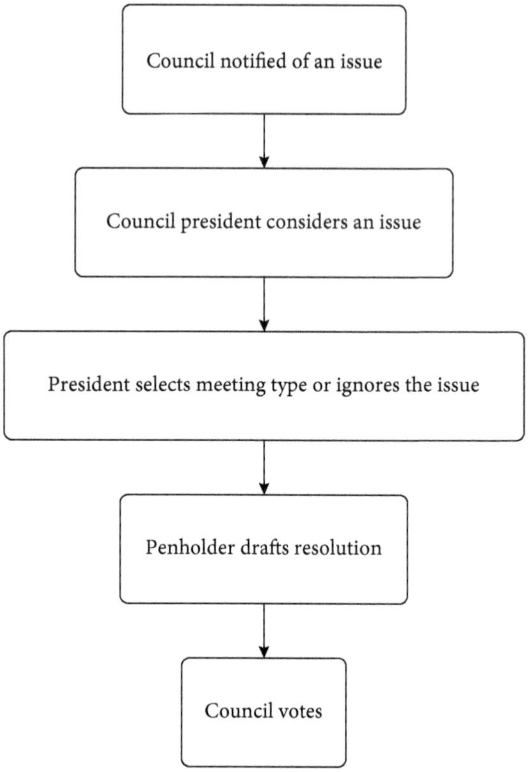

Fig. 1.1 Diagram of agenda-setting in the UN Security Council

public accountability costs to her own advantage, selecting a meeting profile that gets a resolution closer to her most preferred action.

This analysis also reveals an under-appreciated puzzle—if the Council president wants to avoid vetoes, then they should never happen. Why, then, do vetoes occur, albeit infrequently? A logical argument is that vetoes are a surprise, a result of uncertainty as to how member states will vote. We argue that member states are rarely unsure how their colleagues will vote. Instead, we turn again to the public accountability to show that vetoes communicate to external audiences when member states are bucking international norms or opinion—they are opportunities for grandstanding, which can offer domestic and international dividends that make the veto more valuable than simply ignoring the issue. Further, the Council president's cooperation with a grandstanding veto is crucial to observing it since she sets the agenda.

1.3 Roadmap for the Book

At its most basic, our argument is that the small details of procedure have an influence on the large movements of the most prominent security institution in the modern international order. How issues move through the Security Council influences what issues the Council can address and whether it will choose to be relevant. The rest of this book is devoted to developing these arguments fully and providing evidence of their validity.

In Chapter 2, we briefly discuss the history of the United Nations Security Council as well as the rules and procedures that have developed over time to guide its work. In Chapter 3, we lay out a theory of Council agenda-setting that helps to explain whether and how the Council will decide to act on a particular issue. Our belief is that this theory is broad enough to help understand Security Council behavior throughout the organization's history rather than just providing a snapshot of behavior *either* before or after the end of the Cold War. Using this theory, in Chapter 4, we provide an overview of the relationship between preferences and Council actions using aggregate annual data. We also examine factors that influence how the Council decides to discuss an issue using a new dataset of meetings and consultations at the agenda-item level. Chapter 5 tests the effects of outside options on activity inside the Council. In Chapter 6, we explore public and private diplomacy arguments with a case study of the Council's decisions to discuss North Korean nuclear proliferation. Just as private diplomacy can widen the bargaining range in bilateral conflict negotiations, it can have the same effect in multilateral negotiations like those held by the UN Security Council. Chapter 7 provides additional case studies of the Council's handling of Kosovo in 1998 and 1999 and the protection of civilians in armed conflict to explore the logic of the formal model more closely, focusing particularly on the content of the resolutions and the efforts of elected members. In Chapter 8, we discuss the implications of this work and consider what it portends for the future of the organization.

2
The History and Functions of the UN Security Council

International organizations are a reflection of the bargaining process member states engaged in to create them. In this chapter, we will explore how the Allies negotiated particular elements of UN's Charter, focusing on decisions about how to structure the Security Council and what the voting rules would be.

Multilateral organizations are a way for powerful states to delegate control (Ruggie, 1993). Member states (even powerful ones) have incentives to delegate, which include reducing transaction costs, increasing legitimacy, and sharing the burden on costly actions. Scholars of international law point out that procedures for delegating power and influence can affect outcomes in international organizations, especially in the agenda-setting process (Crowley and Jackson, 1996; Schachter and Joyner, 1995). For example, the UN General Assembly and the Security Council have distinct membership, voting rules, and degree of authority delegated to each body. As a result, they produce agendas that reflect these differences (Stiles, 2006).

2.1 The Creation of the Security Council

The founders of the UN envisioned the Security Council as an international organization that could be responsible for maintaining world peace and security (Bailey and Daws, 1995). To fulfill this lofty mandate, the UN Charter lays out an institutional framework that includes six distinct bodies.[1] Of these, the Security Council is preeminent. In Article 24 of the Charter, the member states agreed to place primary responsibility for international peace and security in the hands of the Council (Sarooshi, 1999). The bulk of negotiations between

[1] The six bodies are the Security Council, the General Assembly, the Economic and Social Council, the Trusteeship Council, the International Court of Justice, and the Secretariat (which includes the Secretary-General and the bureaucracy that supports the organization's other principal bodies).

Bargaining in the UN Security Council. Susan Hannah Allen and Amy Yuen, Oxford University Press.
 DOI: 10.1093/oso/9780192849755.003.0002

the Soviet Union, UK, and US, the primary authors of the UN, concerned control over the Council as well as its powers and responsibilities.

Within the family of UN bodies, the Council is designed to be the center of activity for the organization. History has shown that the Council has not always been at the heart of action. During the Cold War, the Council was often paralyzed by conflicting opinions of the five permanent members and their veto power. Despite a window of optimism in the immediate post-Cold War era, the Council again faced great challenges regarding multilateral response to threats to international peace and security after the US-led invasion of Iraq in 2003. The Council's role continues to evolve.

We will discuss the formal rules of the Council and how the procedures and practices that have developed over time influence both the agenda and activity of the United Nations Security Council (UNSC). According to the UN Charter, any UN member nation can place items on the Security Council's agenda, but the Council decides which items come up for discussion, and only Council members can propose resolutions. Unlike the resolutions passed in the General Assembly, Security Council resolutions are binding, meaning they commit all UN members to action. What led countries to create and/or join an institution like the UN, particularly given the preeminence of the Security Council?

2.1.1 Establishing the UN and the Security Council

From the outset, the UN was an American initiative. Throughout the early 1940s, American President Franklin Roosevelt (FDR) often talked about the need for "Four Policemen"—the US, UK, China, and USSR—to create and maintain order in the postwar world.[2] In his mind, this new international organization would serve as a stationhouse for the four policeman to work out of, with the effectiveness of the organization built on the strength of these four powers (Hildebrand, 1990; Meisler, 1995). Despite FDR's vision, the exact structure of the new institution would be negotiated in active bargaining among the winners of World War II.

On August 14, 1941, Franklin Roosevelt and Winston Churchill introduced the Atlantic Charter. In a joint declaration, they called for the creation of an international institution to ensure economic cooperation and anchor a future permanent system of global security (Mingst and Karns, 1995). In early 1942,

[2] In fact, Roosevelt asked Secretary of State Cordell Hull to organize a team to begin planning for the peace, including the formation of a new international organization, even before the US entered the war (Meisler, 1995).

long before the end of World War II, many allied states affirmed these principles. Initially, Roosevelt applied the name "United Nations" to the 26 nations who pledged to defeat the Axis powers (http://www.un.org). When the Allies met at Dumbarton Oaks in 1944, they discussed details about the membership and structure for a new formal institution.[3] At the Yalta Conference in early 1945, they made additional decisions concerning procedures and voting rules. Finally, in the spring of 1945, all of the countries fighting against Germany and Japan were invited to the San Francisco Conference to finalize and sign the UN Charter.

Each delegation recognized that the primary weakness of the League of Nations was its lack of enforcement power, and they believed this shortcoming could only be remedied if the powerful states had a more influential role in the new organization (Schlid, 1995). Together, the delegations developed the basic structure of the organization—a broad assembly, a smaller executive council, an international court, and a supporting bureaucracy made up of international civil servants. Of utmost importance to the allied nations was working through the details regarding the membership, voting rules, and enforcement powers for the executive council (later known as the Security Council).

In the initial phase of the Dumbarton Oaks Conference, the leaders agreed that the Security Council should work to prevent future world wars, but exactly how the Council would function was still open for debate. What types of international concerns would be the domain of the Council? Would the UN, and the Security Council in particular, discuss, and respond only to threats to international security or should economic and social issues be included as well? The Soviets only wanted the Council to deal with international security, but the British wanted a broader mandate. The British representatives at the conference were concerned about the fundamental differences in the political, social, and economic interests of the Allies, which they believed (correctly) would make permanent postwar cooperation difficult (Schlid, 1995).

From the earliest discussions, the Soviets wanted only the US, UK, and USSR as permanent members. Roosevelt championed China as a potential check to a resurgent Japan. For his part, Churchill pushed for a seat at the table for the French (in part to counterbalance Soviets on the continent) but was less certain of the need to include China. The Soviets doubted that either France or

[3] The initial idea was to include China in the original discussions, but the Soviets did not want to share the table with the Chinese because they had not yet declared war on Japan. As a result, the negotiations were held in two phases with the Chinese arriving after the Soviets left. The second phase was less influential because the majority of the details and main features for the new UN were hashed out in the first phases, and then the agreements were presented to the Chinese who had little to do other than acquiesce (Meisler, 1995).

China qualified as a great power. Despite the fact that Soviet leader Joseph Stalin wanted to limit the permanent seats to three, he was willing to go along with the Western proposals for broader membership (Schlid, 1995).[4]

The three primary players also came to Dumbarton Oaks with differing ideas about how long non-permanent member terms on the Council should be. The British wanted three year terms to give these members experience. The US favored only single-year terms in order to bring a range of states into the Council's deliberations. The Soviets split the difference by proposing two year terms. Eventually, the three delegations reached a compromise that allowed for two year terms with rotating replacement—three new members each year rather than a full turnover of six members every other year (Hildebrand, 1990). After preliminary discussion on the membership and responsibility issues, the US proposed that the five permanent members and six rotating members would make up a Security Council with the authority to maintain international peace and security (Meisler, 1995). Only the permanent members would hold veto power.

2.1.2 Negotiating Over the Voting Rules

Voting as a way to conduct diplomacy is a recent innovation, but doing so in a majoritarian fashion was completely new when introduced in the UN. In the past, diplomacy had always been carried out by consensus; even in the League of Nations every state had a veto (Bailey and Daws, 1995).

Because all three delegations at Dumbarton Oaks viewed peace and security as indivisible, the allies wanted to establish a body that could peacefully resolve disputes before conflicts between states could escalate to war (Hildebrand, 1990).[5] For this reason, each country arrived with a proposal regarding how the Council could engage in the peaceful settlement of political and diplomatic disagreements and differing views on how much authority the Council should have to do so.

[4] The US briefly backed a proposal for a permanent seat on the Council for Brazil for greater geographic representation, but there were a range of challenges to this idea—both among the allies and within the Roosevelt administration, so the proposal was abandoned at Dumbarton Oaks (Hildebrand, 1990; Meisler, 1995). The idea of expanding permanent membership to countries like Brazil, South Africa, India, and others in order to improve geographic representation has been one of the most frequently proposed reforms to the Council structure.

[5] Determining how the Council could be a more effective tool of preventive diplomacy continues to be a challenge. Suggestions appeared in Boutros-Ghali's Agenda for Peace (1992) and the Brahimi Report (2000).

The Soviet Union did not oppose the core proposal put forth by the US regarding the influence and function of the Security Council. In fact, they wanted a stronger Council and advocated for the creation of an independent air corps to be placed at the Council's disposal for rapid response (Meisler, 1995). The British had their doubts about the value of the independent air corps. The delegation from the UK did not think the air corps proposal was feasible, in large part because even in 1944, air power was still largely unproven. Strategic conventional bombing against Japan and Germany had not decisively turned the tide in World War II (Schlid, 1995).

The US contingent also doubted that the US Congress would ratify a UN treaty that included the creation of an independent air corps because of the potential constitutional issues that would arise regarding the deployment of US troops by the UN. To overcome this problem, the Americans put forth a plan that would be more acceptable to the American people. Rather than a standing air corps, the Council could call on members to supply troops and that this proposal would be much more palatable to domestic constituents (Schlid, 1995).

If the Council was authorized to use "all means necessary" to resolve threats to international peace and security, determining the voting rules for the Council would be critical. Because Security Council resolutions are binding on member nations, the strong states were concerned that this could give authority over national militaries to the organization. With this potential threat to sovereignty, all three states insisted that they would not sign on to the new organization without the ability to veto proposed action (Schlid, 1995). As long as these members knew they had a veto, they were confident that the Council could not authorize military action without their support.

All three allies agreed that only the permanent members (and not the elected members) should have a veto, but they disagreed on the extent of that veto power. Cooperation between the US and the Soviet Union would be necessary to maintain postwar peace, and both viewed the UN as the most promising way to bring that about. The Soviets believed that the best way to guarantee this cooperation would be to require unanimity among the permanent members. With this check on the Council's power, they also supported broad powers for the Council.

The differences in the Soviet and British proposal reflected differences in interests for the post-war peace. As the sole socialist power on the Council, the Soviets worried that they would be isolated, and that, without veto power, they would be unable to defend themselves and their national interests. The Soviets also wanted the Council to be far more decisive than the League of Nations and be able to take clear, unanimous action in situations that warranted it.

In contrast, the British did not want the unanimity requirement, but they did envision more limited powers for the Council. They worried the permanent member veto might put these states too far above other members, making membership in the organization undesirable to lesser powers. The British wanted a requirement for two-thirds majority and that the votes of states involved in a conflict would not count (Schlid, 1995). Moreover, the British thought members should recuse themselves from discussions and votes where states had a vested interest.

The US's position on voting and the veto was slower to evolve for several reasons. Staff within the executive branch offered up a range of possibilities, and later, the legislative branch raised additional concerns that had to be addressed. In particular, the State Department worried about how to deal with the British concern that a party to a dispute should not be allowed to vote on matters of interest to that state, which ran counter to the Soviet proposal. On this issue, several compromises were offered and discarded (Schlid, 1995), leaving the matter of voting rules unsettled at the close of the Dumbarton Oaks conference.

One possible explanation for the difficulty in resolving the voting rules issues could be domestic politics in the US. Roosevelt may have feared that an agreement on voting rules could open him up to an attack from either members of Congress or his Republican presidential opponent Thomas Dewey (Meisler, 1995). Others have suggested that the lack of agreement at this stage arose from growing distrust of the Soviets as the war progressed (Hildebrand, 1990). Either way, the US presented a new proposal (backed by Britain) at Yalta in February 1945. FDR worked hard to persuade Stalin to agree to this voting formula, which gave permanent members the right to veto all but procedural issues. In the case of peaceful disputes, permanent members would recuse themselves from voting on issues with which they were involved (Meisler, 1995).

The compromise became known as the Yalta Formula, which is laid out in Article 27 of the Charter. According to the Yalta Formula, a simple majority is required to pass procedural matters and for all other matters (or substantive matters as they have come to be known), a super-majority is needed, and no permanent member can oppose it (Bailey, 1969). Conducting diplomacy by majority vote was a new idea at the time because previously, systems of consensus had been the norm. Voting by consensus safeguarded state sovereignty because no obligations could be forced on a state without consent (Haftel and Thompson, 2006), which was appealing to many state governments.

The weaknesses of such a system had been revealed, however, in the failure of the League of Nations system.

In order to guarantee that the strong states would join the new institution and to avoid potential paralysis of a consensus-based system, alternative voting systems were considered for the new UN. The Allies felt that moving away from consensus voting would allow for speedier and more decisive actions (Wilcox, 1945). The Yalta Formula reflects a desire to find a middle ground between a pure consensus system and a pure majoritarian one. Consensus among the permanent members is required, but only a majority of the total membership is needed to pass a resolution.

Despite the efforts of the Allied powers to design the UN to their advantage, many contentious issues remained for the San Francisco Conference in April 1945, where the framework was introduced to a broader coalition of states, whose support was also needed to make the new organization a success. Despite Stalin's support for the voting rules proposed at Yalta, Soviet representative Vyacheslav Molotov again challenged the Yalta Formula in San Francisco, leading many to fear that the new organization might have to be constituted without Soviet participation.

The Soviet delegation was not alone in raising concerns. The majority of concerns raised at the San Francisco conference came from smaller states. First, they noted that the General Assembly (GA) is an essential body within the organization, but that the resolutions passed in the GA only express the body's approval (or disapproval). The founders viewed the GA, which has a seat for every member nation, as more of a forum for discussion rather than a body for action (Bailey and Daws, 1995). If decisions were made by a majority in the GA that did not include the permanent members of the Council, binding action was unlikely to be taken.

While the small states were concerned about their (limited) place in the new organization, both small and middle powers were critical of the power of the Council and its permanent members. While the GA can offer advisory opinions on matters of international importance, when the Security Council passes a resolution, the full membership of the UN is obligated to "accept and carry out the decisions of the Security Council," according to Article 25 of the UN Charter. Because Council resolutions are binding, the importance of the permanent members' veto power is magnified. Australia led a movement for greater checks on the major power veto (Meisler, 1995). Smaller states feared that the veto would do nothing to check aggressive action by the permanent members while enabling them to act with impunity against other states (Bailey, 1969).

For the first two decades of the UN's existence, the Security Council had eleven members (six elected members in addition to the five permanent ones), and a passing vote on a resolution required seven positive votes. As decolonization increased the number of countries in the world, one of the first reforms introduced to the Council was to increase the number of non-permanent seats. Membership on the Council increased to fifteen in 1965 with ten elected members joining the five permanent ones. Now nine positive votes are needed in favor of a resolution following that expansion.

Elected members to the Council do have some control over the permanent members, though. Because the Yalta Formula does require a majority of votes in favor of a resolution, the elected members can kill any resolution if they vote as a block—the so-called "double-veto." Block voting, however, cannot force passage of a resolution since permanent members still have the ability to veto.

Despite efforts by the smaller states to curb the veto at the San Francisco Conference, the great powers insisted that the veto provision was essential—especially since the greatest burdens for defending international peace and security would fall upon them (http://www.un.org). Eventually, the Yalta Formula was accepted by a vote of twenty to ten (with fifteen abstaining and five absent) (Meisler, 1995). The San Francisco Conference and the signing of the UN Charter signaled what the allies hoped the new organization would be able to do going forward. When we think about the institution and how it functions today, it is important to recognize that it is the product of a historical bargaining process.

At times, the institution has been up to the challenge and at other times, it has been mired in great power rivalry. The Charter describes how the UN, and the Security Council in particular, should work in theory. In the next section, we examine how it works in practice.

2.2 The Security Council in Practice

The Security Council holds primary responsibility within the UN for responding to threats to international peace and security. The enforcement powers of the Council can be grouped under two headings, those for bringing about a peaceful settlement of a dispute or situation (covered in Chapter VI of the Charter) and those for maintaining or restoring international peace and security once a threat to or breach of the peace has been identified (covered in Chapter VII) (Goodrich, 1972). Chapter VI of the UN Charter provides several options for addressing the peaceful settlement of disputes. They can gather information about a dispute, offer mediation to the parties, or call up upon the Secretary-General to use his good offices to assist in resolution. Recommendations and assistance offered under Chapter VI is advisory and non-binding while Chapter VII actions are binding and obligate all members of the entire UN.[6]

The Security Council may also draw upon Chapter VII of the Charter in response to disputes, especially if those disputes have become militarized. Unlike many international bodies, the Council does have some degree of enforcement power. It can impose economic sanctions, such as trade limitations, arms embargoes, financial restrictions (or penalties), and travel bans (Cortright and Lopez, 2000). In addition, the Council can call for collective military action under Chapter VII of the UN Charter. When sanctions or collective military action are authorized under Chapter VII, all members of the broader UN organization are obligated to act—not just the members of the Security Council.

Because of the tensions between the US and Soviet Union during the Cold War, binding action was rare, and the vast majority of action that was taken by the Council occurred under Chapter VI. Prior to 1990, Chapter VII was only invoked twice—once in 1950 in response to the North Korean invasion of South Korea[7] and again in the early 1960s in response to internal conflict in Congo.[8]

The world has changed a great deal since the end of the Cold War. The Council as well as the wider UN community's definition of what constitutes a threat to international peace and security has broadened, and the methods that the Security Council uses to deal with these threats have also evolved. In the early years, the Council was primarily concerned with interstate conflicts, viewing intrastate conflict as outside of their mandate. During this period, limited consensus between the great powers led to a limited role for the Council and more limited commitments via Chapter VI.

In more recent years, fewer conflicts in the world are between states. More are civil wars that occur within the borders of nations. Responding to intrastate wars and the humanitarian crises that accompany them requires more

[6] Initially, most UN peacekeeping missions were authorized under Chapter VI, but more and more the provisions of Chapter VII, which have more "teeth" associated with them, have been used in the creation of new missions. The informal term Chapter Six and a Half has been adopted for missions that fall somewhere between the two.

[7] This Chapter VII action was only authorized because the Soviet Union was boycotting the Council at the time.

[8] The fact that the mission to Congo, United Nations Operation in the Congo (ONUC) cost Secretary-General Dag Hammerskjold his life and nearly ruined the organization financially diminished enthusiasm for Chapter VII action (Einsiedel, et al 2014).

expansive action from the Council and the international community, which has resulted in more Chapter VII actions. This transition has not always been smooth. The permanent members have struggled and, at times, disagreed about what the role for the Council should be in matters of civil war, given the norm of sovereignty. Intrastate conflicts also make it more difficult for the Council to take action that is perceived as impartial by all participants and to which all parties consent. Robust action may seem necessary in response to genocide in Darfur or ethnic violence in Myanmar, but defining a consistent response for every situation has proved challenging for the permanent members.

2.2.1 The Procedures of the Security Council

Formal rules and informal procedures are important for how international organizations function. The UN Security Council uses a mix of formal and informal rules to accommodate the needs and desires of all its members as well as those countries that are members of the General Assembly only. Informal powers and the chance that the permanent members could act on their own (and ignore the UN) do not make the Security Council irrelevant, but they do put some limits on action. Despite having the strength to act unilaterally, powerful states still work through organizations like the UN, taking advantage of both formal and informal practices that only they as powerful states have access to. The powerful states must be mindful that these informal procedures cannot be used too often because they may undermine the legitimacy of the organization (Stone, 2011). One prominent explanation for the persistence of the post-World War II order including the UN is that the powerful states, particularly the US, have exercised strategic constraint (Ikenberry, 1999).[9]

Article 30 of the Charter stipulates that the Security Council shall adopt its own rules of procedure, and in 1946 the Council adopted its formal Provisional Rules of Procedure (S/96). Subsequently the Provisional Rules of Procedure have been modified rarely, and the last revision was made in 1982 (S/96/Rev.7), adding Arabic as the sixth official language of the Council (http://www.un.org/en/sc). These procedures have not changed in a meaningful way since 1982. Changes in the number of meetings or resolutions after the

[9] Ikenberry argues that the US could have dominated the UN Security Council at various points in history, but recognizing the value of the institution, chose not to in order to maintain the stability of the bargain struck in 1945.

Cold War cannot be attributed to formal changes in the rules or procedures of the organization. Prior to 1990, the General Assembly frequently accused the Council of a lack of transparency. In recent years, member states have made efforts to increase the Council's openness.[10]

Chapter II (which includes rules 6 to 12) of the Provisional Rules of Procedure is related to the Security Council's agenda (http://www.un.org/en/sc/about/rules/). The first matter of business in any Security Council meeting is the adoption of the agenda (Rule 9), which during the Cold War was a potentially contentious process that enabled the Soviet Union and the western allies to make politically charged public statements. Rules 10 and 11 cover matters with which the Council is concerned (Highlights of Security Council Practice, 2013). The Security Council retains control over its working methods. The persistent "provisional" status of these rules is a reflection of the fact that the rules are under the control of the Council members themselves and can be changed with relative ease at any time.

When formulating its working methods, the Council established several kinds of meetings that it can hold—each with different allowances for who can attend, who may be invited to participate, and what information gets reported to the broader public. There are four types of meetings: public meetings, private meetings, informal consultations, and Arria-formula meetings.

The two most frequent types of meetings are public meetings and informal consultations. Public meetings are held formally in the Council Chamber at the UN Headquarters in New York. All speeches and discussions in these meetings are a matter of official record published by the UN so that all member states and the broader public can read transcripts of the meeting, including verbatim transcripts of statements offered by each participating delegation. Typically, when people think about Security Council meetings, these are the type of gatherings they envision. This public diplomacy is important for member states to make statements on the global stage and to pass resolutions that are binding for the entire organization.

Secondly, we focus on informal "Consultations of the Whole" to explore when the Council meets privately to discuss issues. Informal consultations are the most opaque form of meeting because no other UN members are invited to attend and no official record is kept (United Nations Security Council, 2012).

[10] In response to concerns about a lack of transparency in the working methods of the Council, several presidential notes have been issued in the past decade to clarify the procedures of the UN Security Council—most recently in 2013. The notes have focused on issues such as the exact process for appointing chairpersons for subsidiary bodies, scheduling of meetings and periods of open debate, the process for removing items from the Council's agenda.

The *UN Journal* began publishing the topics for these consultations in 1994, but the substance of these meetings is still largely unknown. In these sessions, Council members hash out disagreements on particular issues or reconcile disagreement between competing draft resolutions. This private diplomacy is important for building consensus and resolving disagreements that member delegations would prefer not to air in public.

In addition, two other types of meetings are possible, but they occur much less frequently. The Council can go into a private sessions, but this is rare. Traditionally, these meetings were used only to discuss and elect the next Secretary-General. More recently, private meetings have been employed to discuss peacekeeping logistics with troop-contributing countries. For these meetings, the Secretariat keeps a record, but the transcripts are not made public.

Finally, there are Arria-formula meetings, which are informal gatherings for Council members, other UN delegations, members of the Secretariat, and other stakeholders to have private discussions. These are neither publicly announced beforehand, nor are they recorded. Arria-formula meetings happen relatively infrequently (United Nations Security Council, 2012). This is the newest and most flexible meeting format. Recently, they have taken the form of inviting non-state actors, particularly non-governmental organizations, to an informal discussion of a particular issue (Daws and Sievers, 2016). In 2015, six informal interactive dialogues were held with regional organizations or other similar partners and a total of seventeen Arria-formula meetings were held (the greatest number in recent years) (*Highlights of Security Council Practice*, 2014).[11]

In addition to considering the types of meetings the Council can hold, we also must think about the potential outcomes. When the Council is meeting in public, the Council can take several types of action. The most familiar of these is to pass a resolution, which can occur only in a public meeting. For a substantive resolution to pass, nine Council members must vote affirmatively

[11] Informal interactive dialogues are a still-evolving working method for the Council. In 2009, when the African Union and League of Arab States appealed to the Council for the opportunity to discuss the ICC's warrant for the arrest of Sudanese President Omar al-Bashir, many Council members disliked the idea of holding a formal public meeting for this purpose. Eventually, the Council decided to meet with the representatives in a conference room (not the Council chamber), and a hastily written note saying "informal interactive discussion" was placed on the door. There is no formal definition for this format. The 2012 handbook on Security Council working methods describes this type of session as "an informal private meeting of the Security Council members convened in order to hold an off-the-record discussion with one or more non-Council member states. The informal dialogues are presided over by the Council president and take place in a meeting room other than the Council Chamber or Consultations Room." (securitycouncilreport.org).

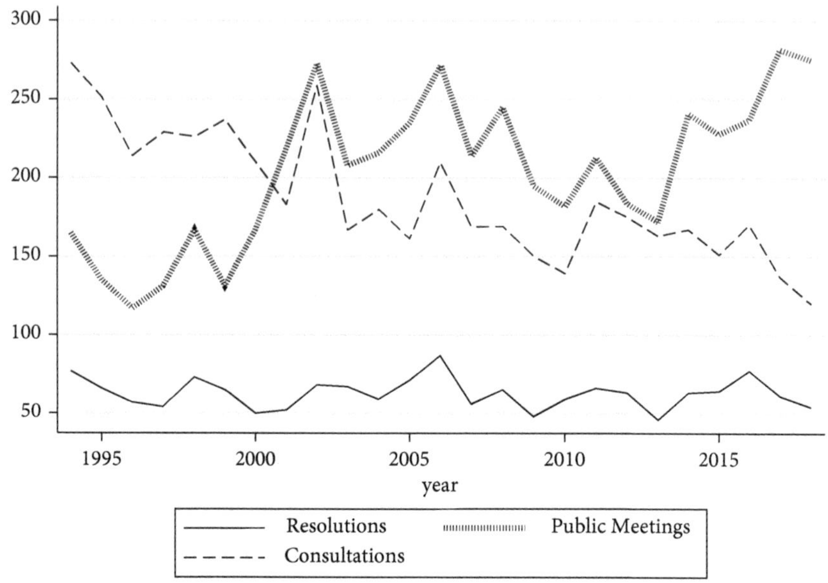

Fig. 2.1 Security Council actions, 1946–2015

on the measure and none of the permanent members can cast a negative vote (Article 27).[12]

Another Council outcome is a presidential statement. These formal public statements are issued by the Council president and are adopted by consensus at a formal public meeting of the Council (http://www.un.org). Presidential statements are not binding the way resolutions are, but they represent a consensus of all Council members and often include recommendations to other member nations or members of the Secretariat. Finally, the Council may also issue notes, letters from the president, and press statements, but these tend to be informational and are not formally adopted by the Council members. All of these informational tools, however, are thought to convey the consensus of the Council.

Since the end of the Cold War, the Council has been much more active—holding many more formal meetings and passing a greater number of resolutions. The Council has engaged in more binding action during this time period. In 2018, 50 percent of the fifty-four resolutions explicitly called on Chapter VII of the UN Charter, which is binding for all UN member states. The increased reliance on Chapter VII has led China to express reservations or abstain in some circumstances when voting on these binding resolutions (Voeten, 2001).

[12] On procedural matters, negative votes by the Security Council do not count as vetoes.

Some peacekeeping missions like United Nations–African Union Hybrid Operation in Darfur (UNAMID) are only partially authorized under Chapter VII in response to Chinese concerns. Other missions have become progressively more robust and have transitioned from Chapter VI to Chapter VII, like missions in Sierra Leone and the Democratic Republic of the Congo.

Security Council activity has increased over time, but so too has the range of issues the Council tackles. During the 1990s, the Council moved away from solely a national security-based approach and began to focus more on human security concerns. With this new emphasis on the security of individuals, discussions of civil conflicts, human rights, economic security, and repression by domestic political actors moved from the edges of the Council's agenda to the center. Because plenary time (the time available for the Council to meet) is scarce, the Security Council cannot debate and respond to all international crises. Determining which issues will get attention is a critical first step in the process of Security Council action.

2.2.2 The Agenda and Agenda-setting Power

Not all threats to peace and security receive the same attention and treatment from the Council. The power to bring issues to the attention of the Security Council is broad, so how does the Council choose what issues to act on? According to the UN Charter, any member nation of the UN can bring a concern to the Council (Article 35(1)). Beyond that, a state need not even be a member of the broader UN institution to do so (according to Article 35(2) of the UN Charter). Article 99 also gives this power to the Secretary-General. No one, however, can force the Council to act on an issue.

In the early years, the tensions of the Cold War often stymied efforts to gain agreement between the powerful nations of the Eastern and Western blocs, which limited the issues the Council was able to take action on. Despite acknowledging likely threats to international peace and security, the rival states were unwilling to delegate power to the Secretary-General to act in such situations (Bailey, 1994). More recently, limitations on resources and, at times, political will have constrained the Council's response.

States and other actors within the UN's system bring issues to the Security Council for a variety of reasons. In some circumstances, states want action. In other cases, states may feel unable to do anything on their own, but public opinion demands that something be done. Bringing a matter to the Council is a way for states to tell their people that they did their best to take international action (Bailey, 1994: p. 112).

Because the formal power to call attention to issues in the Security Council is so broad, the more important stage of the agenda-setting process involves scheduling meetings and proposing resolutions. Only states with a seat on the Council have these powers, which limit and manage the flow of issues put before the group. As a result, Council member states have tremendous power to focus on (or ignore) issues as they see fit, but no single Council member has greater agenda-setting power than another member.

The agenda of the Security Council actually has two parts—the Summary Statement of the Security Council and the provisional agenda for each meeting.[13] The first part of the agenda, formally known as the Summary Statement of Matters on Which the Security Council is Seized, is all the topics that have been brought to the official agenda, but which were never fully resolved. These are issues, that for whatever reason, the Council discussed at some point in time, and may discuss again. An example of this type of agenda item is "The situation in Cyprus," which was first discussed in December of 1963 and continues to be discussed in the context of the ongoing peacekeeping mission on the island. On the other hand, there are also topics included that have been postponed and that the Council has not chosen to formally close. One such item is "Letter dated 11 July 1960 from the Minister for Foreign Affairs of Cuba addressed to the President of the Security Council."[14] Hurd (2008) notes that at the start of 2005, the Summary Statement contained 147 items, some nearly as old as the UN itself. Efforts to pare the agenda to the most relevant items has decreased that number to sixty-four items in 2016.

The second part of the agenda is the functional part. For each session of the Council, the Secretary-General creates a list of potential issues including a range of current crises or issues that might be topics for the upcoming meeting. According to Rule 6 of the Provisional Rules of Procedure of the Security Council, "the Secretary-General shall immediately bring to the attention of all representatives on the Security Council all communications from States, organs of the UN, or the Secretary-General concerning any matter for the consideration of the Security Council in accordance with the provisions of the Charter" (http://www.un.org).

Members of the Council also influence the working agenda. In terms of day-to-day impact, a critical actor is the President of the Security Council—a position that rotates each month among the members. At the beginning of

[13] Interestingly, in 1946, a committee of experts was asked to examine the provisional rules of the Security Council. In their report, they noted that the term "agenda" is not well defined and is used ambiguously throughout the document.

[14] There are several agenda items like this one associated with the conflict between the US and Cuba that have persisted on the Summary Statement for decades without additional discussion due to objections by the US.

each month, the Council president in consultation with the Secretary-General produces an informal calendar (or programme of work) that indicates the topics and corresponding dates for meetings in the coming month.[15] Most of these topics are already listed on the Summary Statement. Many of the meetings to be scheduled flow directly from previous decisions by the Council—for example, discussions of mandate renewal of peacekeeping missions or reports by the Secretary-General that were requested by the Council within a specified time frame (Sievers and Daws, 2014). The Council's schedule is roughed out by the president at the beginning of the month, presented to the other Council members, and is published on the UN's website, but the course of world events may cause meetings to be added and moved as necessary.

Based on the Programme of Work, the Council president formulates a provisional agenda for each particular meeting and determines the order of voting to approve the agenda (Bailey and Daws, 1998). According to Rule 7, at the start of every Security Council meeting, members discuss this provisional agenda and vote on it in order to make it the official agenda (Hurd, 2008), and only items which have been brought to the attention of representatives via Rule 6 or that the Council has already considered can be included on the agenda. Provisional agendas are often published in the UN Journal but only after they have been approved by the Council in prior consultations (Sievers and Daws, 2014). If differences of opinion concerning the agenda cannot be hammered out in informal consultations, the agenda must be put to a public procedural vote.[16] These votes were a frequent part of Security Council activity during the Cold War, but they have nearly disappeared in recent years. Without the rivalry between the Soviet Union and the US, members seldom take to the floor to challenge the basic structure of the agenda.

In the early days of the Council, a meeting was convened any time an issue was presented to the Council and then to formally debate the appropriateness of taking up the matter if any Council members expressed doubts. As mentioned previously, the formal powers to propose topics for the Council's agenda are very broad. Historically, the Council has rejected a few proposed topics. Those decisions seem to vary by case and have typically reflect concerns that were more political than legal (Sievers and Daws, 2014).[17]

[15] Other members of the Council are also often consulted when these programmes of work are created.

[16] Procedural votes typically arise when either Council members cannot agree on how to formulate the description of the agenda item or when Council members disagree about whether or not to convene a Security Council meeting on a given topic (Sievers and Daws, 2014).

[17] Proposed items have historically been rejected for the following reasons (whether singly or in combination): A lack of clarity in the proposal, no clear threat to peace, fears that a decisions by the

Similar to the lack of clarity about whether or not the Council can refuse to call a meeting on a proposed issue, removing issues from the agenda is complicated. No clear provisions exist in the Charter to remove items from the agenda—even individual members of the Council itself cannot do so, which is the why the US has been unable to remove complaints against itself filed by the Castro regime in Cuba. Items only come off the agenda when resolutions are passed, when all proposals on the matter are rejected, or by an explicit decision by a majority of the Council to remove the issue (Bailey and Daws, 1998). Removing issues can provoke strong reactions, and thus the Summary Statement has become a "catalogue of simmering arguments" (Hurd, 2008: p. 144). Some smaller states see symbolic power and importance in keeping issues on the agenda. In 1996, the Security Council attempted to create a new procedural rule allowing that "matters that had not been considered by the Council in the preceding five years would be deleted from the list of matters of which the Council was seized." Non-permanent members of the Council protested before the rule could even go into effect. As a compromise, any item up for deletion can be retained at the request of any UN member state, and some states like Pakistan, who actively works to keep India/Pakistan issues on the agenda, regularly file their requests more than a year in advance to maintain their symbolic place on the agenda (Hurd, 2008). On the other hand, these stale issues are seldom reopened by the Council.

2.2.3 The Role of the Veto

The veto is one of the most defining institutional rules of the Security Council. The veto (or the threat of veto) influences both the Council's agenda and the outcomes of the discussions resulting from that agenda. Because the permanent members all possess veto power, certain matters will never come before the Council at all. On other issues, draft resolutions fail to gain sufficient support to come up for a vote. The Soviet invasion of Afghanistan received little to no attention from the Council. The same is true for US action in Vietnam. Even after the political balance shifted following the fall of the Soviet Union, some issues are still off limits like political control of Tibet and the human rights of the Uyghurs in China. Debate in the Council in 2014 surrounding events in Crimea was distinctly shaped by Russian veto power.

Council might have a harmful effect or interfere with outside processes, inopportune timing, and that the proposal is being made primarily for propaganda reasons (See Sievers and Daws (2014), pp.213-15 for a fuller discussion).

In the League of Nations, decisions were made by consensus. There, every member nation possessed the power to kill any item, which is, in essence, a *delaying* power. Those who have the ability to veto resolutions can demand policies that meet their minimum preferences, regardless of the majority opinion. Veto power gives a member the ability to delay passage of any policies until an alternative is introduced that meets their minimum demands. As the number of veto states increases, policy gridlock becomes more likely (Tsebelis, 2002). As more states have veto power and thus have minimum demands that must be satisfied, the more difficult it will be to find any resolution that suits them all. The fact that all members of the League of Nations had veto power greatly hindered the organization's ability to make any decisions or pass any binding resolutions.

The advantage of giving certain states veto power, however, is that it guarantees that those key states' concerns are considered in the drafting of all resolutions. Having members with veto power reduces the range of possible alternatives to the status quo and narrows the range of choices for consideration. This is important for the UN, an organization that originally served fifty-one member states and currently includes 193 member states. Without a veto system, debate and negotiation among those 193 members could lead to nearly unbreakable gridlock. Representatives of the US, Britain, and to a lesser degree the Soviet Union recognized the importance of the veto provision as they negotiated the creation of the UN because of the possible need for the great powers to opt out. "The veto is the safety valve that prevents the United Nations from undertaking commitments which it presently lacks the power to fulfill" (Jessup quoted in Mahbubani (2004)).

As discussed previously, many states were concerned that the veto would allow the great powers to enforce their will over the weaker states, but in the minds of the organization's founders, the veto was about the great powers committing to work together to defend peace and security on behalf of the weaker states (Claude, 1963). Negotiators at the San Francisco Conference suggested that without the veto, the stronger states would be unwilling to commit to the organization over the long term. Nearly seventy years hence, none of the great powers have left the organization, so perhaps the veto power has held the organization together (Mahbubani, 2004). Despite the likelihood that the veto has kept the Council together, it is a negative power rather than a positive one.

Despite the influence veto power conveys, it has been used rarely. Between 1990 and 2018, veto members cast a total of forty vetoes in public meetings, or just over one per year (http://www.un.org).[18] During this same period, the number of resolutions exceeded sixty-three resolutions per year.

Vetoes have not completely disappeared since the end of the Cold War, but the threat of the veto is often sufficient to table an issue or a resolution. France issued an explicit threat of veto in the diplomatic follow-up to Resolution 1441 on Iraq in 2002 when the US and UK sought greater support from the Council for military action (Hulton, 2004). In 1999, China used its veto in the Security Council to prevent the mandate renewal for United Nations Preventive Deployment Force (UNPREDEP) in the former Yugoslav Republic of Macedonia (Press Release SC/6648), ending the Council's first efforts at preventive peacekeeping, which had been introduced in Secretary-General Boutros Boutros-Ghali's *Agenda for Peace* in 1992. More recently, in 2019, the Russian Federation vetoed several draft resolutions demanding action in response to use of chemical weapons by the Syrian regime led by Bashar al-Assad.[19]

In recent years, vetoes have been cast for one of two reasons. First, a sponsor may underestimate the strength of a permanent member's objections, incorrectly assuming that the member would likely abstain or grudgingly vote for the draft resolution. The majority of resolutions are drafted by one of the Western Three who work to craft documents that will be acceptable to all members, especially the P5.[20] An example of underestimating the power of veto threat was Russia's 1993 veto on a proposal for peacekeeping funding for Cyprus, a long-running Security Council endeavor. In many cases, however, the sponsors likely know prior to the vote that the resolution will fail but decide that a public record of their position and the votes (for and against their position) is important (Sievers and Daws, 2014). Examples of this type of behavior include a 2012 vote on Syria that was vetoed by both China and Russia.

Overall, in the post-Cold War era, the Council has demonstrated a greater inclination toward consensus decision-making. Not only did the rate of vetoes decrease, more decisions from the Council were issued through presidential statements, which require consensus.[21] More vetoes or threatened vetoes have been utilized during informal consultations during the post-Cold War period

[18] One additional veto was cast in a private meeting on the issue of reappointment of the Secretary-General.

[19] Neither France nor the UK has cast a veto since 1989.

[20] In the Council, a penholder nation is designated for many issues and that country is in charge of drafting all resolutions on that topic.

[21] These statements are read at public meetings of the Council and have been agreed upon by all members in advance (Hulton, 2004).

(Mahbubani, 2004). While more agreement has emerged during the post-Cold War era than during the Cold War, there are signs of increased contentiousness among the permanent members in recent years. More vetoes have occurred in second half of the 2010s, with the average rising to 3.2 per year between 2015–2019.

While many feel that the veto has paralyzed the Council when its influence is needed most, others suggest that the veto has had exactly the influence it should—limiting action by the UN when its most powerful states could not come to an agreement about the best action to take.

2.2.4 How has it Worked?

Over time, the Security Council's influence on international peace and security has waxed and waned. Bailey (1994) notes that when the Security Council considers action, member states weigh the relative strength of two principles from the UN Charter—the principle that the UN shall not intervene in matters which are essentially within domestic jurisdiction unless the Council has decided to utilize enforcement measures (Article 2.7) versus the principle that members states shall work together to achieve universal respect for human rights and fundamental freedoms (Articles 55c and 56). Initially, the Council viewed non-intervention as the top priority, but there was a shift following the end of the Cold War. In the 1990s, the second criterion was given priority. At present, the relative weight of these two principles is not completely clear, but the Council leans toward giving priority to the second criterion (Bailey, 1994).

According to Stone (2008), when states delegate power to an international organization, they are not concerned so much that the institution itself will act beyond its mandate. The greater fear is that the organization will be captured by the most powerful state, and that state will overreach. To some degree, activity and activism of the UN has fluctuated with interest from the US. While the UK is the permanent member most likely to utilize the Council for diplomacy, its influence is not as strong as its trans-Atlantic partner (Tardy and Zaum, 2015). When the US has been engaged, the Council has taken strong action. Between 1991 and 2014, more than 40 percent of the resolutions passed were binding Chapter VII resolutions (Wallensteen and Johansson, 2015). At other times, the US has marginalized the Council, working through NATO on Kosovo in 1999 and opting to invade Iraq in 2003 without authorization from the Security Council. In the early years of the Syrian Civil War, the Obama administration showed some interest in coordinating international response through the Council, but divergent preferences with the Russians made this a non-starter.

In the twenty-first century, one area where the Council has found unity of purpose has been terrorism, as consensus arose in the aftermath of the terrorist attacks of 9/11. The physical proximity of the UN's New York City headquarters made real to delegates the sense that global terrorism poses a clear threat to international peace and security. In the immediate aftermath, the Council invoked the US' right to self-defense via Article 51 of the UN Charter, providing a legal basis for the US invasion of Afghanistan (Stahn, 2003). Beyond that the Council also passed Resolution 1373, which obligated all states in the UN community to take action against global terrorism. Curbing the financing of terrorism is a cornerstone of the resolution, and one that all Council members support.[22]

Division again arose, however, when the US called upon the international community to take the War on Terror beyond Afghanistan and into Iraq in 2003. While the US brought its concerns about Iraq and weapons of mass destruction before the Council, the other members did not feel that it constituted a sufficient threat to international peace and security to warrant invasion. The US opted to invade without approval from the Council. International public opinion supported the Council's decision not to go along with the invasion plans, but many seemed to hold the Council responsible for failing to prevent it (von Einstiedel, Malone, and Ugarte, 2015). The largely unilateral decision by the US created and continues to create friction among the members of the Council.

Clearly the tensions of the Cold War hobbled the UN, and the Security Council in particular. As hostility between the US and the Soviet Union was peaking in the late 1950s, the Council conducted only limited business. In 1959, the Council only met a total of five times (Mingst and Karns, 1995). In that same year, only one resolution could be agreed upon, and it was procedural rather than substantive nature. The Council had received a request for assistance from the government of Laos, and Secretary-General Dag Hammarskjold was asked to examine the matter further because the Council was unsure whether to place the matter on its agenda. The conflict in Laos between the communist Pathet Lao and Royal Lao Army supported by the US complicated the issue for the Council members. Eventually, the Council passed a resolution creating a sub-committee to further review the report and other received documents. At this time, they could only agree to examine the issues

[22] See https://www.securitycouncilreport.org/monthly-forecast/2019-03/counter-terrorism.php.

further, particularly those regarding potential incursions from North Vietnamese troops, and even on this procedural point, the USSR opted to vote no (http://www.un.org).[23]

On the other hand, another way of reading the Council's actions during the Cold War is to say that the institutional design worked. The organization did not commit itself to any action that the major powers could not agree on. The one major exception is the Uniting for Peace Resolution (UN General Assembly (UNGA) Resolution 377) passed in the General Assembly in 1950 as a means of circumventing repeated vetoes by the Soviet Union during the Korean War.[24] Under the United for Peace resolution, "the Assembly may take action if the Security Council, because of a lack of unanimity of its permanent members, fails to act in a case where there appears to be a threat to the peace, breach of the peace or act of aggression" (A/RES/377).

Historically, the permanent members have kept the Council at bay on tricky issues of strategic concern to themselves. The US kept the war in Vietnam off the Council's plate and US interest in Israeli politics has limited the attention given to the Arab-Israeli conflict.[25] One resolution was proposed concerning Soviet involvement in Afghanistan; it was immediately vetoed, and the issue was never brought up in the Council again (Wallensteen and Johansson, 2004). This has continued in recent years as conflicts in the Ukraine and Tibet have not appeared on the Council's agenda.

When great power agreement is impossible, the Council often improvises. Peacekeeping, which has become a fundamental part of the Council's mission and identity, was developed in large part as a response to the lack of great power unity on how to respond to regional conflict (Mingst and Karns, 1995). In the early years, UN peacekeeping was characterized by neutrality, consent, and non-use of force. The Council was careful not to overstep and infringe on the norms of national sovereignty and non-intervention. A neutral peacekeeping mission that had permission to intervene (via the principle of consent) made it possible for the organization to respond without bringing Cold War tensions

[23] Negative votes by permanent members on procedural issues do not invalidate decisions. During the Cold War, procedural votes were frequently taken and recorded. In recent years, however, procedural votes have been infrequent. Most procedural decisions such as the adoption of the agenda, an invitation to an individual to participate in Council meetings, adding a new item to the seizure list or the suspension or adjournment of a meeting are now arrived at by consensus (http://securitycouncilreport.org).

[24] Interestingly, the procedure laid out in the Uniting for Peace Resolution has only been used a handful of times to move issues through the UN system and around deadlock in the Security Council. The last time it was used was more than thirty years ago when Zimbabwe convened an emergency session of the UNGA concerning the "Question of Namibia."

[25] Only one Security Council resolution has been passed concerning the Arab-Israeli conflict, and it was passed in 1948 (Resolution 54) (Wallensteen and Johansson, 2004).

into the mix. Until the 1990s, P5 countries did not send peacekeeping troops for fear that a mission's neutrality would be compromised.

Peacekeeping has evolved more quickly since the end of the Cold War. Part of this evolution has resulted from the change in discourse about the nature of security. Prior to the 1990s, security was typically considered to be a state-centric concept. Strategic national interests were key considerations in discussions about security. More recently, the concept of security has been applied more frequently at the individual level. Human security, first defined by the United Nations Development Programme in 1994, includes not only specific violence, but also generalized threats like those which arise from economic, food, health, or environmental insecurity and threats to personal, community, political security, or human rights violations (United Nations Development Programme, 1994). Changing the focus away from the state has also enabled the Council to justify weakening the norms of sovereignty and non-intervention as they authorized more peacekeeping missions to respond to intrastate conflicts. Over time, discussion about human security and the importance of states protecting their citizens expanded into the development of the Responsibility to Protect (R2P) policy, which asserts that the international community has an obligation to respond where nations states are unable to (or fail to) protect their people from massive loss of life (A/RES/60/1). Following the R2P doctrine, the Security Council authorized the 2011 NATO–led military action in Libya to protect human lives.

Both the substance and process of the work of the Security Council are constantly evolving and changing in response to events in the world around it (Mahbubani, 2004). From a procedural standpoint, in order to keep up with the changing international reality, the members of the Council periodically supplement the Provisional Rules of Procedure of the Security Council through adopting and publishing specific new working methods (http://www.un.org/en/sc). Recent efforts in this direction have focused on requests from the broader UN community to increase transparency concerning the decision-making process of the Council.

Britain and France have been the most active members of the Security Council, but the US continues to be the most influential followed by Russia and increasingly China (Mahbubani, 2004). The Western Three still draft most of the Council outcomes (including resolutions, presidential statements, or press statements), as one of these three is the penholder on most situation-specific issues on the Council's agenda.[26] The words of the Council usually begin with

[26] See Security Council Report, http://securitycouncilreport.org, for a full description.

a draft from these countries and are then amended by other members states. This has been the traditional arrangement for most of the history of the Council. In fact, it has only been in recent years with the increased workload of the Council, that elected members have been asked to serve as penholders on specific recurring thematic issues.

The practice of the Western Three countries serving as the primary penholders for the Council began as one of expediency. The permanent members have larger and more expert staffs. Because of their continuity on the Council, they hold an advantage over elected members in terms of both institutional knowledge about particular issues as well as Council procedures. Initially, this system was highly informal and the leadership of the Western Three largely went unquestioned. More recently, elected members have challenged the system as they often felt short-circuited in draft negotiations, which often were being conducted among the permanent members. As the agenda of the Council has expanded and as elected members have demanded a greater role, more elected members have been taking up the pen. A prominent example has been the rotation of multiple elected members over nearly a decade serving as penholders on the humanitarian aspects of the conflict in Syria. Expanding the opportunities for elected members to influence the writing of resolutions can help increase the legitimacy of the Council as well as its representativeness.

Since the end of the Cold War, there has been a greater focus in the Council on operational decision making and less on posturing and position-taking, particularly among the permanent members (Hulton, 2004). As a result, the Council has been able to partially fulfill the founders' vision of providing collective security (Mahbubani, 2004). The success of the 1991 Persian Gulf War and the Council's continuing commitment to peacekeeping are evidence that the Council can and does work together under certain circumstances to safeguard international peace and security.

The challenges persist, however. The failure of the UN Security Council to halt mass killings in Syria and Myanmar point to weaknesses in the system. The interests of the P5 have not been perfectly aligned in the post-Cold War era and will likely continue to diverge. Permanent members still use the Council as a forum for sorting out the disagreements among themselves. Debate in the Council over Russian interference in Crimea in 2014 led to brash political statements that could have been stolen from Cold War debates. US Representative Samantha Power stated that "the Russian Federation was known for its literary greatness, yet today its representative had shown more imagination than Tolstoy or Chekhov in extolling the conduct of the 'so-called referendum.'" Her French counterpart Gerard Araud said that "France almost felt pity in listening to Russian diplomats and seeing Moscow so willing to grasp at straws."

One of the biggest questions non-permanent member states continue to raise about the Council in the post-Cold War era is that of Council reform. While the make-up of the Council reflected the political realities of 1944, many question whether they continue to reflect the state of the world in 2020. Many believe the Council is past due for more membership changes. A working group was created by the General Assembly in 1993 to consider the question of increasing the members of the Security Council. More recently and more publicly, in 2005, then Secretary-General Kofi Annan proposed two models for Security Council reform. Proposals have been made to bring countries such as India, Brazil, Japan, Germany, and South Africa onto the Council as permanent members to increase representation. World leaders even held a world summit on the issue and passed a consensus statement on the issue, but no action has been taken. More recent discussions in 2008 and 2015 within the UN General Assembly have gained little traction with the majority of member states.[27] At the end of the day, any Security Council reform will require support from the P5 countries. While some of them have expressed support for the idea of reform, none have been willing or interested in taking the lead of this issue which could potentially lead to decreased influence for themselves.

The agenda-setting process laid out in the UN Charter for the Security Council offers the opportunity for a wide range of actors to bring issues up for consideration. Over time, however, as the Council's view of its mandate has broadened, the member states have been more strategic about how and when they will take up particular issues. Although the Security Council does not have procedures that look precisely like those of a national legislature, decisions about scheduling plenary time play an important role in defining the Council's agenda and greatly influence the decisions that are (and are not) made by the UN Security Council.

In this chapter, we have explored the bargaining process that led to the creation of the UN Security Council and that shaped the rules and procedures that continue to govern it today. We have also provided a brief history of the institution and its functioning since its inception. In Chapter 3, we present a generalized model to understand the process by which the Security Council tackles the threats to international peace and security that come before it.

[27] See https://www.securitycouncilreport.org/monthly-forecast/2019-09/in-hindsight-security-council-reform.php.

3
A Theory of Institutional Behavior

The United Nations Security Council is an active body. Meetings happen daily, and proposed resolutions pass much more often than they are vetoed. The domestic and international media regularly report on events happening in the Council in response to international crises and developments affecting peace and security. This activity suggests that the UN and the Security Council are primary fora of diplomatic activity. The bureaucracy supporting the Council has grown, coalescing into a steady institution at the center of international peace and security. Likewise, member states have invested more in their diplomatic missions over time, decisions that suggest they see benefits to devoting resources to participating in the UN system.

Increased activity and investment in institutions, however, does not guarantee that member states will always get what they want, nor does it imply perfect harmony among them. The process of moving from an agenda item to action on any issue is complex, the result of strategic behavior among the decision makers. This is particularly true for the Security Council, where resolutions are binding and can impose substantial costs on member states. Council actions mobilize human and material resources and can even define limits on foreign policy for all or certain member states. In other words, when the Council requires action, it is almost certainly *costly* action in some form. Security Council resolutions are important. So why are some issues chosen for discussion, while others languish on the agenda? What factors and forces do Council members consider when they decide what to discuss? There are many strands of theory to explain behaviors inside the Council. Drawing on existing and new theoretical work, we present new arguments to explain how the Council decides what issues to discuss and how to discuss them. We argue these decisions turn on expectations about the likelihood of agreement, the details of the agreement, and the makeup of the Council at the time, particularly the delegation holding the presidency.

Bargaining in the UN Security Council. Susan Hannah Allen and Amy Yuen, Oxford University Press.
 DOI: 10.1093/oso/9780192849755.003.0003

3.1 Bargaining Inside the Institution

As we described in Chapter 1, we see bargaining within an institution as part of the broader bargain among states that supports the current international system structure. In fact, the institution itself represents an agreement among member states. As we noted previously, institutions set rules that define parameters on what they discuss, who decides, how they decide, and how implementation proceeds. Chapter 2 describes in detail the minutiae of Security Council rules and procedure, but here, we examine the rules and apply insights from legislative bargaining theories to understand how the Security Council functions and what effects the structure has on what they discuss, what resolutions pass, and when states bypass the institution.

The business of maintaining international peace and security has evolved into a complex political process involving not only a codified voting procedure but also an agenda setting component that sorts what issues the Council takes up each month. We develop a theory of institutional behavior to cover a wide range of actions in the Council that incorporates both spatial and sequential modeling techniques. Spatial models are a simplified way to visualize a range of possible policies between two extremes. Policymakers bargain over these options to try and get the policy they most prefer. Sequential models are a structured way to examine a series of decisions. In these models, the choice of one decision maker is contingent upon what choices they or others made before and what they expect to occur later.

Prior models of the Council have tended to examine the policy outcomes with a spatial framework, but these types of analyses are notoriously difficult to test on a large scale because pinpointing existing and alternative policies on a policy space in a consistent way that allows comparison across time has proven extremely difficult. They also do not consider the process the institution imposes on decision making, which itself is strategic, and influences the outcomes we observe. We modify and build on past models in two ways. First, we consider the basic structure of Voeten (2001) and expand the spatial analysis to increase the scope of the theoretical model. In his original specification, Voeten simplified his analysis to cases of deadlock in the Council to illustrate the effects of the threat of unilateral action. Our expansion relaxes that simplification to cover a wider range of possible situations in the Council, which allows us to develop testable hypotheses about the relationships among Council members, meeting selection, and voting behaviors. We then revisit one of the most important features of Voeten's original specification—the uncertainty about commitments to outside action. We explore this uncertainty empirically, with testable hypotheses regarding the sources of uncertainty, in Chapter 5.

Next, we explore the strategic environment surrounding the Council as it relates to external observers and the process the Council uses to consider, discuss, and vote on pressing issues on its agenda. For this analysis, we develop a sequential, strategic model that includes anticipated reactions to possible Council output. A developing literature explores the informational role the Security Council plays, particularly for domestic and international audiences. However, Security Council members can also manipulate the strategic environment inside the institution in their favor, depending on which observers they want to influence. The following chapters test these ideas in turn with new data on actions taken in the UN Security Council and case studies that trace and explain the behavior inside the Council.

3.1.1 The Council as a Tool for Powerful States

When and why does the Security Council act? An array of explanations for many facets of this question abound in the literature, beginning almost immediately from the inception of the United Nations Charter.[1]

One of the most widely assumed features is that the Security Council is a tool of the US, used to manage global affairs in the way hegemonic stability theory describes.[2] Specifically, post-World War II, the US held the position of hegemon, or near-hegemon, and built a system of institutions to manage such issues as the international monetary system (Bretton Woods institutions like the International Monetary Fund and the International Bank for Reconstruction and Development (World Bank)), international trade (the General Agreement on Tariffs and Trade), and peace and security through the UN. The history described in Chapter 2 and many other tomes on the UN and the Council suggest a great deal of give-and-take in the negotiating process around the UN, its main bodies, and the decision-making rules. Thus, its structure

[1] Interestingly, much of the literature on the UN in the late 1940s and for much of the 1950s was preoccupied with the UN's failure to do what it was intended to do, that is, act quickly to prevent aggression. The impression of a weak UN started quite early in its tenure, but that characterization depends very much on what one thinks the UN is supposed to do and whether, given the existing climate among the great powers, it is achievable (Jebb, 1952). The impression that the UN was an American tool for managing global politics is much less clear in early writings and analysis of the UN (see for example Cohen (1951)).

[2] For an example of the Council as a tool of the US, see Bennis (1996) and Gibbs (1997). Kindleberger (1973) and Krasner (1973) give the original specification of hegemonic stability theory.

is the result of hard deliberation among the three primary victors in World War II, rather than a system imposed by a hegemon.

The behavior since, however, may also give the impression that the US uses the Security Council as a tool to achieve its goals. Starting with Korea, action in the UN seemed to occur at the behest of the US, an impression that persists today. The UN resolution on Korea passed in the absence of the Soviet representative in the meeting, actions taken in the US sphere (i.e., Western Hemisphere) only happen with the American blessing and are rare events,[3] the US routinely vetoes resolutions condemning Israel, a close ally, and the list of events that serve US parochial interests is long. Even modern institutions scholars echo this impression:

> International organizations are compelled to navigate the treacherous vortex created by US power. If they stray too far from the current, they become irrelevant to US policy, and may find themselves adrift; yet if they are captured by the US policy preoccupations of the moment, they risk losing their legitimacy. An example of the first tendency is the United Nations Security Council, which the United States has marginalized when it failed to support US policies in the former Yugoslavia and Iraq. (Stone, 2011, 2)

A related line of inquiry follows how the US uses various institutions and forms of aid to leverage its foreign policy goals in an international form of logrolling. The central claim in this line of research is that the US trades forms of aid (direct aid or through other institutions like the International Monetery Fund (IMF)) for votes from less powerful nations in various international institutions, including the Security Council (Andersen, Hansen, and Markussen, 2006; Bueno de Mesquita and Smith, 2010; Dreher, Sturm, and Vreeland, 2009*a*, 2009*b*; Kuziemko and Werker, 2006; Vreeland and Dreher, 2014). One interesting implication of this body of work is that the institutions themselves do not guarantee the US control. Instead, other forms of power *external* to the institutional rules give the US its power inside institutions. As Stone (2011) argues, there are limits to both how much the US can exert this influence and how much other members can manipulate formal and informal rules to make US influence more costly, resulting in the kinds of institutions we see today, with tangles of formal and informal rules that affect the choices and output of any international institution.

[3] Large-N empirical evidence shows that UN action in the Americas is the least likely region to receive UN intervention (Gilligan and Stedman, 2003).

Focusing on US influence, however, misses many other instances where the veto-wielding members of the Council have exercised influence as well. A branch of research on the actual output of the Council (peacekeeping missions and sanctions) focuses more broadly on the interests of the veto-wielding members as the primary drivers of activity inside the Council, often at the expense of weaker UN member states (De Jonge Oudraat, 1996; Gilligan and Stedman, 2003; Neack, 1995).

These studies that uncover how powerful states wield their influence within institutions all highlight how that influence undermines the *legitimacy* of international institutions. The implicit assumption is that there is some independent understanding of what makes an institution legitimate, so we can therefore determine *whether* an institution is legitimate. What is the standard against which we judge the legitimacy of an institution? Some approaches look at whether the institution meets its stated goals, for example, is the UN able to manage threats to peace and security successfully?[4] Others, such as the literatures previously described, look at the institution's ability to pursue actions independent of great power interests, which is quite an interesting notion since the post-World War II institutions were all built to give proportionate influence to the great powers to keep them committed to participating inside these institutions in the first place (Bosco, 2009; Jessup, 1949). Still others look to an institution's representativeness, that is, how democratic is it? Is representation equal (e.g., one state, one vote)? The implication here is that the more democratic an institution is, the more legitimate it is. As the enormous literature on democracies shows, however, more representative institutions may run up against effectiveness, a problem that contributed to the destruction of the League of Nations.[5] The concept of legitimacy, then, is set on shifting ground.

Bargaining theory offers no direct link to what we might understand as a legitimate outcome. We typically invoke our normative values for this task, but we might also consider one additional, less strict form of legitimacy, which is legitimacy by consent. Legitimacy by consent means that agreement about a course of action confers legitimacy on that action. It does not require that agreement be unanimous among all member states, merely that the agreement be reached through previously agreed rules of decision making. This notion of legitimacy avoids the conflict between equality and effectiveness

[4] This is most obvious in the UN peacekeeping literature (e.g., Doyle and Sambanis (2006); Fortna (2008); Gilligan and Stedman (2003)) and diplomatic writings of actual UN policymakers, particularly career bureaucrats (e.g., Boutros-Ghali (1999); Corwin (1999)).

[5] O'neill (1996) conducts a very interesting study on expanding the veto-wielding members in the UN Security Council which highlights this deadlock effect as well.

should it arise, allows for the fact that effectiveness is determined by more factors than the institution controls and is therefore too stringent a standard, while also capturing what may be the most fundamental feature of a legitimate institution—agreement. The recent literature on the signaling value of working through an institution adopts this understanding of legitimacy, which we detail further in Section 3.2.

3.1.2 A Spatial Model of Council Bargaining

The UN Security Council has a complicated decision-making process. As described in Chapter 2, there are specific, codified rules on voting procedures, membership in the Council, and agenda setting. There are also a variety of informal procedures, known as the provisional rules, which have changed only a little since the UN's founding, while some features, like the informal consultations, have come into greater use over the years. Fundamentally, our question is, under what conditions does the Council take action? For the spatial modeling we use in the following section, the action in question is when the Council will move the policy from the status quo position, an action we refer to as a status quo override.

A simplified look at how the preferences of Council members shape potential resolutions is useful. Voeten (2001) formalizes these features in a spatial model aimed at exploring how the possibility of action taken *outside* the purview of the UN Security Council affects the possibility of a status quo override when the Council is otherwise deadlocked, that is, the status quo policy falls between the two most extreme Council members, so any new policy will be vetoed without some outside consideration introduced into the bargaining. We adopt the same basic structure in this first analysis, but we relax the conditions that create deadlock to explore policy generation in all possible situations in the Council to derive testable hypotheses from broader conditions. Voeten's model gives us important insights into cases like Haiti and Kuwait, where outside options were fairly credible, but the analysis does not explain many other actions and resolutions in the Council where no outside options are credible and yet, resolutions and even peacekeeping occurred. For example, East Timor eventually received a UN peacekeeping mission, United Nations Mission in East Timor (UNAMET) despite having no significant third parties to provide military support for the independence movement. Our expansion offers an explanation for these actions as well. Next we convert insights from Voeten's specification into testable hypotheses about outside options and behavior inside the Council.

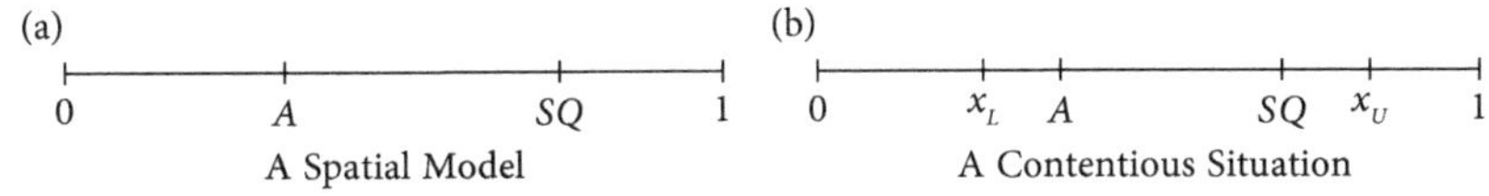

Fig. 3.1 Baseline spatial models of the UN Security Council

We begin with a unidimensional policy space arrayed from zero to one along which each member of the Council's most favored policy falls.[6] We can also represent the status quo (*SQ*) policy on this line as well as any proposed new policy (*A*) for comparison. We also place the ideal points of the two most extreme members on the policy space, x_L for the lowest extreme member and x_U for the highest extreme member. This setup is conventional for simple spatial modeling and is how Voeten (2001) starts his analysis of politics inside the Council. Voeten defines the payoffs to each Council member as the negative Euclidean (straight-line) distance between the member's most preferred policy and the agreed policy.[7] Thus, the farther away the realized policy is away from the preferred policy, the lower the payoff to the Council member.

Cooperative Conditions

Voeten's analysis makes an additional simplifying assumption upfront that limits his analysis to situations in which the status quo falls between the two most extreme veto members, a situation we call *contentious*, because the two extreme members prefer the status quo to move in opposite directions if it moves at all, making a new policy impossible to achieve without other

[6] The policy space represents a continuous range of policies for a given issue. The unidimensional nature of the policy space implies that there are two extremes with a range of options in between, so a unidimensional policy space is represented by a line. This is a very common assumption in bargaining analyses, though it is possible to consider multidimensional policy spaces as well. The unidimensional policy space might include different options depending on the issue under discussion; for example, considering a peacekeeping mission in a civil conflict might range from doing nothing, to sending a political mission, to deploying a small Chapter VI mission, to mobilizing a Chapter VII enforcement mission, and the various details that are more or less intrusive to the conflict. If the issue is about nuclear proliferation, then the policy space might range from doing nothing, to diplomatic pressure or increase to imposing sanctions, or even outright invasion. There are many facets to even these policies, but we can imagine them as roughly more or less intrusion. Further, there are often reasons to think the policy space is actually multidimensional if the Council is attempting to address several issues simultaneously or trading favors across more than one issue. Multidimensional policy spaces become very complex very quickly, so for tractability, we stick to one dimension.

[7] This payoff specification simplifies the analysis. Other spatial models employ a quadratic loss function specification for its curvilinear properties, which offer more flexibility in the policy space analysis. Both formulations assume particular shapes to the utility function, with the linear shape assuming that each step away is the same drop in utility as the step before it, while the quadratic loss function assumes that the farther away a policy is from an ideal point, the faster the drop off in utility. We stick to Voeten's specification where we expand on his model for comparison and move to the more flexible specification in a separate formal model in Section 3.2.5, from which we derive insights for the discussion of public costs.

influences. For our purposes, we want to understand how the Council functions and what output makes it through this very convoluted process, so our theory cannot be limited to only the contentious situations. A simple remedy is to consider what happens when the status quo falls outside the policy range between the two extreme veto members. These more *cooperative* situations occur when the status quo falls to the same side of all veto members, which we illustrate with Figure 3.2.

Assuming symmetric preferences,[8] when SQ is outside the range between the two most extreme veto members, some alternative policy (A) will always pass, as long as it falls in the range between SQ and A_m, where A_m is the mirror image of the SQ location around the veto member nearest SQ and defines the outer range of acceptable alternatives to the status quo. Naturally, this advantages the nearest veto member; however, all members get more utility out of the new policy. It also implies that when the status quo is outside the range between the extremes, there is some clustering of the permanent members. We can use this property to derive some expectations about the likelihood of a cooperative situation that will lead to an alternative policy to the status quo.

An SQ that falls in the regions shaded with slanted lines is a cooperative situation, so the larger those regions are, the more likely a cooperative scenario is. Figure 3.3 illustrates the difference. In scenario (a), the distance between the two veto member extremes is large, so the space outside of that range is small. If we assume that SQ is uniformly distributed (has an equal chance of falling

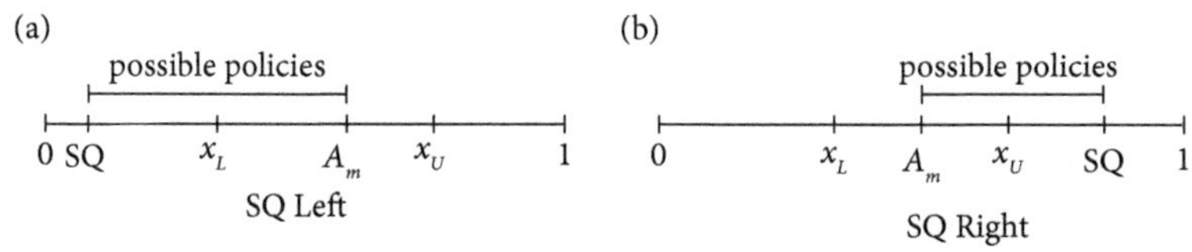

Fig. 3.2 Cooperative situations

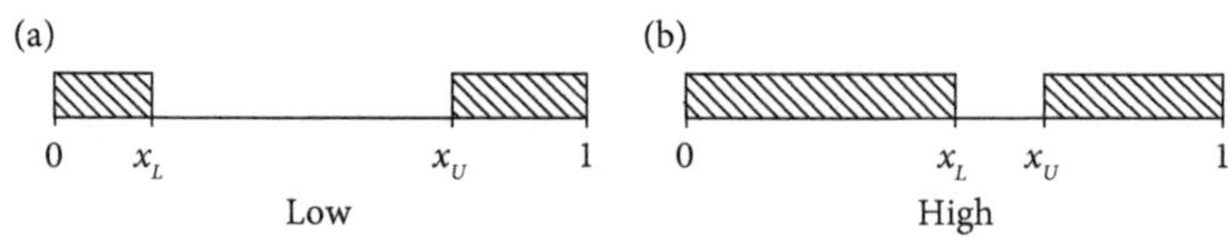

Fig. 3.3 Likelihood of a cooperative situation

[8] Symmetric preferences implies that the rate at which the Council member's payoff declines is the same whether the alternate policy is moving to the left or the right of the member's most preferred policy.

anywhere along the policy space), then it's simply less likely that a cooperative situation exists. Scenario (b), however, is one in which there is more space for SQ to fall outside the range between the extreme veto members, so a cooperative situation is more likely. In other words, the closer the veto members are clustered in their preferences, the more likely the status quo falls where every member would benefit from a new policy. This relationship implies our first testable hypothesis.

Hypothesis 1 *When the permanent members' preferences are closer together in a given year, more cooperation can happen, resulting in more interactions and more resolutions.*

The decision to hold a meeting under these conditions is straightforward. When all veto members would prefer a new policy to the status quo, the Council will hold a meeting. A further consideration is warranted however, since there are so many issues on the agenda and finite plenary time. We would expect the Council to prioritize issues that are most pressing, such as crises unfolding or issues in which a P5 member holds a particular interest. It is also important to note that cooperation does not rely on the Council members holding the same or even very similar preferences, merely that there are situations where the status quo falls outside of the spread of P5 preferences, and in those cases, they will be much more likely to reach agreement on a resolution.

Contentious Conditions (Voeten's Model)

The dynamics of status quo override become more complex when the situation is contentious between the veto players in the Security Council. Voeten (2001) explores this situation in great detail. Here, we review and summarize his primary analysis of the effect an outside option has on policy and generate testable hypotheses for observable behavior.

The contentious situation reflects the conditions modeled in Figure 3.1. In this model, there is no status quo override because any movement of the policy in a favorable direction for one veto member results in a loss of utility for the other member. Thus, without some other factor, the status quo persists. Voeten considers an important outside option: unilateral action by one of the veto members.[9] His model sets the two most extreme members at the two most extreme points on the policy spectrum such that $x_L = 0$ and $x_U = 1$.

[9] Voeten conceptualizes this as action taken by a superpower, but outside options can also be action taken by a regional institution or an ad hoc coalition.

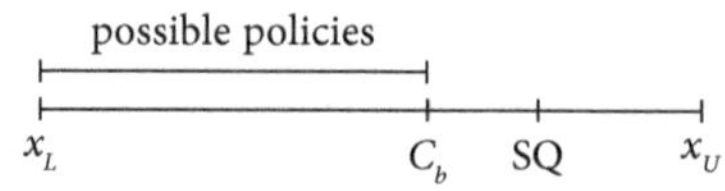

Fig. 3.4 Range of agreements with an outside option

Suppose the veto member with the outside option is represented at x_L.[10] Suppose further that there is a cost, C_b, to going it alone. This cost might include anything from material costs for being a lone intervener to the international costs that might accrue later on other issues where cooperation might be useful.

For the veto member with the outside option to choose to work inside the institution instead, the institutional payoff must be better than the unilateral payoff:

$$x_L - C_b < x_L - A$$

Since x_L is set to zero, the costs of unilateral action must be greater than the value of the alternative policy ($C_b > A$) for the veto member to choose to work within the institution. Thus, the costs to unilateral action can serve as a critical point on the policy space denoting what policies would be acceptable to the veto member considering outside options; any policy to the left of C_b would not be vetoed. The other extreme veto member would also accept any policy in the range $x_L < x_U$, because the right-most veto player is comparing the new policy to the unilateral intervention outcome (x_L), so all policies greater than x_L are strictly better than allowing unilateral intervention.

Finally, in the complete information case, from a repeated Rubinstein bargaining perspective, the realized policy would always be C_b because the two most extreme veto members know that any other offer would be vetoed by the other side and countered. Thus, the solution is to select the only offer acceptable to the two most extreme veto members.

In the original article, Voeten offered some compelling cases to illustrate the strategic dynamics captured in this spatial model, but what are the broader implications for Council behavior in terms of meetings and resolutions? Because we cannot accurately measure all of the possible alternative policies and compare to the status quo situation, we must focus instead on the observable actions that occur in the Council, specifically meetings and resolutions. The

[10] Voeten denotes the member with the outside option as a superpower, x_S, but substantively, this merely needs to be any veto member with a strong enough interest to act outside of the Council. There are many cases where veto members have opted to do so, though the US is the most frequent unilateral intervener. Further, his challenger x_C, is equivalent to our x_U.

logic presented in these formal derivations implies two hypotheses regarding the relationship between the likelihood of unilateral intervention and actions taken in the Council.

First, the possibility of unilateral intervention changes the dynamics of the Council. A simple policy model (Figure 3.1b) shows that an alternative policy is compared to status quo policy in circumstances in which there is no outside option such as unilateral intervention. One insight from Voeten (2001) is that the comparison is no longer between a new policy and the status quo but instead between a new policy and the most extreme policy that would be set by the Council member conducting a unilateral intervention. When the status quo is between the two veto member extremes, the policy is stable, unless there is an outside option. In these cases, the likelihood that the Council meets increases because the issue will move to a more extreme position if no compromise happens inside the Council. Further, because real situations involve uncertainty over whether unilateral intervention will actually take place, the more likely they think a unilateral intervention is to happen, the more likely they will meet to discuss the issue, at least to get more information and possibly to reach compromise short of unilateral intervention.[11]

Hypothesis 2 *A meeting for a particular issue is more likely when the preference of a veto member with an outside option is one of the two extreme preferences.*

Hypothesis 3 *A meeting is more likely when there is an increasing likelihood of unilateral intervention by one of the veto members.*

We could extend this logic further to relate it to resolutions, however; the spatial models presented in previous theory assume a pared down set of actions to examine fundamental steps in the bargaining process. Chapter 2 gives a detailed description of the formal and informal rules guiding Council actions including the different meetings that can occur as part of the bargaining process. Some meetings, such as those convened only to cast official votes, are merely placeholders where the compromise has already been struck. In the modern era, the bargaining really happens in the longer formal meetings

[11] Voeten (2001) solves an incomplete information model to derive the beliefs that must hold for potential intervener to make an offer and for the other members to accept the offer based on their beliefs about the credibility of the threat to intervene unilaterally. Veto members accept the policy offer when their belief that the potential intervener will back down is less than $\frac{c_B}{x_{SQ}}$. (In Voeten's specification, she uses $c_A + c_L$, splitting the costs for other modeling purposes. Our C_B term rolls them together.) As the costs of intervening increase, the policy offer moves more in favor of the opposite most extreme veto member, making action inside the Council more likely.

or the consultations. Delegations share more information through the meeting process, which shapes the content of a resolution before they vote on it. Without considering the constraints on each delegation, we cannot be certain that expectations about intervention will systematically lead to more or fewer resolutions.

We will now examine an understudied constraint in the Security Council, domestic and international *public costs*, a term we use to distinguish from the more widely used term, audience costs. Audience costs also refer to public reaction, in either domestic or international settings, to behavior that informs observers about some otherwise unknown characteristics about an actor. The concept of audience costs has taken on a more specific meaning in some literatures to refer to "the ability of a government to create a situation … in which it would pay a domestic political price for backing down" (Trachtenberg, 2012: abstract).[12] To avoid confusion with the concept used in regime-type signaling arguments, we define public costs to capture a specific, anticipated cost that states bear when an action reveals a state as one type or another; for example, will China take a hard line on North Korea or push back against Western pressure? Further, these costs are only possible if negotiations occur in a public setting that reveals the veto members' true underlying preferences and reservation values. We show how these external costs affect bargaining inside the institution and the kinds of processes they use to discuss issues in the Council.

3.2 Diplomacy and Public Costs

In addition to debates on independence and assessments of institutional outcomes, a third literature considers a function that institutions perform that is not written into the mission statement or list of sweeping goals an institution adopts as its *raison d'être*—informing domestic publics about the value of a particular policy proposal. Interactions between states have consequences for domestic constituents and international audiences. This literature approaches the relationship between domestic audiences and governments, with international institutions acting as information arbiter in between. That is, institutions can help less informed domestic audiences determine whether their own government's foreign policy goals are reasonable.

[12] It is unfortunate that this concept has become so closely associated with a particular form of costly signaling in democratic regimes since the concept of anticipated consequences for public action is enormously important in understanding any political behavior.

States develop and follow policies that are costly to them in the hopes that the benefits of the effort will outweigh those costs. Some of these costs are direct. How many citizens will be at risk as a result of a given policy? How much money and materiel will a policy expend? Costs for following a particular policy can also be indirect, however, and these indirect costs can have significant impact on future direct costs if, for example, the international policy is unpopular at home. International reactions can also impose costs, for example, with future international policies losing support from allies leading to smaller coalitions or high-cost unilateral action. States can take actions to try and reduce these costs, and one possibility is by providing more information about the legitimacy of a policy by gaining the approval of an international organization. Deciding to pursue policy through an institution or unilaterally is an important, strategic question examined in recent analyses.

This literature, however, focuses on how institutions can affect the relationship between a state contemplating a particular policy and relevant observers *outside* the institution that may decide to impose costs on the state. We contend that the impending public costs also influence what happens *inside* the institution. The benefits of signaling good policy to an external audience through institutional approval may undermine the ability of a delegation to negotiate a resolution closer to its most preferred policy. We develop a new strategic model to explore these dynamics.

3.2.1 The Informational Role of Institutions

An institution's ability to convey reliable information is dependent upon how legitimate that institution is perceived to be. In Section 3.1.1, we considered some of the ways the broader institutional literature defines the concept of legitimacy and offered a basic notion, that institutional legitimacy is derived from agreement that arises out of a bargaining process using a pre-determined set of rules for decision making. A robust literature on the informational role an institution can play relies on a similar understanding of legitimacy. This line of argument suggests that leaders go to institutions because multilateral approval is a mark of agreement among states with quite different interests. For example, Ian Hurd describes how regional peacekeeping has been criticized as neo-imperialist, an effort to exert control in nearby regions rather than a concerted effort to quell a resumption of fighting but resorting to approval in the Security Council helps reduce these charges (Hurd, 2002). The implication is that approval granted by an international institution for actions that may have self-interested motivation signals that there are other, acceptable justifications for action beyond mere parochial interests. Again, the normative understanding is important here, but the *agreement* among states is what confers the legitimacy (Finnemore, 2003; Hurd, 2008). Claude (1966) argues directly that conferring legitimacy is one of the primary functions of the UN.

Thompson (2009) adopts this same position regarding the Security Council, primarily because the Council's permanent members are known to hold quite disparate preferences over many important issues, such as the balance between interventionism and sovereignty. Agreement inside the Council means states that are not considered particularly like-minded feel the action is justified despite the variety and sometimes contradictory nature of their interests. Often, this logic is tied to the rationale of reducing international public costs to get cooperation through the institution as a cost-sharing mechanism. Third states, though, do not want to join efforts that primarily serve the self-interest of the state proposing the policy, so the institution helps signal the worthiness of the cause because working through an institutions brings its own, sometimes significant, set of costs (e.g., reduced options, delays, political capital, etc.) (Thompson, 2009).

Focusing specifically on institutional signals to domestic audiences, some have argued that institutions can serve to reduce principal-agent problems between informed leaders and less informed publics who must pay the costs for foreign policy (Chapman, 2007; Cortell and Davis, 1996; Smith, 1998). Recent formalizations of these dynamics show how domestic political considerations interact with the messaging capabilities of international institutions. Fang (2008) models this relationship directly to show how an international institution can help reduce electoral consequences of failed international policy, and that this possibility incentivizes leaders with private agendas (i.e., motivations that are not good for the domestic voting population) to mimic leaders who do not have a private agenda and instead prefer to pursue the most beneficial policy for the voting population. A related analysis considers variation in the type of institution as well as the type of leader. As Chapman (2007, 2011) argues, the ability of an international institution (specifically the Security Council) to send an informative signal to the domestic population about a leader's policy, the institution must send a message that *contradicts* the type of institution it is perceived to be. For example, if the Council is perceived to be conservative, then it only credibly signals when the policy it approves is sufficiently revisionist in nature to illustrate that the leader's policy is legitimate.

These studies have demonstrated the outward signaling value the Council provides to domestic and international audiences around the legitimacy of coordinated action. When Council members are able to reach agreement, audiences can make assessments over whether actions are justified. Our approach, however, examines the inward effects of the public costs on the ability of the Council members to reach agreement in the first place. In Section 3.2.2, we examine the inverted dynamic that arguably affects the quality of the signal external audiences receive and further whether anticipated public costs affect whether the Council deliberates in public or private.

3.2.2 Politics Inside the Institution

Delegations send signals to multiple audiences. Beyond the domestic constituencies and international actors, they are revealing information to their bargaining partners inside the institution. The signaling among bargaining partners has been most thoroughly studied in crisis bargaining absent an institutional context, but the literature does examine how domestic audience costs can alter bargaining dynamics with international actors (Fearon, 1994*a*, 1994*b*; Schelling, 1966; Schultz, 1999). Evidence abounds that institutions influence domestic audiences and domestic audiences influence institutions in other contexts outside the security realm. We show how these same dynamics carry over to security institutions and identify the conditions under which Council members will use commitment tactics (leveraging domestic/international public costs) to influence negotiations inside the Council and when they will opt for more cooperative tactics designed to avoid those public costs to reach agreement.

3.2.3 Leveraging Public Costs Inside the Institution

Bargaining is an expected part of cooperation within the normal operation of international institutions. Agreement, however, is not reached simply because members of an institution share broad goals of cooperation. Members often have different preferences over how an issue should be resolved, even if they agree something should be done.

Signaling models have been widely used to illustrate how certain costly actions can convey information that is otherwise unobservable.[13] For example, in the realm of conflict, costly signals might include mobilization signaling

[13] E.g., Fearon (1994*a*); Schultz (1999, 2005).

resolve; taking a public stance may also generate reputation costs for a leader (Lupton, 2020; Schelling, 1966). In the context of institutional bargaining, delegations can tie their own hands by going public with their positions, generating reputation costs from either domestic or international observers that could lead to direct costs (Putnam, 1988; Snyder and Diesing, 1977).[14]

A natural expectation from these analyses is that delegations that have larger public costs can push the negotiations in their favor. From a spatial modeling perspective, high public costs would force any agreement to be closer to the ideal point of that delegation. Strategic logic would predict that delegations would try to leverage better offers as they work out resolutions inside the Council, so long as it does not destroy a favored deal, by debating issues in a public meeting; however, we know that the Council often avoids public discussion or even any record of discussion using private consultations instead of public ones. The structure of agenda setting allows the Council president to choose the meeting format, suggesting that there may be a strategy to meeting selection that would affect the bargaining outcomes.

3.2.4 Avoiding Public Costs Inside the Institution

Secret diplomacy has a long history and was an important part of the French system of diplomacy that dominated Europe from the seventeenth century to the end of the World War I (Nicolson, 1954). Only with Woodrow Wilson's call for the creation of the League of Nations and openness did public diplomacy emerge. If the institution is focused on preventing conflict as well as the provision of information, secrecy may be an important facet of the organization's function. As Morgenthau (1967) notes, the primary objective of diplomacy is the "promotion of the national interest by peaceful means." Under what conditions will leaders choose to conduct their diplomacy in private, given that most of the research on crisis diplomacy suggests that public signals are the key to commitment? Kurizaki (2007) notes that the costs generated by going public simultaneously reveal information but also risk escalation. Leaders may prefer to use private diplomacy when they fear escalating a crisis or when the escalatory costs are higher than the informational benefits (Leventoğlu and Tarar, 2005). In the case of an institution like the Security Council, the

[14] Those direct costs might be some form of accountability or removing a leader from office, but they may also reduce cooperation or threaten other policy goals. These kinds of direct costs are not existential for a leader, but they are still costly and are certainly considered in decision making, as our cases illustrate.

alternative is often "do nothing," which means the issue is not addressed within the Council, and any attempts to settle an issue must be done outside of the UN's purview, which can be particularly costly to member states that choose a unilateral approach or a coping strategy to let the issue lie. Stasavage (2004) also makes a similar argument about international institutions that greater transparency can lead to worse outcomes because the negotiators are bargaining under the eye of constituents who can hold them accountable. They differ from our approach in that they model the uncertainty between representative and constituency; we model how those anticipated costs affect bargaining at the international level.

Private diplomacy should not be dismissed as purely cheap talk, especially because it can be shown to increase the range of acceptable agreements (Kurizaki, 2007). Private negotiations can allow for face-saving outcomes—like occurred in the Cuban Missile Crisis—which would be difficult if all negotiations were to be held publicly.[15] For private diplomacy to work, all parties must agree for the negotiations to remain private; this is not true of public diplomacy. Overall, private diplomacy is informationally inefficient, but not necessarily ineffective because it enables states to avoid escalatory maneuvers that result when public threats increase the costs of concessions and withdrawal to a level that makes fighting nearly inevitable.

Further, the recent literature on the role institutions play that considers the reverse relationship between institutions and domestic constituencies is relevant once again here. Fearing domestic costs for policies that a leader prefers but cannot easily convince the domestic constituency to support, a leader may appeal to an international institution for support. Under certain conditions, international support may be a signal that a particular policy is legitimate in the eyes of the international institution, which can signal to domestic audiences the worthiness of the policy (Chapman, 2007, 2011; Fang, 2008). In these cases, the public meeting can be a show of international unity designed to mitigate domestic political backlash for a policy that might have significant detractors at home.

Ultimately, delegations must decide whether they will pursue *commitment tactics*, which emphasize gaining leverage for intra-institutional bargaining or *cooperative tactics*, which seek primarily to mitigate domestic and international public costs for the sake of reaching agreement within the institution. While most of the literature on public costs focuses on the information

[15] A related argument suggests secrecy can help increase cooperation when information is proprietary or sensitive because actors are more willing to share in a secure environment (Carnegie and Carson, 2020).

asymmetry that they influence, we treat potential public costs as a choice in the Council—under what conditions will the Council work in public and leverage the effects of external public costs, and when will they choose to avoid them? We argue that one of the primary drivers of this decision is the expected likelihood of agreement under each scenario. We will now develop a simple formal model to examine how the primary actors decide on a meeting, decide how to vote, and how these decision affect the location of the agreement on a policy space. For the Security Council, resolutions are the agreements; the Council votes on them according to rules established in the UN Charter. The resolutions can contain material changes in policy that mobilize soldiers and money, alter jurisdictions and monitoring, and allocate resources to broad ranging problems, so they are non-trivial expressions of activity. Measuring and comparing the details of all resolutions, however, is not possible because there is no uniform scope and scale that can be used across issues to compare actual and proposed agreement terms. Existing measures of preferences in the UN, such as the Bailey, Strezhnev, and Voeten (2017) ideal points, offer only an annual measure of the general preferences of UN members across a range of issues. Our needs are more specific, in that we need to examine preferences on a particular issues. For this, we use qualitative analysis in Chapters 6 and 7.

3.2.5 Council Meetings and Information Flow

What can a meeting tell us about bargaining tactics? As the agenda-setting literature suggests, even agreeing to discuss an issue is a strategic decision. Because the Council also has a range of meeting types that differ in the amount of information communicated to outside audiences, meetings capture whether the Council wants to reveal the discussion taking place or keep those details confidential.

The Security Council retains control over its working methods, a set of rules that govern day-to-day procedures. These rules have remained "provisional" in status, a reflection that the rules are under the control of the Council members themselves and can be changed with relative ease at any time. Within these working methods, the Council has established several kinds of meetings, each with different allowances for who can attend, who may be invited to participate, and what information gets reported to the broader public. For our purposes, we are interested in two kinds of meetings. The first is the formal public meeting. These meetings are a matter of official record published by the UN so that all members of the UN and the broader public can read transcripts of the meeting, including the statements offered by each participating delegation. We focus on informal consultations to capture when the Council meets privately to discuss issues. Informal consultations are the most opaque form of meeting because no other UN members are invited to attend and no official record is kept (United Nations Security Council, 2012). Public meetings and informal consultations are the most frequently used forms of meetings, and their relative frequency has changed significantly over time.

The type of meeting, then, serves as a proxy measure for which strategy the Council ultimately pursues. If a public meeting is held, particularly one in which debate takes place (distinct from formal, public meetings in which only the vote is held), then the president of the Council decided to make these exchanges known to the public. This informs domestic and international audiences of what each Council member is willing to say publicly and is a way of invoking public costs by indirectly engaging the relevant audience prior to a decision being reached on the issue, according to the commitment strategy. Conversely, a public meeting may also be a way of demonstrating to domestic audiences that there is international consensus on a course of action. Finally, if the Council president calls an informal consultation, then all Council members are expected to keep the positions discussed private, or at least, without an official record. Observing an informal consultation is consistent with the cooperative strategy of attempting to reach compromise without invoking potential domestic and international public costs in the mix. This formulation treats meeting types as revealing different amounts of information. Where public meetings reveal all, informal consultations reveal activity but not positions, and the absence of a meeting leaves audiences in the dark.

We use a model with three stages to examine how issues move from the wide agenda reflected in the Council's weekly summary statement to the programme of work, the actual meeting agenda of the Council. As described in Chapter 2, the Council president sets the meeting agenda with assistance from the Secretary-General. Thus, in the first stage of the model, the Council president decides whether to hold an informal consultation, public meeting, or no meeting at all. In the second stage, a *penholder* delegation drafts the actual resolution text that the Council votes on in the third and final stage with an eye toward what will pass and what policy they most prefer.[16] We assume the penholder is a permanent member since historically it usually is.[17] We examine the agenda-setting process first without the possibility of an outside option. We then consider the situation in which one of the permanent members will

[16] Council votes are always taken in a public meeting. To simplify the model, we refer to public meetings substantively as those in which debate is open and recorded to distinguish them from consultations. Thus, in the model structure, if the Council president selects a consultation that moves to a vote, the vote occurs in a follow-on public meeting.

[17] Writing a resolution often involves all sorts of informal diplomacy, legal analysis, and logistical analysis. It is resource intensive for diplomatic missions; thus, capacity is a factor in why there is usually a permanent member involved in drafting resolution text.

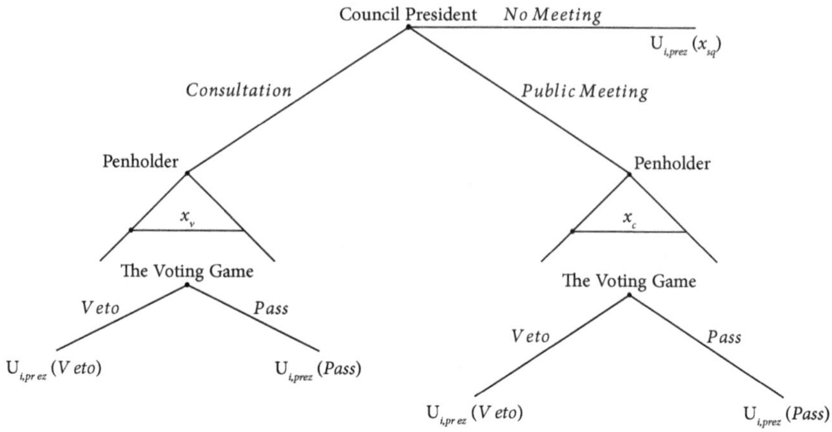

Fig. 3.5 An extensive form game of UN Security Council agenda setting

Table 3.1 Parameter legend

$U_i(x_{sq})$	Quadratic utility for Council Member *i* of status quo policy
$U_i(x_v^*)$	Quadratic utility for Council Member *i* of policy in public meeting
$U_i(x_c^*)$	Quadratic utility for Council Member *i* of policy in consultation
g	Multilateral costs, costs for implementing new policy
d	Cost for wasted plenary time, incurred only if discussion ends in threatened or realized veto
n	Unity cost, incurred for casting a veto
A_i	Public costs for actions taken through the Council
z_i	Public costs for not acting through the Council

act unilaterally if no action is taken in the Security Council, referring to this actor as the intervener and denoting it with subscript 0.

We use quadratic loss functions to define utilities for each actor in this analysis.[18] A quadratic loss function represents a curve that decreases from a peak value, where that peak value is the utility a delegation would get if policy is set at its ideal point. The farther away from that ideal point a policy is, the less utility the delegation gets from that policy. We index each veto member's preferences and unique costs with subscript *i*, such that $i \in \{1, 2, 3, 4, 5\}$.

Each decision taken also has specific costs associated with it. In the informal consultation process, a resolution that passes bears a multilateral action cost,

[18] Analyses in prior sections used Voeten's (2001) linear specification for consistency. Our analysis benefits from the continuous, differentiable nature of the quadratic loss function, with only a slight increase in the complexity of the solution, which is fully detailed in the Appendix A.

g, which is the same for all Council members.[19] These costs may be expensive, involving heavy outlays of troops and funding or they may be smaller costs, involving some diplomatic action with no material input, but they are assumed to be larger than zero. If the Council vetoes a resolution, the policy remains at status quo and all Council members pay an opportunity cost, d, representing the wasted plenary time in the Council. Any veto member who *casts* a veto additionally incurs a small, internal unity cost, n, representing the risk to reputation or future cooperative behavior in the Council on issues it cares about. In other words, a veto member who votes to pass a resolution even when another member vetoes it gets a slightly better payoff for voting to pass.

Following a public meeting, there are different, external public costs, that affect the payoff of each permanent member individually. There are two constituencies to consider in this scenario. There are some who might be dissatisfied if action happens through the Security Council; we represent this cost as A_i. There may also be a constituency that prefers action through the Council, so they would impose a cost, z_i, if veto occurs. Casting an actual veto also imposes the same internal unity cost, n, in the public meeting scenario.

Finally, any outcome that ends with no resolution, whether a veto or a decision not to have a meeting at all, leads to status quo policy and associated costs, if a meeting occurred. Figure 3.5 shows the extensive form game and reflects consolidated, simultaneous voting games at the terminal nodes. Tables 3.2 and 3.3 specify the payoffs for the outcomes in each voting game.

We solve this game with a subgame perfect Nash equilibrium concept. At the third node, the subgame is a simultaneous voting game in which the Council delegations are voting on a single resolution policy that the penholder has already chosen. There are two pure strategy Nash equilibria at this node, one in which everyone votes to pass a resolution and one in which a single delegation vetoes and all others vote to pass. The veto outcome reflects the fact that if any delegation casts a veto, all other delegations will prefer to vote to pass the resolution. A veto means all delegations get the veto outcome, status quo policy, but voting to pass in this case avoids the reputation costs (n) of voting against a resolution after going through the meeting process. That is, voting to pass a resolution if any other veto member casts a veto yields slightly higher utility for the same outcome.[20] As long as each delegation has

[19] It is unlikely that multilateral costs, g, are the same for all Council members. We assume g is the same across Council members for notational simplicity. Because we derive constraints in terms of g, we can actually see how different values of g for different members would shift the overlapping ranges of acceptable resolutions in the curve plots below (Figures 3.6a–3.9), rendering the assumption benign for our analysis.

[20] Vetoes are rare, and double vetoes are even rare, but they do happen. In this first iteration, vetoes never occur in this game because the Council president opts not to discuss issues that will not

Table 3.2 Payoffs in the consultation voting game

	Veto | All Pass	Veto | Veto	Pass | All Pass	Pass | Veto
Member i	$U_i(x_{sq}) - d - n$	$U_i(x_{sq}) - d - n$	$U_i(x_v^*) - g$	$U_i(x_{sq}) - d$
Council president	$U_{prez}(x_{sq}) - d - n$	$U_{prez}(x_{sq}) - d - n$	$U_{prez}(x_v^*) - g$	$U_{prez}(x_{sq}) - d$

Table 3.3 Payoffs in the public meeting voting game

	Veto | All Pass	Veto | Veto	Pass | All Pass	Pass | Veto
Member i	$U_i(x_{sq}) - d - n - z_i$	$U_i(x_{sq}) - d - n - z_i$	$U_i(x_c^*) - g - A_i$	$U_i(x_{sq}) - d - z_i$
Council president	$U_{prez}(x_{sq}) - d - n - z_{prez}$	$U_{prez}(x_{sq}) - d - n - z_{prez}$	$U_{prez}(x_c^*) - g - A_{prez}$	$U_{prez}(x_{sq}) - d - z_{prez}$

greater overall utility for a new policy than the status quo outcome, each will vote to pass a new resolution. These conditions are met when the new policy is closer to each member's ideal point, the costs of wasting plenary time are sufficiently high and the Council sees it as reasonably important to work together such that the action justifies the multilateral cost each member must bear.[21]

garner agreement. We relax this specification in a following section to examine vetoes in a complete information setting.

[21] The constraints on this decision are that

$$g < d + n - x_i^2 - 2x_i x_{sq} + x_{sq}^2 \tag{3.1}$$

for veto members following a consultation and

$$g < d + n - A_i + x_i^2 - 2x_i x_{sq} + x_{sq}^2 + z_i \tag{3.2}$$

for veto members following a public meeting, and that the resolution fall within the upper and lower bounds set by the veto member's ideal point and its distance (and reflected distance) from the status quo point, with adjustment based on costs. Further, the proposal under consideration must fall within the policy range defined below for each player. In the consultation scenario, this means

$$x_i - \sqrt{d - g + n + x_i^2 - 2x_i x_{sq} + x_{sq}^2} < x_v^* < x_i + \sqrt{d - g + n + x_i^2 - 2x_i x_{sq} + x_{sq}^2}, \tag{3.3}$$

and for the public meeting scenario,

$$x_i - \sqrt{d + z_i - g + n - A_i + x_i^2 - 2x_i x_{sq} + x_{sq}^2} < x_c^* < x_i + \sqrt{d + z_i - g + n - A_i + x_i^2 - 2x_i x_{sq} + x_{sq}^2}. \tag{3.4}$$

These functions are fully derived in the Appendix A. Figure 3.6 illustrates these decisions spatially.

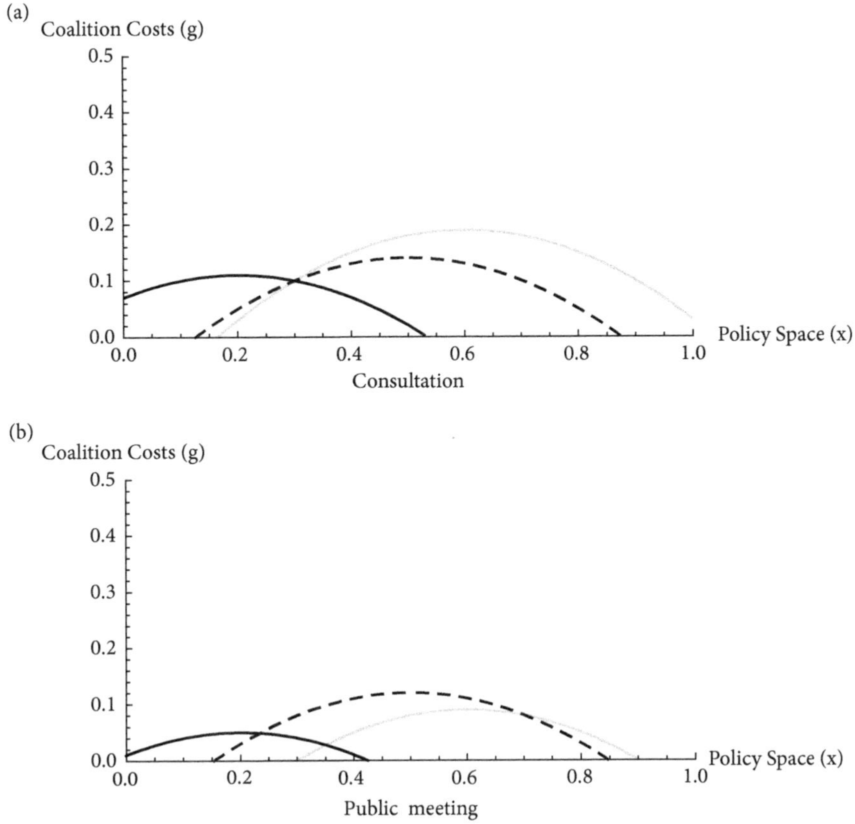

Fig. 3.6 The two plots reflect the different curves that result in different meeting settings (left-most member in black, middle member dashed and right-most member in grey). In both meeting settings, rising multilateral costs (g), narrow the range of possible alternative policies, converging on the status quo. With these public accountability costs, the range of possible policies in the public meeting is even more severely restricted.
Note: The left-most member (black line) prefers a policy at .2 with $A_1 = .1$ and $z_1 = .04$. The right-most member (grey line) prefers a policy at .6 with $A_2 = .15$ and $z_2 = .05$. The middle member (dashed line) prefers a policy at .5 with $A_3 = .08$ and $z_3 = .06$. We set $x_{sq} = .3$, the opportunity costs $d = .08$, and internal unity costs $n = .02$.

Figure 3.6a is a graphical representation of the dynamics drawn from the model where the veto member accepts any policy under its curve for a given coalition cost. These curves represent the boundaries of acceptable agreements for each actor, given a level of multilateral action costs (g). The black line represents the left-most extreme veto member (.2), the gray line represents the right-most extreme veto member (.6), and the dashed line represents a veto member with a preference between the two extremes (.5). We include only three players for visual clarity. The scenario is one in which there are veto players on opposite sides of the status quo, and including an opportunity cost. The y-axis represents rising coalition costs, g. As g increases, all of the veto members' ranges shrink such that above a particular value of g, here around .1, there is no agreement that all would pass. Further, as the coalition costs increase, the range of agreements converges on the status quo.

In the public meeting scenario, the public costs incurred for different, public behaviors can significantly alter the range of acceptable agreements. It is possible for the public costs paid for vetoing a resolution to overwhelm the utility for the status quo policy, yielding more flexibility regarding passage.[22] On the other hand, public costs incurred for passing a resolution may also greatly influence the location of the passage cutpoint, severely restricting the range of acceptable agreements. The difference in the public meeting is that these costs will vary across veto members, because each will incur different public costs depending on the issue, action, and domestic situation of the veto member. Ultimately, the larger the public costs for passage, the narrower the range of acceptable agreements, all else equal.

Proposition 1 As $z_i - A_i$ *increases, the range of acceptable agreements for member i also increases.*

Further, in relating the public costs for veto against the ones for passage, each mitigates the effect of the other, but if the public costs for passage overwhelm those for veto ($A_i > z_i$), then the larger the net costs, the more constrained the agreement range. This implies that the veto member with the largest net public costs for passage will be the most constrained, which reduces the range of acceptable agreements. Figure 3.6b shows the impact of public costs on each veto member's range of acceptable alternatives. Using the same preferences as in Figure 3.6a and adding in specific public costs for each veto member, the curves change dramatically, no longer crossing at the status quo because the public costs are unique to each player. According to the model, for a resolution to pass in a public meeting, one of two things needs to be true: (1) the costs incurred for vetoing a resolution must be far greater than the costs for passing it or (2) if the costs for passing a resolution are larger than the costs for vetoing,

[22] Formally, from Equation 3.2, as the net difference between z_i and A_i increases, the ceiling on g increases, expanding the curves in Figure 3.6b and widening the range of acceptable agreements.

they must be small enough to still yield a positive utility just by getting a better alternative policy in place.

In the actual process, a penholder delegation leads the resolution writing process.[23] Essentially, the penholder sets the content in the resolution that the Council will vote on. If the voting game following a consultation and/or a public meeting has overlapping agreement ranges for all five veto members, then the penholder can select a resolution that will pass from within that range such that the resolution maximizes its own utility within the confines of the agreement ranges of all five veto members.[24] If the outcome from the voting game is a veto, however, the penholder can select any resolution. To simplify the analysis, we suggest that the penholder would select its own ideal point in those cases, in case of an error in casting a vote by the vetoing delegation.[25]

The Council president chooses whether and what kind of meeting to schedule based on what the subgame perfect behavior would be in the following stages. Thus, she compares the policies that result from each process and chooses the one that provides the most utility to the president's delegation. One straightforward result in this model is that if any meeting is expected to end in a vetoed resolution, the Council president will elect not to discuss the issue when the delegation holding the presidency gains no benefit for allowing the veto.[26]

[23] For a quick overview of the penholder position in the Security Council, see this summary from the Security Council Report, a non-profit, non-political transparency organization supported by twenty-five UN member states who are not permanent members of the Security Council, http://www.securitycouncilreport.org/monthly-forecast/2013-09/in_hindsight_penholders.php.

[24] If the penholder is also a veto member and if the voting game has a pass equilibrium, then there exists a policy that the penholder will select and vote for in the third stage. If the penholder is an elected member, the penholder is still constrained by the veto members' ranges and cannot "go rogue" and kill a resolution that the veto members would agree to because one of the veto member delegations would simply write the resolution instead, circumventing an elected member penholder, who would not be able to veto it.

[25] This is a trembling-hand Nash refinement. It is possible to interpret actions in the Korean War along these lines. Since January of 1950, the Soviet representative had been boycotting the Council for refusing to expel the Nationalist Chinese delegation in favor of the People's Republic of China. At any time, the Soviets might have returned to vote, and surely would have vetoed the resolutions regarding Korea and providing support to repel the North Korean invasion. The US submitted a resolution prescribing multilateral support for South Korea while the Yugoslav delegation submitted one calling only for cessation of hostilities and UN mediation. The American draft was approved seven to one with two abstaining and the Soviets absent, while the Yugoslav draft was rejected (S/PV. 474). The Soviets knew these actions were happening, but they held out hope that the vote would be considered illegitimate, as revealed in a cable the Soviets sent to the Council following the resolution vote on June 27 claiming it was an illegal vote (United Nations Security Council, 1950). By the articles in the charter at the time, however, the vote was valid, so the Council carried on, and the Soviets learned from this tactical error. These events took place prior to the 1965 expansion of the Security Council and the voting rule change from seven votes in favor to nine in favor and without a veto cast (A/RES/1991 XVIII).

[26] We detail the conditions under which vetoes occur in a later section that discusses grandstanding in the Council.

Hypothesis 4 *When both public meetings and private consultations are expected to end in veto, the Council president will not put an issue on the agenda for discussion, given* z_i, $A_i > 0$.

Holding the Council presidency can potentially yield influence on the content of a resolution or even whether an issue will be taken up in the Council. The Council presidency rotates alphabetically, so there is no strategic process for determining who will hold the presidency. Further, because there are ten elected members and five permanent ones, the majority of the time the Council presidency is held by a delegation without veto power. This position represents a periodic opportunity to shape the Council's agenda and the output without requiring a veto power. Manipulating the working agenda does not guarantee the president will get her most preferred outcome, then again, neither does holding a veto. For elected members, the presidency offers more direct influence than being a sitting member without agenda-setting authority.

This analysis, though a simplified representation of the Council process, offers some important implications for understanding Council behaviors.[27] First, the process carves a space for elected members to exert some influence over the issues the Council discusses despite lacking veto power, but there are limits to consider as well. An elected member cannot stop discussion of an issue it would like to avoid when it does not hold the presidency. An elected member can, however, introduce an issue it wants to discuss during its month in the presidency that others have avoided in their months.[28] Canada has done this multiple times while holding the presidency.[29] It is also possible that veto members pressure elected members to put items on the agenda that they otherwise would not. While we found no evidence for this, it is admittedly difficult to observe. Given that the veto members themselves will hold the presidency in the future with certainty and given a more friendly president may be next to set the agenda, the urgency to pursue a pressure campaign is

[27] This formal structure does not directly incorporate the informal contact that these delegations share on a daily basis, which undoubtedly helps shape the work of the Council. As any study of international organizations or even domestic legislatures acknowledges, backdoor channeling happens in all of these contexts. We argue that informal contact justifies our assumption that the delegations are able to determine preferences and cutpoints with greater accuracy given the constant contact across a range of issues that the delegations experience daily.

[28] It is important to recognize that delegation capacity is an important consideration for an elected member to choose to raise an issue that has otherwise been ignored. For example, in 2016 the United States Permanent Mission employed 161 people while Ireland maintained a permanent mission with 11 people (ST/PLS/SER.A/306).

[29] See Chapter 7 for details on how Canada pushed through a discussion and resolution on the responsibility to protect (R2P) initiatives culminating in the passage of Resolution 1674 in 2005.

more complicated that it first seems. We do not model that dynamic, however, it deserves attention in future research.[30]

Second, it is possible for the delegation holding the presidency to leverage or suppress the influence of external public costs as a way to maneuver the content of a resolution. Beyond selecting an issue for discussion, the type of meeting can affect how delegations bargain over the content in a resolution, particularly what kinds of concessions and promises can be made in the eye of the public versus behind closed doors. North Korea's sixth nuclear test, conducted on September 3, 2017, elicited just such a calculation. The Council received a public briefing on the situation on September 4 in which reports verified an underground thermonuclear test. Statements during that meeting offered corroborating insights into why the negotiations over a response happened in consultation rather than a public meeting. First, the US Ambassador, Nikki Haley, emphasized this point, "The Security Council has spoken with unusual unity and consistency on North Korea," (S/PV.8039, p. 3–4). In the same meeting, however, the Chinese delegation proposed a solution, a suspension-for-suspension program in which the North Koreans suspend their nuclear development while the US discontinues large-scale military exercises with South Korea. The US anticipated this proposal and resoundingly rejected it before the Chinese delegation even spoke, setting the groundwork for a public split. The US wanted the Chinese to suspend all fuel sales to North Korea to put pressure on the regime to discontinue the nuclear program (Sanger and Sang-Hun,September 5, 2017). A week later, the Council met in consultation behind closed doors and negotiated the resolution that passed later that afternoon. Resolution 2375 included neither the suspension-for-suspension plan nor the complete fuel cutoff floated by, arguably, the two extreme position holders. Instead, it included level fuel sales to North Korea only and a series of stark sanctions on goods North Korea exports, a compromise position worked out privately in the consultation. The consultation shielded both the US and China from staking and holding public claims and instead afforded some flexibility to walk back from the possibility of no response from the Security Council. In this case, inaction from the Council seemed the worst possible outcome for both the US and China, reflected in their unified condemnation of the nuclear tests.

[30] Indeed, we do know that the veto members with connections to other institutions sometimes leverage that connection to influence how elected members vote, but that is a different behavior than agenda-setting. See, for example, Dreher, Sturm, and Vreeland (2009*a*), (2009*b*) and Vreeland and Dreher (2014).

Relatedly, the public costs can have a large impact on what deals delegations would be willing to accept. If the public strongly supports action through the Council, the delegation will be obliged to consider a wider range of proposals than it would in a closed setting. Conversely, if the external constituency prefers the Council not to act, then a public meeting process will restrict the range of agreements compared to a consultation process.

We derive two hypotheses from the formal solutions in the model. First, Hypothesis 5 reflects the fact that, all else equal, the presence of public costs paid for passing a resolution that did not match external constituent (whether domestic or international) expectations, is going to narrow the possible range of acceptable resolutions. As these ranges shrink, they become less likely to overlap. This result does not imply that no agreement is possible under any circumstances, it simply implies that those circumstances are less likely to exist, thus a veto decision for any single veto member is more likely. The model shows that Council presidents would rather pursue resolution success over failure or else not pursue discussion at all, a result that matches interviews we conducted at the UN in the Security Council Affairs division in the Department of Political Affairs. This dynamic, then, implies that consultations, not beholden to public costs, are more likely to be chosen as public costs increase for a public meeting. If the public costs for veto outweigh the costs for passage, the opposite dynamic prevails, widening the agreement range in a public meeting compared to a consultation. This scenario allows a Council president to leverage those public costs to get a reluctant veto member to play along more than it would in a private setting, essentially bringing public opinion to bear.

Hypothesis 5 *All else equal, and given a Council president seeking agreement, when the public costs for passing a resolution in the Council are larger than the public costs for veto, the likelihood of consultation increases because they constrain possible agreements, making a resolution harder to pass. Conversely, when public costs for veto are larger than those for passage, the range of possible agreements is wider in a public setting, making it more likely the Council president will select a public meeting.*

These effects highlight the Council president's role in the agenda-setting process. The presidency rotates alphabetically through the full council membership, so very frequently, an elected member holds the position, creating a way for the E10 to influence the process at particular junctures in the calendar. This structure means that a Council president has some influence even without carrying the veto. A Council president can neither prevent an issue from ever being discussed nor ensure that an issue is handled in the way she most prefers, but a strategic president can sway the discussion more toward her preference just by determining the meeting flow. Thus, the model shows that the Council president chooses the meeting profile that results in a Council policy that maximizes her expected utility. If agreement is possible, then she chooses the resolution closest to her preference, otherwise, she chooses not to discuss the issue at all.

Hypothesis 6 *The Council president is more likely to choose the type of meeting (consultation, public or none) that results in a proposal closest to the president's preferred resolution.*

Hypotheses 6 relies on spatial modeling insights to compare preferences and actual agreements along a spectrum. This technique of modeling is widely used in legislative politics, but it is notoriously difficult to measure quantitatively and compare on a common scale. Instead, we explore this hypothesis with qualitative work, which allows us to focus on the details of an issue and its many complicating facets to try and establish preferences, compare possible agreements and review the positions of the veto members in various policy statements inside and outside the UN's framework.

Adding an Outside Option

One of the fundamental aspects of Council decision making is the possibility of a superpower resorting to an outside option of unilateral action beyond the purview of the Security Council. Formally, this alters each player's comparison from one between an alternative policy and the status quo to one comparing an alternative policy to the superpower's ideal point set using outside means. The result of Voeten's analysis was to shift a situation in which no agreement could be reached to one in which a new policy would pass within the Security Council. We reanalyze our model and include an intervener with a credible outside option specified and denoted by the subscript 0 to consider how the decision process might change in this situation.

A credible outside option shifts the locus of agreements from the status quo to the intervener's policy preference point, just as happen with Voeten's model, creating the possibility that the range of observed outcomes will look very different to outcomes without an intervener. Figure 3.7 offers a comparison plot between a consultation and public meeting, where the solid black line and solid gray line represent veto members and the dashed line is the intervener. In the consultation scenario, the veto members' curves cross at the comparison point, in this case the intervener's most preferred policy. From there, the curves are differentiated by each veto player's most preferred policy. Because the intervener's costs for no agreement mean incurring the military costs for war, the intervener's curve moves more independently of the veto members, so it can define an agreement boundary under some conditions, while the most extreme veto members set the agreement boundaries under others. As the costs of war for the intervener increase, its willingness to accept agreements inside the institution that are farther from its ideal point increases, all else equal. The effects of the public costs on the veto members' choices are similar to the situation without an intervener.

Beyond a different locus around which the delegations define their acceptable alternative policies, the process proceeds quite similar to a situation in which there is no outside option. The penholder still sets the policy that maximizes its own utility within the range of acceptable agreements for the veto members (including the intervener). The Council president will choose whether to schedule a consultation, public meeting, or ignore an issue based on the payoffs from each scenario. Involving an intervener, however, means a delegation in the presidency could get a free policy change closer to its ideal point even if agreement within the institution is possible simply by refusing to discuss the issue. In fact, if a veto is costly to the Council president in both the private and public meeting processes, then the president has an incentive to ignore an issue, even when an agreement in the Council is possible. The logic is counterintuitive. The president is weighing an agreement bearing all the costs of a resolution inside the Council against the outcome for ignoring the issue. If the Council discusses the issue in a public meeting or consultation, the range of possible agreements is wider because just having the discussion ensures that the Council members factor in the costs of veto in their acceptable agreement ranges, making them wider. The Council president also has these considerations, but she is comparing the range of agreements that she would accept in the public meeting and consultation to the range of agreements that make ignoring the issue more profitable than working through the institution.

Proposition 2 *If* $d, z_{prez} > 0$, *there exists a range of resolution agreements that would be accepted in the Council, but the president would not select for discussion.*

A graphical representation illustrates the ranges under comparison in Figure 3.8. We assume that the Council president is also a veto member for

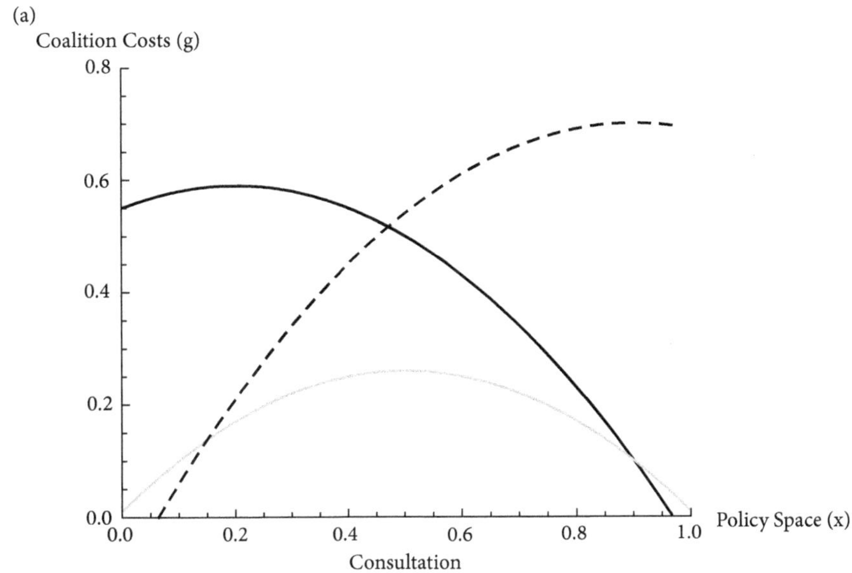

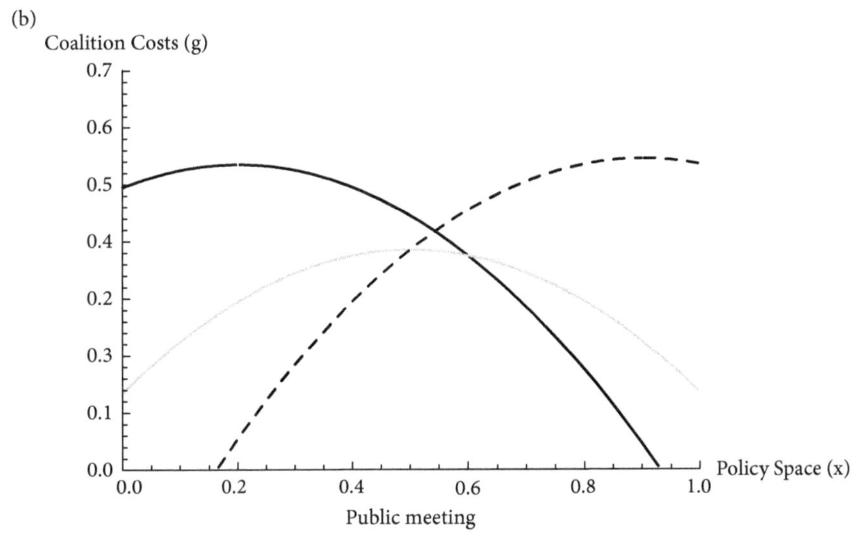

Fig. 3.7 These curves represent agreement ranges for two veto members and an intervener (dashed line) in two meeting scenarios. An intervener with an extreme ideal point significantly widens the range of options for the veto members; however, the intervener is also willing to compromise when the costs of going it alone (m) are high.

Note: We assume values of $x_0 = .9$, $A_0 = .1$ and $m = .7$ for the intervener (dashed line), $x_1 = .2$, $A_1 = .1$ and $z_1 = .18$ for the first veto member (black line) and $x_2 = .5$, $A_2 = .02$, $z_2 = .28$ for the second member (grey line). We set the unity cost $n = .02$.

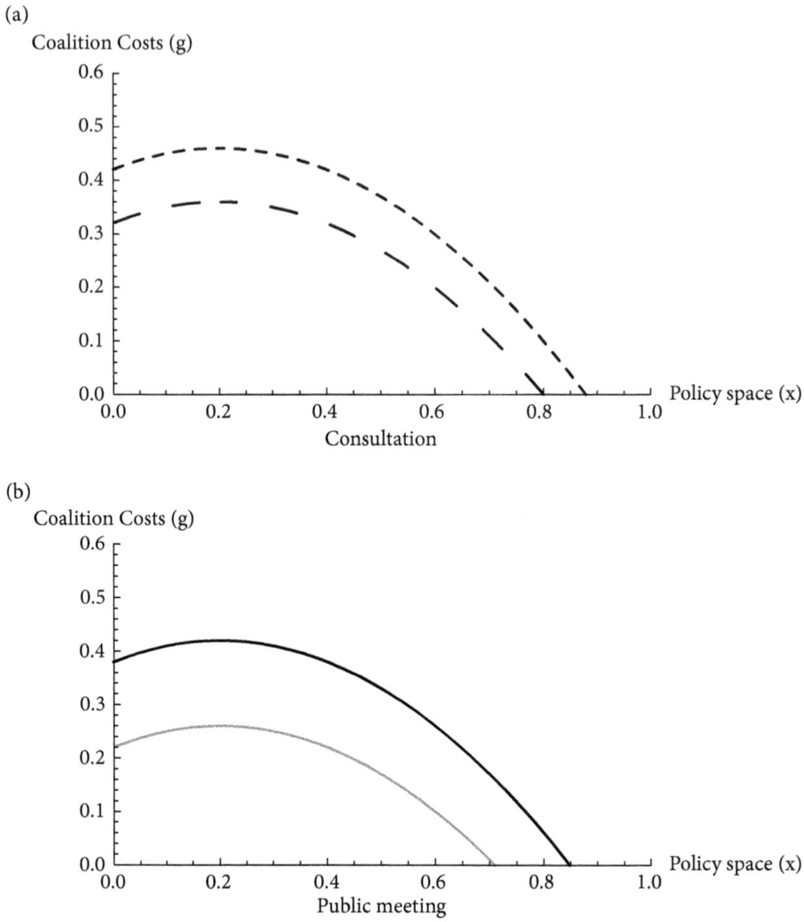

Fig. 3.8 These curves represent when resolutions are possible but ignored. When the anticipated resolution policy falls between the curves in each graph, it is better for the Council president to allow the intervener to act unilaterally, avoiding the multilateral and meeting costs that would accompany action through the Council.
Note: We assume the following values: $x_{i,prez} = .2$, $x_0 = .8$, d, $A_{i,prez} = .1$, $z_i = .06$ and $n = .02$.

consistency. Each graph overlays the range of agreements that are acceptable to the veto member in a meeting (the area below the tightly dashed black line in Figure 3.8a and the solid black line in Figure 3.8b) and the range of agreements that are preferable to the veto member at the first node, where she decides whether to hold a meeting at all (depicted by the widely dashed line in Figure 3.8a and the gray line in Figure 3.8b). The region of each graph between the two curves shows resolutions that would be acceptable in the meeting but are not better than ignoring the meeting for the Council president. In other words, it is better for the president to ignore an issue if the anticipated resolution policy realized lands between the curves for a given multilateral cost. Because the policy would end up close enough to the expected resolution policy without incurring the costs associated with the resolution, the president can simply allow the intervener to proceed. As the Council president's ideal point moves closer to the intervener's ideal point, the curves shift toward the x-axis, meaning they contract. Thus, the closer the Council president's ideal point is to the intervener, the more likely she will choose to ignore an issue with an outside option.

Grandstanding

During the Cold War, the relationship between the US and the Soviet Union clearly had a restraining effect on Council activities. Following the UN intervention in Korea in 1950, the Soviets maintained a presence on the Council and voted accordingly. The impression of deadlock in the Council, however, is a bit exaggerated. The Council still passed more resolutions than vetoes in most years, but it is clear that activity in the Council was less frequent and that the ratio of vetoes to resolutions was higher than it is today.

Conventional wisdom tells us that the distribution of preferences during the Cold War explains the patterns of resolution and vetoes because the Western Three held preference so far removed, spatially, from the Soviet Union and China. Aggregate, annual measures of ideal points confirm a more heterogeneous set of preferences during this period, but the model of Council agenda-setting we have presented shows that divergent preferences are not enough to explain the larger ratio of vetoes. Recall that the model can end in a resolution that passes or fails *or* it can end with issues languishing on the agenda that are never discussed in the Council. This means that divergent preferences might end in a pattern of vetoes, or it can end in a pattern of no meetings. So what else explains the variation in meetings and veto ratios? As specified, the model biases outcomes toward avoiding confrontations in the form of a veto. The payoff structure penalizes all Council members for a veto (in the form of opportunity costs) and further penalizes the vetoing member with a reputation cost. We know that vetoes happen, and it's plausible that they occur unexpectedly, like the Chinese veto against extending the United Nations Preventive Deployment (UNPREDEP) mission in 1999. We argue, however, that often they are perfectly anticipated and serve a different purpose, to publicly state a position in opposition to other Council members' preferences. We refer to this as grandstanding.[31]

Because the model already incorporates public costs for both veto outcomes and resolution passage, we need to relax a single constraint to make vetoes observable in the model. Whereas we assume $z > 0$ in the first analysis, allowing $z < 0$ introduces a positive utility boost for a veto outcome when z is negative. Thus, under some conditions, the benefit of a veto outweighs the reputation cost and can generate a scenario in which a public meeting happens, the veto members stake positions, and a vote yields a failed resolution. The vetoing delegation gets an audience boost in utility for that outcome.[32] In other words, there is another factor beyond preferences that drives Council action all the way to a veto – public costs. Recall from above, divergent preferences may yield weaker resolutions or no meetings at all, not just vetoes. So some other factor may also be important, a factor like domestic opposition to the policy under consideration in the Council at the moment.[33] Figure 3.9 overlays the decision curves at the last stage and the first stage for the Council president when $z_{prez} = -.2$. Compared to Figure 3.8b, Figure 3.9 shows that the gray curve now encompasses the black curve, meaning there are resolutions for which the Council president will agree to a public meeting but will veto in the last stage. The difference between the scenarios in Figures 3.8 and 3.9 are that the president's payoff for allowing the veto to occur is larger than the payoff to ignoring the issue. Further, if we decoupled the president from the vetoing member (say in a situation in which the Council president is not a veto member), then both would have to gain some net positive utility for an observed veto to choose to hold a meeting and cast a veto. The voting game in the last stage still results in only one member vetoing since there is still a reputation cost to being the vetoer that reduces the utility for a veto outcome.

[31] In fact, with the daily interactions among delegations in the Council and the highly informal communications around issues, it's difficult to imagine that the Council members cannot be sure how their fellow delegations will vote. The question then is, why do they decide willingly to push the issue all the way to a veto? Our explanation is that they get a utility boost from their domestic or international audience for rejecting the new policy publicly. Groseclose and McCarty (2001) offer an analysis of the politics of blame in the American politics literature that expands on the logic we describe here.

[32] There is still only one vetoer in the voting game since one veto rewards all who benefit from a veto, even if they are not the ones who cast the veto. In fact, those with a veto boost gain while avoiding the reputation costs, just as in the original specification.

[33] This refinement is relatively unsophisticated; however, it introduces results that are observed in the Council and incorporates insights from analyses of signaling to outside audiences, particularly as Chapman (2007, 2011) argues that support or refusal from the Council can be meaningful to publics trying to decide whether to trust their own policymakers. Vetoing a policy in the Council can alter support for a policy—especially if a veto member chooses to pursue an action outside of the Council.

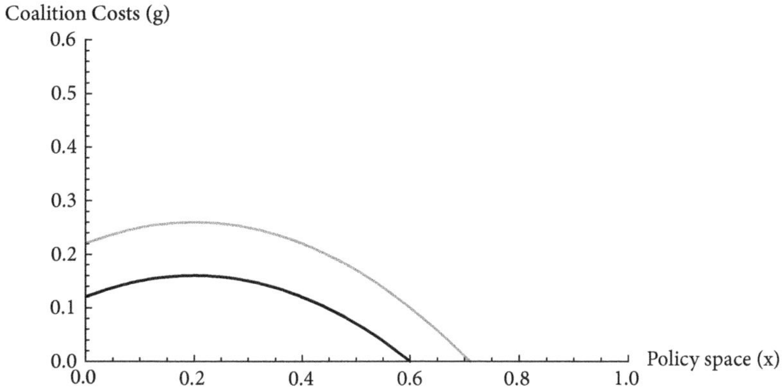

Fig. 3.9 A Grandstanding Scenario

Relaxing the restriction on the z parameter reveals another way that the Council president has leverage when we include public accountability into the model. In this scenario, a veto generates a public benefit, so while it shifts curves the same way A_i does, we interpret it as boosting a delegation's payoff when a resolution visibly fails in the Council. A recurrent example of this is when the US is forced to veto resolutions condemning Israel for various actions against Palestinians, most recently in June 2018, but consistently since the 1970s.[34] The issue of Palestine has frequently split the Western Three, sometimes with France voting for the resolution while the UK abstains and the US vetoes while other times, the US is alone in its dissent. These episodes are very public declarations that the US holds an outlier position on this issue.

This dynamic is characteristic of, but not limited to, the Cold War era. We can see this boost in utility for a veto with France's threat to veto a war resolution in the Council in early 2003 regarding Iraq. While there were complex issues driving French preferences over military action in Iraq, polling evidence shows a clear, domestic benefit to threatening a veto in the Council because a majority of French citizens polled in a Pew study did not support military action in Iraq (*A Year After Iraq War: Mistrust of America in Europe Even Higher, Muslim Anger Persists*, 2004).[35]

[34] The one exception was a US abstention to a resolution on the "Palestine Question" in 2016 condemning Israeli settlements in contested areas. The stated justification for abstaining instead of vetoing was the resolution's emphasis on reducing terrorism and violence against civilians (UN Press Release SC/12657).

[35] Further questioning in the Pew poll showed that French citizens disliked President George W. Bush as the problem rather than the US as a whole, suggesting personal blame and a wish to thwart his efforts in Iraq.

The analysis in this section thus far has focused on public costs and the presidency, but we emphasize that the president operates within the confines of what is passable. The preferences of the permanent members figure prominently in this determination, which is why the voting game is built into the meeting selection model. Veto players must be accommodated in policy bargaining, and since the Security Council has five veto players, each must view the policy inside the Security Council to be better than the status quo situation and better than what unilateral action outside the institution would produce. Hypotheses 2 and 3 capture these issues for the likelihood of resolutions, but we need the meeting choice analysis to help us explain how the Council gets to a resolution vote or not and why the Council chooses to meet publicly or privately.

In the meeting choice game, the Council president is strictly better off avoiding issues that are so contentious that no agreement is possible among the permanent members. Functionally, meetings on issues that have no chance of passing waste time that could be devoted to issues on which the Council might be able to act. As the institutional signaling literature suggests, however, actions in the Council can also inform domestic and international audiences about many aspects of an issue and the options available to address it, including revealing delegation preferences to domestic and international audiences in the form of public bargaining. Thus, there are times when the permanent members might wish to keep their preferences private or times when they might wish to try and leverage public costs.

3.2.6 Alternative Explanations

Here, we consider alternative explanations for the behaviors we observe, the decision to hold a meeting, and whether that meeting is on the public record or not. Two major approaches and one less prominent but still important perspective are relevant here. First, is the argument that the US delegation leads the UN body with direct and indirect methods of influence. This strand of reasoning runs through several research areas relating to the Council, from peacekeeping missions and where they are sent to questions on why elected members choose to run for a seat in the Council (Andersen, Hansen, and Markussen, 2006; Bennis, 1996; Dreher, Sturm and Vreeland, 2009*a*, 2009*b*; Gibbs, 1997; Kuziemko and Werker, 2006; Stone, 2011; Vreeland and Dreher, 2014). Areas that seem unrelated are nonetheless connected by an argument that the US is the weight-bearing member and therefore wields enormous control inside the Security Council, irrespective of procedure and rules. It's plausible that the US exerts pressure on the other delegations to bring up issues or kill issues that it does not want to discuss. If this is the case, then the meeting agenda would follow American interests quite closely. The discerning test is whether delegations can raise issues that the US does not want to discuss, and further, whether a compromise can be reached. An alternative angle to consider is whether the US can raise issues that are expressly forbidden by other Council members. We entertain this idea most directly in the case studies where we can trace the direct and indirect influence of the US delegation in actions beyond formal statements and voting records. A strict interpretation of this perspective would predict American dominance on issues brought up in the Council and resolutions that reflect the US' most preferred policy for any given issue. A more nuanced understanding of this argument would be that the US wields influence where it can through multiple means of getting other Council members to agree with its stance, thus resolutions would lean toward the US more and the agenda would roughly follow the pattern of changing US interests over time. Depending on the degree of the lean, however, this more nuanced interpretation begins to dovetail with our analysis in what patterns we might expect to emerge just from the standard operating procedures of the Council as written in the Charter and the provisional rules.

The second approach comes from the Cold War perspective that behavior in the Council was for the benefit of the home audience (Putnam, 1988). For example, the Soviet Union might speak in a public meeting to demonstrate disagreement with the American delegation, and even if a vote was carried out, would veto. The US adopted the same tactics, as did the other western veto members to reinforce the divide between the Soviets and the West. Under conditions like these, there is no consideration for the benefits of cooperating on issues (Snyder and Diesing, 1977). Instead, the Council members want to use those public costs to stake their position and refuse to budge, but this approach also leads to all public meetings and many, many vetoes. In fact, the only agreements would be ones where the delegations could not muster public costs or where the audiences all want the exact same policy; both are rare conditions. Further, what does an explanation like this mean for the Council today? It seems most connected to the policy signaling role the Council plays for audiences who might be less informed about the legitimacy of their leader's foreign policy (Chapman, 2009; Chapman and Reiter, 2004). These claims about actions in the Council are less competing explanations to ours and more complementary in that they rely on some of the features we highlight to explain how the Security Council might influence external audience opinion.

Instead, we examine how external audience opinion influences actions inside the Council.

Finally, the activities of the institution may simply be directed by what is happening in the world as it addresses events related to the Security Council's primary purpose, maintaining international peace and security. This perspective suggests a very functional and reactive orientation where action in the Council happens in response to crises: military, humanitarian, natural disasters or otherwise. Related to this, but somewhat different, is the expectation that the increased bureaucratization of the UN in general has generated much of the activity we observe. There are now committees on the Security Council, new (separate) divisions within the Secretariat that support peacekeeping and peace-building efforts that gives the Council a bureaucratic, automated character. This last perspective is hardly considered in the political science literature on the Security Council because we view it as such a politicized arm of the UN. Indeed, it was built to be so, but there is no doubt that studies also consider action in the Council to be reactive when they measure crisis occurrence or bureaucratic when they account for standard review practices for peacekeeping missions (Allen and Yuen, 2014). We consider these explanations as well in our analyses.

3.3 Observable Implications and Research Design

The models we've presented in this chapter identify several factors that explain activity in the UN Security Council. We first examine the distribution of preferences using basic spatial modeling. From this, we determined there could be two states of the world, one in which the veto members all prefer some change in policy in the same direction (the status quo policy falls to one side of all the veto members), which we consider to be a more cooperative setting, and one in which the status quo falls between the veto members' most preferred policies, which we call a contentious scenario. We noted that cooperative scenarios imply that the veto members are more closely clustered together, so we expect more cooperation on average when they hold preferences that are close together. We also revisited Voeten (2001) to examine what factors could make a contentious scenario more cooperative. The prospect of unilateral action on the part of a major power can have this effect, according to his spatial model. We qualify and extend the logic to explain action in the Council, that is, that as the likelihood of unilateral action increases, the Council will be more likely to take up the issue for discussion. Both of these insights lend themselves to large-N statistical tests, which we conduct in Chapters 4 and 5 using aggregate annual data and new monthly, agenda-item data in the former and estimates of the likelihood of an outside option in the latter. While spatial theory has implications for what a resolution would look like given the possibility of unilateral intervention, measuring policy locations across issues in a way that allows for cross-issue comparison is not possible, so we use qualitative methods of analysis which allow for detailed comparison of each delegation's position and the final resolution text.

We also presented a new model of the Council's agenda-setting process. Prior models of the Council pay close attention to the veto-wielding members, but the process provides opportunities for elected members to influence the Council's agenda in ways previously ignored in the literature. Further, we incorporate domestic and international public costs to examine how outside pressure affects the range of agreements that can arise inside the institution. The model shows that a delegation in the Council presidency can select particular issues and direct the method of discussion down either a public or private path. These two paths shape the possible range of outcomes, depending on the relative public costs along the public path. We illustrate these influences with three cases, the pattern of discussions around North Korea's nuclear testing and missile development, strategic meeting selection and grandstanding in Kosovo, and the Council's decision to take up the protection of civilians in armed conflict (the Responsibility to Protect issue).

4

Anticipating the Deal: Agenda-Setting in the UN Security Council

Why are some threats to international peace and security handled in the Security Council while others are not? During the Arab Spring, why was the Council actively involved in the politics of Libya while it was nearly silent after the 2013 coup in Egypt? In the last chapter, we presented several hypotheses that address the question of what the Council chooses to discuss. Here, we test two insights from those models using new data on Council behaviors. Our focus is on the decision-making process that leads to issues being discussed in the Council. First, we explore how differences of opinion between the permanent members affects the agenda. Intuitively, we assume that tensions and disagreement between the permanent members will affect when action will be taken within the Council, but we employ newly collected data to test Hypothesis 4 empirically.

Often, studies of the Council focus on resolutions. We take a step backwards to the agenda-setting process that leads to the resolutions that the Council votes on. No resolution can pass on an issue that is not placed on the Council's agenda. Every member of the Council has the opportunity to influence the agenda when they serve as Council president. The presidency rotates alphabetically, giving every member—permanent or elected—a voice in what the Council discusses and debates.

A great deal of scholarly attention has focused on the powerful permanent members and how they utilize the Security Council, and given the data limitations of past analyses, it can be difficult to test whether the agenda-setting process is meaningful or merely reproduces what the permanent members want. The Security Council Agenda Item Data (SCAID) allows us to explore whether the institutional features allow for different patterns of behavior for different presidents. We do this by comparing how permanent member presidents behave compared to elected member presidents. Because of the previous focus on the permanent members, less is known about the behavior of elected

Bargaining in the UN Security Council. Susan Hannah Allen and Amy Yuen, Oxford University Press.
© Susan Hannah Allen and Amy Yuen (2022). DOI: 10.1093/oso/9780192849755.003.0004

members, and annual data provided no avenue to know when an elected member was directly responsible for action in the Council or not.[1] In this chapter, we analyze whether or not elected members make different decisions than their permanent member counterparts regarding agenda-setting using new monthly data. Elected members have limited time on the Council and less influence on Council outcomes. We believe these factors should make their agendas look different from the permanent members. If E10 agendas look different than P5 agendas, then these findings would suggest that elected members do have some independence from P5 preferences because the institutional rules allow it.[2]

Do elected members place the same types of items on the agenda? Elected members might have greater concerns about security threats nearby. Unlike permanent members, they lack the ability to project power all over the globe. Their domestic populations would want to see them advocating for the Council to assist in addressing violence that may be nearby. If this is true, then elected members would put more geographically proximate countries on the agenda than permanent members will.

On the other hand, elected members might be interested in using the Council to advance their foreign policy goals. They may choose to put issues on the agenda associated with countries who have similar policy preferences to them in an effort to solve conflicts in ways that help an ally or state with demonstrated shared interests. Bringing the troubles of a politically aligned nation to the Council draws global attention to the problem, potentially yields some action, and if not, may present the opportunity to shame powerful nations who refuse to compromise on a form of action.

Elected members also might use their agenda-setting power to advance thematic issues like human security, climate change, and the plight of refugees. With limited time and resources, the Council cannot respond to all issues, so the strategic choices Council presidents make about which issues to place on their calendar tell us a great deal about their decision-making process.

[1] Mikulaschek (N.d.) on the influence of African members on the Security Council is a notable exception.

[2] Because there are no easy ways to measure public costs quantitatively or place policy options and preferences on a universal policy space, we must test some of our ideas using indirect methods. Thus, while we are primarily testing how the likelihood of veto affects whether an agenda item is discussed in the Council—the selection effects in Hypothesis 4—we are also testing one element of Hypothesis 6, that some Council presidents do in fact have different interests than the veto members, and they show up in the Council's agenda.

4.1 The Activity of the Council

Since the end of the Cold War, the UN Security Council has been much more active (Figure 4.1)—holding more formal meetings and informal consultations as well as passing a greater number of resolutions. The Council has engaged in more binding action during this time period as well, passing at least 145 Chapter VII resolutions during the 1990s alone. These resolutions are not just binding for Council members, but all members of the UN.

The end of the Cold War kicked off a new era of cooperation in the Security Council, but political tensions between the permanent members have not disappeared completely since then. Regardless of the international climate, the Council has remained a center of international diplomatic activity as Figure 4.1 illustrates. There is a brief dip after 2003: US and UK's failed efforts to bring the Security Council in on the invasion of Iraq that led to the overthrow of Saddam Hussein, but activity rebounded quickly. Tensions between members over the Syrian civil war have persisted but seemingly have not stood in the way of the Council taking action on other issues. In 1988, the Security Council met publicly fifty-five times and passed twenty resolutions. In 2018, the Council met publicly 275 times and passed fifty-four resolutions.

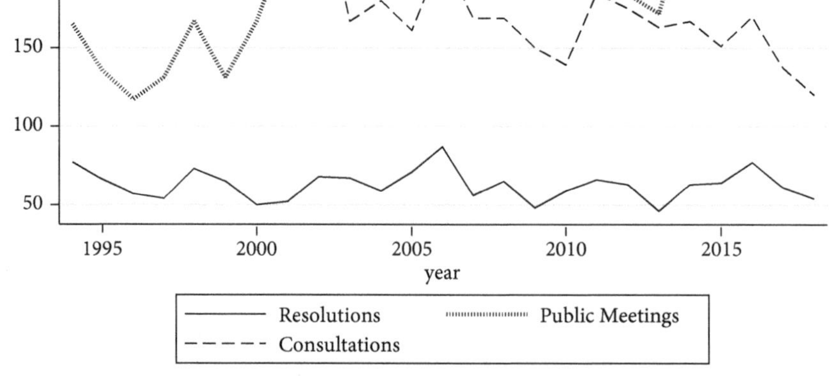

Fig. 4.1 Security Council Activities, 1985–2015

Despite this uptick in activity, not all threats to international peace and security have received attention (or equal attention) from the Council. Not all issues that are discussed by the Council result in resolutions. To understand these patterns of behavior, we must dig further into the process by which issues are selected for discussion.

4.2 Setting the Agenda

How does the Council decide what to discuss? The selection of agenda items shapes the resolutions that pass. In Chapter 3, we formalize the agenda-setting process to explore what determines whether an issue is ever taken up by the Security Council. In this chapter we focus on two central influences: the preferences of the permanent members and those of the Council president.

Hypothesis 4 argues that issues likely to end in veto are less likely to be selected for discussion in any meeting type. Thus, we can examine data at the issue level (rather than at the annual level presented in Figure 4.9). These tests will be specific to particular national issues. We focus first on the relationship among the permanent members to test whether or not agreement about countries that are the subject of potential agenda items increases the likelihood that meetings or consultations are scheduled related to that agenda item.

We also considered the role of the Security Council President—a monthly, alphabetically rotating position in which both elected and permanent members periodically sit. Since there are ten elected members, most of the time an elected member is the Council president. On the other hand, each elected member only serves as president once or at most twice during their time on the Council.

Each month the president sets the Programme of Work (the official term for the Council's working agenda). Plenary time (the available time for the Council to meet) is finite, and no agenda-setter wants to fill that time with discussions that will end in deadlock. Discussing issues that are doomed to fail represents a waste of precious time that could be devoted to other issues that might have some chance of generating a resolution that the members agree on.

Past scholarship on the elected members has focused primarily on how seats on the Council might generate side payments connected to how that member votes in the Council, though David Malone does mention that holding the presidency might also be a motivation to run for a Council seat (Dreher, Sturm, and Vreeland, 2009*a*, 2009*b*; Kuziemko and Werker, 2006; Malone, 2000). Shifting this focus, we assume that serving as the Council's president for a month and setting the agenda can be a valuable political opportunity for an elected member. Since this opportunity is limited, they are unlikely to schedule issues that they know will lead to resolutions that will not pass.

A country's time as president is limited, and the space on the Programme of Work is limited. On average, fourteen public meetings are held each month along with thirty-two consultations. More notably, resolutions do not pass with greater frequency when elected members hold the presidency—roughly five resolutions pass per month throughout the period, regardless of who the Council president is. In terms of the volume of work, the Council's actions are consistent regardless of which nations hold the presidency. Presidents must choose carefully what issues to place on the agenda if they hope to advance their policy preferences.

4.2.1 Tracing the Council's Agenda

To understand how the UN Security Council makes choices about agenda-setting, we need more information about the process. For each year, we collect the Security Council's Summary Statement of Matters on which the Security Council is Seized for the years between 1994–2015, which helped us track which agenda items were on the Council's master agenda in a given year (and thus could potentially be on the Programmes of Work in that year). As discussed in Chapter 2, the Summary Statement is one of the two parts of the Security Council's agenda, and it is a complete list of all the topics that have ever been brought to the attention of the Council but have not been deemed fully resolved. While the UN has made this information available on its website, the data has not been collected systematically and analyzed. Our data collection efforts make this analysis more expansive than existing data allowed, offering new quantitative data on the Council agenda, across years and issues.

After creating a list of possible agenda items, we turn to the UN Journal. Provisional agendas appear in the *UN Journal*, a publication of the UN that details all the meetings of major bodies that are expected to happen at UN Headquarters in a given day. Using the journals, we were able to see when the Security Council planned to meet on particular agenda items and when items were first brought to the Council's attention.[3] Beginning in 1946, the Journal was published in hard copy form but more recently, the Journal has been

[3] Date of the first appearance of agenda items was cross-checked using the UN Security Council Repertoire, which is available online and contains a table of first appearances (http://www.un.org/en/sc/repertoire/data.shtml).

made available each day online (https://journal.un.org). From the journals, we code which agenda items were the topic of both formal public meetings and informal private meetings. Journals have been digitized back to 1993, but the primary topics of informal consultations were not listed in the Journal until 1994, which frames our time period.[4]

With these daily records of Council meetings, we then count the number of meetings held on a particular agenda item by month and by year. For the analyses in this chapter, we use the monthly data. These data cover more than two decades from 1994–2015, which is an interesting period in the Council's history. This period encompasses the initial post-Cold War enthusiasm for the Council, the frustrations following peacekeeping failures in Rwanda and Somalia, a resurgence in peacekeeping, the Council's reaction to the US invasion of Iraq in 2003, as well as its struggles to respond to the Russian presence in Ukraine and the Syrian Civil War. With this waxing and waning of action in the Council, there is significant and important variation in the frequency with which the Council takes up issues, the types of issues discussed, and the means by which the Council responds to particular issues.

After collecting all of the provisional agendas, we then double-check the occurrence of meetings and coded output (votes, resolutions, presidential statements, etc.) using the meeting records on the Security Council's website, the Security Council's Annual Report, and the Security Council's Repertoire, which details Council actions by issue area, and agenda item in roughly three-year increments. This site was also helpful to clarify exactly which agenda item a particular meeting or resolution should be associated with in a very small number of cases when there were multiple relevant agenda items active in a given year and the referent was unclear.[5] All told, we collected information on 364 distinct agenda items, which over time, account for 32,940 agenda-item-months.

Many agenda items sit dormant on the Council's Summary Statement and never appear on the Council's monthly programmes of work throughout the whole period of study like "The Hyderabad question" or "Complaint by Cuba." On the other hand, some agenda items like "The situation in the Middle East" are active (at least one consultation or meeting is held) in 62 percent of the

[4] All Security Council meetings of both types often list "other matters" as possible topics, which allows for member states to discuss topics outside of those specifically named on the agenda if necessary. As a result, our data probably do not represent a comprehensive list of all topics discussed at all meetings for our time period, but based on the publicly available information, we are able to provide a representative pictures of the way that the Security Council allots its scarce plenary time.

[5] Ambiguity arose in less than 2 percent of cases and was associated with issues that had multiple related agenda items.

months in our data. For the full sample presented here, about 13 percent of the agenda item-months have some type of activity.

The agenda items considered by the Council vary greatly and fall into two major categories: thematic issues and national issues. Thematic issues are those dealing with social, political, military, or economic issues that are not tied to a specific member nation. An example of a thematic issue is "Children and armed conflict." This agenda item was introduced for the Council to respond to the issue of child soldiers in warfare, first addressed with UN Security Council Resolution 1261, prohibiting the targeting and recruitment of children in war. The resolution names no specific nation but broadly prohibits several practices related to children as victims and combatants in warfare. An example of a national issue would be "The situation in Cyprus," which first appeared on the Council's agenda in 1963 and continues to be a topic of discussion for Council members because of the continuing peacekeeping efforts of the United Nations Peacekeeping Force in Cyprus (UNFICYP). Looking at the characteristics of the issues themselves, some are going to warrant faster consideration than others, depending on the nature of the issue. We expect that national issues will receive more frequent attention than thematic as this type of issue is more likely to be connected to an international crisis or event demanding the Council's immediate attention. In this chapter, our primary interest is in the national issues, and they will be our focus in the initial analysis. Thematic issues will be considered later in the chapter.

The degree of agreement that permanent members have regarding particular issues influences whether or not an item will appear on the agenda or not. When a threat to peace and security arises, permanent members want to help resolve crises when possible, but the variability in their preferences can make this difficult. If one permanent member strongly favors the government in a civil conflict while another favors rebel factions, it is unlikely that the Council will be able to pass a resolution or create a peacekeeping mission to assist in the peace process in that country.

To measure the preferences of the P5, we begin by looking at the foreign policy similarity between each permanent member and the subject nation of the agenda item. The rates of common voting in the UN General Assembly between each P5 country and the subject country are summed and divided by five for an average rate of voting together. We use this as an average measures of political similarity between the subject country and the permanent members. As the average political similarity increases, we expect the Council to be more likely to act. We use S-scores based on common voting in the General Assembly following Signorino and Ritter (1999) to calculate our average affinity and variance measures. S-scores tell us the percentage of the time that two states vote together on issues in the General Assembly. For each national item listed in the Summary Statement, we collect the S-score between that country and each permanent member of the Council and take the average.[6]

While the average feelings of the permanent members tells us something important about the likelihood of Security Council action, variability in those preferences may also be important. If the Western Three have very similar policy profiles to a subject nation but Russia and China have very dissimilar profiles, the average could still be relatively high. Therefore, we also look at the variation in preferences of the permanent members, calculating the coefficient of variance for the average S-scores. The coefficient of variance is a standardized measure of dispersion (calculated as the ratio of the standard deviation to the mean) and expresses how spread out the S-scores are around the mean. We assume that when the permanent members have more divided feelings about a subject country and thus greater possibility for disagreement and no resolution, they will opt not to take up an issue. Thus, as disagreement increases, the likelihood that a particular agenda item will be discussed in a given month decreases.

Analyzing the Agenda

Turning to the substance of the agenda, we analyze which issues are considered in a given month and what type of meeting(s) are scheduled. For nearly all legislatures, meeting time is limited. Looking at how that scarce resource is allocated tells us about the priorities and preferences of the members. The primary agenda-setting power in the Council lies with the ability to schedule discussion among the members. Any country that is a member of the UN can place an item on the Council's agenda, but only members of the Council can influence the programme of work, which is outlined each month by the Council's president. Without discussion, an issue will never be brought to a vote.

For this analysis, we consider whether meetings are held on a particular topic. The outcome is an ordered outcome variable that runs from 0 (no action on this agenda item) to 3 (at least one consultation and one public

[6] We find similar results when we use the ideal point data created by Bailey, Strezhnev, and Voeten (2017), but interpreting the variance measure is more difficult because ideal points tell us about distance from an arbitrary anchor point (the Western order), which is already expressing some information about variance. For this reason, we have opted to go with the S-scores for clarity of interpretation. The S-scores tell us the similarity between the target country and the permanent members, which we believe is more relevant to the core theoretical concepts we are interested in.

meeting were held), running from no time invested in the issue to multiple sessions held on the topic in the month.[7] The middle categories represent only a consultation—the least frequently occurring outcome—and only a public meeting. We order the categories in this way because we believe that the public meetings represent investment of both plenary time and reputation as states are forced to take public positions on issues in public meetings.

In addition to considering the impact of the preferences of the permanent members, we also look at whether or not the preferences of the Council president matter. Those measure are calculated in the same manner as described above for permanent members. In addition to those affinity measures, we also consider the potential impact of geography. Using data from Haveman and Hummels (2004), we include the logged distance between the capital of the subject country and the Council president. We expect that presidents may be more interested in discussing threats to international peace and security in their own regions in hope of faster resolution. We anticipated that this may be particularly true for elected members who may want the threat neutralized but lack the wherewithal to do so unilaterally—unlike the permanent members.

One of the most active areas of Security Council work is peacekeeping. Creating and maintaining a peacekeeping mission requires the passage of UN resolutions and meetings to discuss re-affirming or refining mission mandates, so we also consider whether or not a particular agenda item is associated with an ongoing peacekeeping mission. Because Security Council activity waxes and wanes, we account for the relative activeness of a particular Council session by the number of resolutions passed in a year.

We also consider the impact of time. The time that an item has been on the agenda influences the likelihood of discussion. On average, older items are less likely to be put on the agenda than items related to more current/recent crises. We also control for changes in UN Security Council activity over time (since the end of the Cold War) but do not include them in these figures for space and clarity.[8]

For easy interpretation of our analysis, we present coefficient plots throughout this chapter. These plots show the relative impact of each variable. The vertical line represents zero (or no effect). The dots are the estimates of the size of the effect, and the lines out from those signal the 95 percent confidence interval which help us know whether we can be confident that an effect

[7] Multinomial models are also included in the Appendix B. Because interpretation of these models is more complex, we opted to present the ordered models in the text. The results in the multinomial models are very similar to the inferences that can be drawn from the ordered models.

[8] The full results can be found in the Appendix B.

is different from zero. We cannot be certain about an independent effect if the confidence intervals cross the vertical line.

Figure 4.2[9] presents the results for all presidents. In a given month, the amount of plenary time afforded to a particular agenda item is determined by the preferences of the permanent members foremost. The power of the veto influences not only what passes in the Security Council, but also what appears on the agenda. The more the permanent members disagree about a country that is the topic of an agenda item, the less likely that item is to show up on the agenda. Presidents recognize that issues with a high level of disagreement among the permanent members are unlikely to be fertile ground for policy making. As a result, these issues are not often put on the agenda.

As expected, agenda items associated with countries where active peacekeeping missions are located are more likely to have more plenary time allotted to them. Although the lethality of conflict in Cote d'Ivoire in the early 2000s was much lower than the lethality of conflict in Nepal at the same time, no meetings were held specifically on the topic of conflict Nepal between 2000

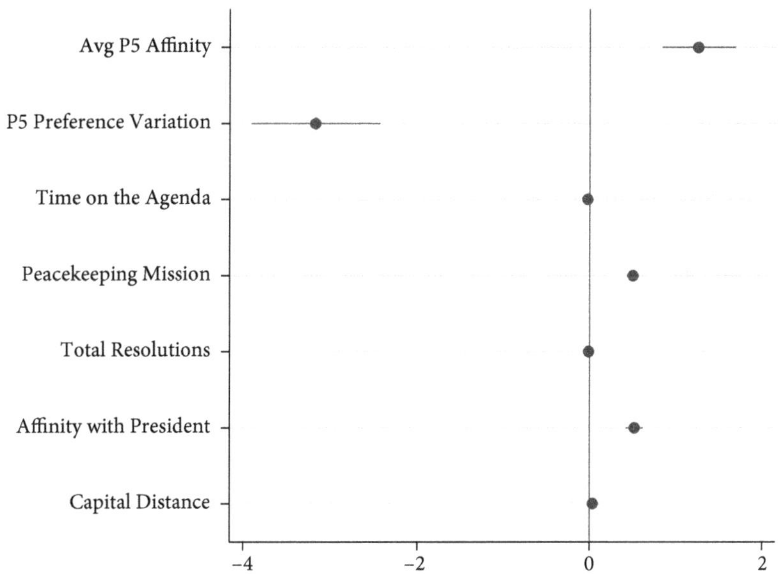

Fig. 4.2 Estimated coefficients and confidence intervals from an ordered probit model of meeting time devoted to an issue in a given month (where 0 is no action, 1 is only a consultation, 2 is only a public meeting, and 3 is both a consultation and public meeting), 1994–2015

[9] Regression output in Table B.1 in the Appendix B.

and 2006. In part because there was a peacekeeping mission in Cote d'Ivoire, forty-five consultations and sixteen public meetings were scheduled to discuss the situation there in 2003 and 2004 when Mission in Cote d'Ivoire (MINUCI) (then transitioning to United Nations Operation in Côte d'Ivoire (UNOCI)) was in the field there.

Turning to the factors related to the Council presidents, we see that when setting the agenda, presidents are more likely to place items on the agenda related to countries where they have similar foreign policy priorities. Geography also has a small positive influence but opposite to our expectation, presidents seem more inclined to include agenda items relating to countries *farther* from home on the agenda, which is a bit surprising. Rather than calling for international response to events in their home regions, presidents are interested in bringing more distant issues to the Council.

Figure 4.2 presents some evidence that Council presidents do have an influence over what gets discussed. To take the analysis a step further, we also looked at the determinants of the agenda for permanent members in comparison to elected members.

Figure 4.3[10] presents results for the permanent member presidents and Figure 4.4[11] does the same for the elected member presidents. When we compare the results for permanent members and elected members, we do notice some differences in what they prioritize when they set the agenda. Permanent members know their baseline preferences have to be taken into account because of their veto power. As a result, they seem to be less concerned about allocating discussion time to countries with similar foreign policies. Permanent members also get multiple bites at the apple as agenda-setter. They get to do so nearly every year.

Permanent members do have distinctive patterns in their agenda setting, however. These are strong states, and within their own regions, they often hold a great deal of political sway. When threats to international peace and security arise in their own regions, they may respond to those unilaterally or want to keep them off the Council's agenda in order to maximize their own influence. The Monroe Doctrine is a long-standing example of a state's desire to minimize the influence of other powers in their neighborhood. This inclination has only grown stronger as the US has become more powerful. Geography does matter to the permanent members when they serve as Council president, but they choose to include subject countries that are farther away rather than close by.

[10] Regression output in Table B.2 in the Appendix B.
[11] Regression output in Table B.3 in the Appendix B.

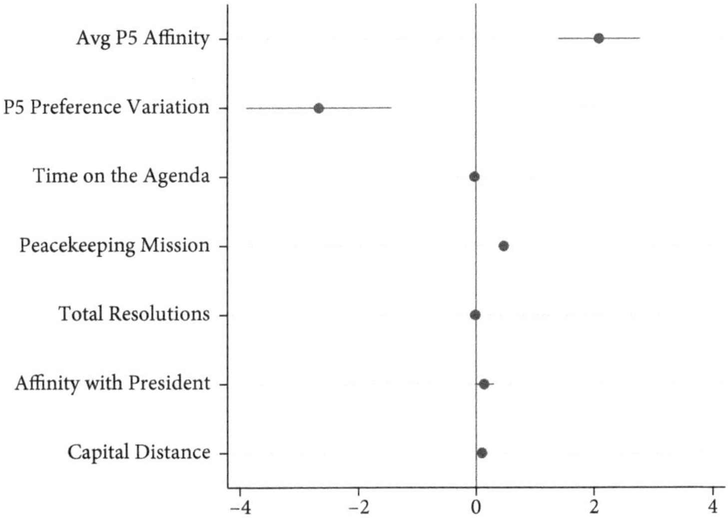

Fig. 4.3 Estimated coefficients and confidence intervals from an ordered probit model of meeting time devoted to an issue in a given month—P5 presidents only (where 0 is no action, 1 is only a consultation, 2 is only a public meeting, and 3 is both a consultation and public meeting), 1994–2015

Turning to the elected members, they place more similar nations on the agenda rather than more proximate or more distant ones. This political rather than geographic focus may reflect the fact that their incentives are slightly different. During their two-year stint on the Council, they will have one or two chances (depending on where they fall in the alphabetical order) to serve as Council president and influence the agenda directly. Elected members have a shorter time horizon for influencing the actions of the Council.

This more limited window of opportunity seems to influence how they use their agenda-setting power. They might want to do something in their region, but if it's a non-start for even one of the permanent members, what's the point of putting that issue on the agenda? Elected members appear to be focusing on national issues they care about and where movement is possible.

To draw more meaningful inference regarding these results, we have also calculated substantive effects in order to compare the magnitude of the influence of these factors. Because the coefficients in regression models with ordered outcomes like those presented here cannot be intuitively interpreted, Figure 4.5 and Figure 4.6 show how the impact of presidential affinity differs on the way that permanent and elected members allot Council discussion time.

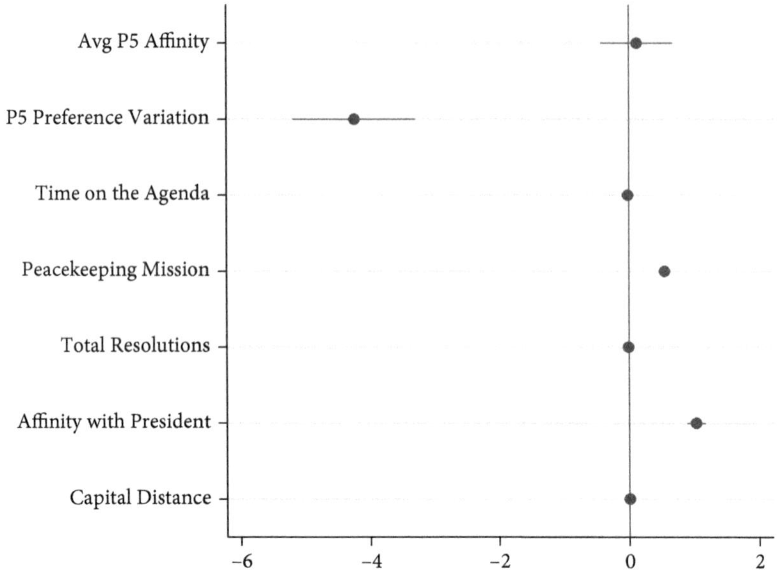

Fig. 4.4 Estimated coefficients and confidence intervals from an ordered probit model of meeting time devoted to an issue in a given month—elected ten presidents only (where 0 is no action, 1 is only a consultation, 2 is only a public meeting, and 3 is both a consultation and public meeting), 1994–2015

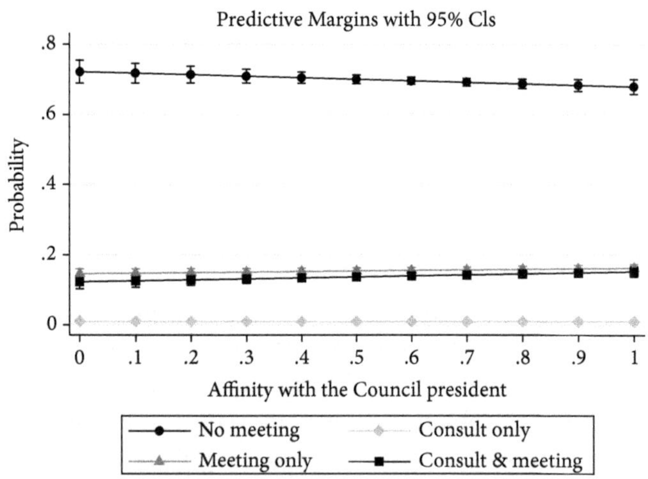

Fig. 4.5 Substantive impact across differing levels of voting similarity for P5 presidents, 1994–2015

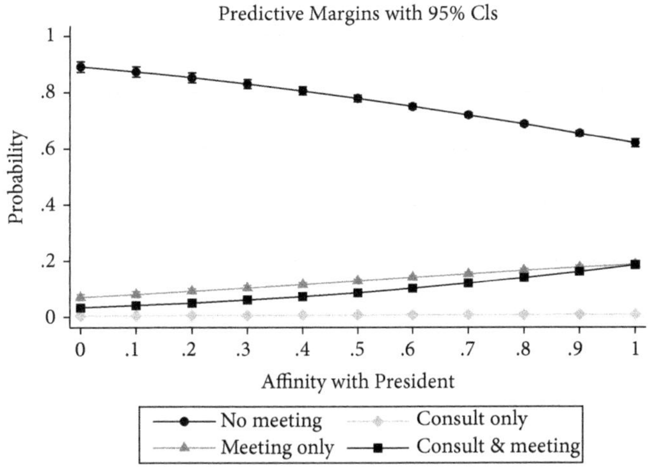

Fig. 4.6 Substantive impact across differing levels of voting similarity for E10 presidents, 1994–2015

For permanent members, affinity makes little difference on agenda-setting decisions. For elected members, greater affinity makes a meeting more likely to be scheduled.

In both of these figures, several things are clear. First, no meeting is the dominant category. For most agenda items in a given month, no discussion is scheduled. Only twenty to twenty-five public meetings are scheduled in an average month, and for many years, we consider there are more than 150 potential agenda items. We know that not all threats to international security are discussed in the Security Council, but this should also highlight the fact that the Council cannot discuss all the threats on its agenda. The time and resources for discussion are limited. That is why it is important to think systematically about the factors that influence which issues get discussed when.

Secondly, for permanent member presidents, moving from low affinity between themselves and the subject country to high affinity does not make much of a difference in the likelihood that plenary time will be scheduled. On the other hand, affinity makes a much bigger difference for elected member presidents. As agreement increases on a given topic, the likelihood that no meeting will occur on that topic drops dramatically. There is a corresponding rise in the likelihood of either a meeting or meeting and consultations rises as agreement increases.

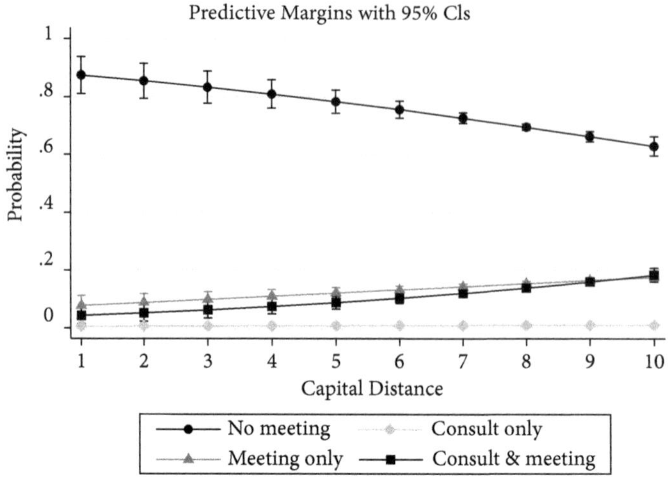

Fig. 4.7 Substantive impact across differing capital distances (in 1,000s of miles) for P5 presidents, 1994–2015

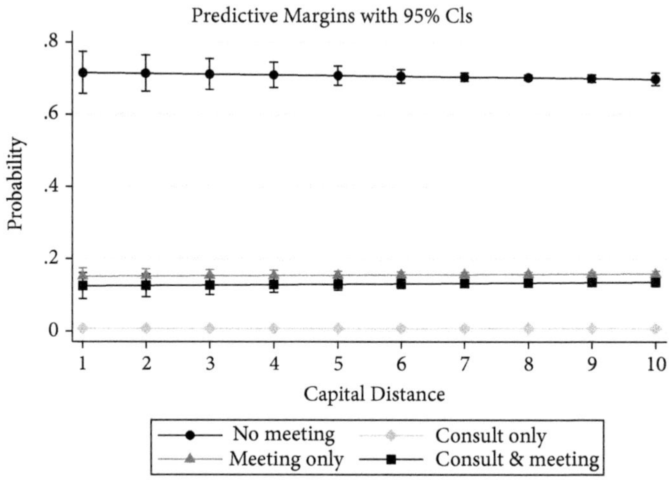

Fig. 4.8 Substantive impact across differing capital distances (in 1,000s of miles) for E10 presidents, 1994–2015

Figure 4.7 and Figure 4.8 show how the impact of capital distance differs for permanent member presidents on the way they allot Council discussion time. Here the patterns are basically reversed. As the distance increases, the permanent members are more likely to schedule meetings, but capital distance has no meaningful effect for elected member presidents. Elected presidents are not putting threats in their region on the agenda more, which is a bit surprising.

Permanent members are placing threats outside of their regions on the agenda, suggesting that they want to handle regional issues on their own, but want to influence the way distant threats are handled.

4.2.2 Thematic Issues

Thus far, we have focused on one of the two types of agenda items that the Council considers—the national issues (or those items specifically associated with a particular country). The Council also considers thematic or cross-national issues. In 2019, twenty-seven percent of the public meetings held by the Council covered this type of agenda item. The thematic issues discussed in recent years cover a broad range of topics including climate change, human immunodeficiency virus/acquired immune deficiency syndrome (HIV/AIDS), non-proliferation, as well as a number of human security issues.

This broad thematic agenda is another change since the end of the Cold War. Prior to the 1990s, the Council focused tightly on issues of war and peace. As the international community's definition of security has broadened, so has the agenda that the Council sets for itself. In the twenty-first century, the Council is a place where global norms are debated and, in some cases, built (Keating, 2015). For example, the Council's Resolution 1325 has framed and broadened international discussion about gender equality and peace for the past twenty years.

Much of the enthusiasm for taking on these non-traditional threats to security has come from elected members and various Secretaries-General, beginning with Boutros Boutros-Ghali. For the elected members, thematic issues offer an opportunity to engage in some policy entrepreneurship on the Council (Keating, 2015). While the permanent members tend to dominate discussion and procedure on the conventional business of the Council, thematic issues offer elected members an opportunity to enhance their profiles during their presidency month(s) (Keating, 2015). We explore Canada's efforts to promote the thematic idea of the responsibility to protect (R2P) in greater detail in Chapter 7.

Looking at the frequency of meetings on thematic and national issues, we compare monthly agendas to see whether this is another way that elected and permanent members use their agenda-setting power differently. Anecdotally, we know that some elected members have advanced thematic issues (Thorhallsson, 2012), but systematic evidence of this trend has been less clear.

For national issues, permanent members and elected members look nearly identical. There is no meaningful difference between the number of meetings on national issues. The month of the year matters more than what type of state holds the presidency when predicting the number of national issues scheduled. Summer months tend to be a bit slower, which is not particularly important or interesting substantively.

The picture looks different, however, when we consider thematic issues.[12] Controlling for time since the end of the Cold War (and the rise of thematic issues), we find that permanent members schedule just over two thematic issues per month while elected members schedule just under three. In a given year, an average of eight more meetings are held on thematic issues, pushing forward high-level consideration of and response to some of the broadest threats to humanity. The Council held seventy meetings in 2019 on thematic issues—an increase of eight more meetings is meaningful.

4.2.3 The Occurrence of Vetoes

Vetoes are a rare occurrence in the post-Cold War Council, especially in comparison to the early days of the institution. Between 1994 and 2015, a total of twenty-seven vetoes were cast. Given that we analyze more than 32,000 agenda-item months in this chapter, vetoes are very unlikely to happen. Even if we think of the data by presidencies (each month), vetoes occurred in less than 10 percent of the months during this time period. Because plenary time is scarce, our basic model predicts that vetoes should not occur. Yet, we do occasionally see them, and our model in Chapter 3 suggests that if they are not due to uncertainty, then they must be a form of grandstanding.[13] Our initial intuition was perhaps that permanent members, with longer time horizons and more frequent influence over the Council's agenda, might be more likely to call for votes that would result in vetoes. There is no meaningful difference, however, in the frequency of vetoes when permanent members hold the presidency versus when elected members do so. Not surprisingly, the best predictor of these rare events is the level of disagreement between the permanent members, but this relationship is weaker in the post-Cold War period than it was during the first forty-five years of the organization. While not a novel prediction, when the permanent members are in greater agreement (both annual and by issue), vetoes are less likely to occur. Our explanation of grandstanding

[12] See the Appendix B for negative binomial estimates.

[13] Based on press releases and the lengthy speeches that accompany a vetoed resolution in the public meeting, surprise vetoes appear to be incredibly rare, even in our tiny set of vetoes, justifying our characterization of most vetoes as grandstanding.

sets a high empirical bar for testing because of the combination of factors that must occur. To predict vetoes at that level, we would need to be able to measure Council member's issue-specific ideal policies more directly (as well as the expected public costs associated with the issue), and no such data exist. Instead, we rely on the case studies to provide evidence for our arguments around grandstanding.

Another interesting regularity to note is that vetoes have only occurred on national issue resolutions, not thematic issue resolutions, which may suggest another area of influence for elected members. Any number of reasons might explain this difference—the norm building and lobbying efforts may be more extensive because thematic issues transcend a particular national emergency, there may be more flexibility in the possible agreements because the scope on thematic issues may be wider. In all, thematic issues deserve more attention in future research.

4.2.4 Resolutions and the Permanent Members

Having first considered the make-up of the agenda, we now turn to resolutions. Resolutions are the best known and easily observable actions of the Security Council. These observable actions represent a bargain struck by the members of the Security Council, but they are also a product of the agenda selection process. No resolutions can pass on issues that do not make it onto the Council's agenda.

Here, we highlight the influence of the preferences of Council members on the number of resolutions passed per year. In Chapter 3, we examined Voeten's original spatial model, which assumes a contentious framework for the Council in which the status quo (SQ) of a particular issue fell between the two most extreme Council members' policy preferences. We expand the analysis to consider the conditions under which we might expect more cooperation, particularly since we observe that the Council's activity and resolutions increased so substantially following the Cold War. The expanded model shows that as the Council members' preferences fall closer together in the policy space, it becomes more likely that an issues that makes it to the Council's agenda will fall outside of the Council's policy range. When this happens, all Council members have an incentive to change the policy, thus agreement should be more likely. This logic is the primary basis for Hypothesis 1.

During the Cold War, the general perception was that the amount of activity occurring in the Security Council was largely determined by the degree of agreement (or disagreement) that could be reached between the US and the Soviet Union. Using data on the number of resolutions passed in each year from 1971–2015, we look at how variability in preferences between the five permanent members might help us to explain the amount of activity in the Security Council over a longer period of time. The preference measure tells us how much Council members agreed in a given year.

This represents a test of Hypothesis 1. We expect that as disagreement (or preference variability) increases, the number of resolutions will decrease in a given year.

To test this hypothesis, we counted the number of resolution passed each year over this forty-five-year period. Using statistical analysis (in this case, negative binomial regression to account for the fact that the outcomes are all whole numbers),[14] we estimate the number of resolutions passed in a given year.

For this analysis, we include the total number of items on the agenda in that year, the number of vetoes cast, as, well as the spread of preferences among the permanent members. In this analysis, there are no subject countries to anchor our comparison. For this reason, we use the ideal point measure rather than

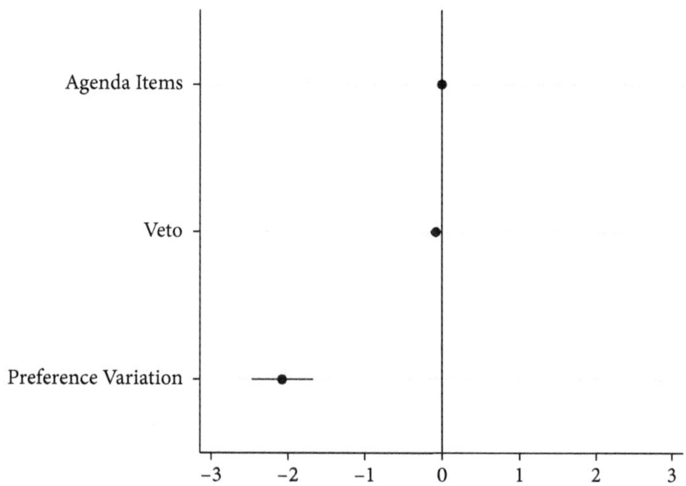

Fig. 4.9 Estimated coefficients and confidence intervals from a count model of the annual number of resolutions passed by the UN Security Council, 1971–2015

[14] The Council cannot pass half a resolution or a quarter of one, so our analysis takes this fact into account.

the S-scores. The ideal point data are estimated using votes in the UN General Assembly to provide a representation of how far (or close) a particular member state's position is to the prevailing Western Order led by the US (Bailey, Strezhnev, and Voeten, 2017). These measures tell us whether a particular country's policy preference is close to or far from the preference of the US.[15]

To measure the degree of disagreement, we take the average policy position of the permanent members and divide it by the standard deviation. This coefficient of variance lets us know whether the preferences of the permanent members are tightly clustered around the average or spread out. The higher the coefficient of variance is, the greater the disagreement is among the P5. These measures are similar to the issue based measures discussed for the first analysis, but here they are an annual measure of agreement.

Results from Figure 4.9[16] illustrate the impact that P5 agreement has on the number of resolutions passed each year since the People's Republic of China began occupying the Chinese seat on the Council in 1971. This figure clearly demonstrates that as P5 preferences diverge and disagreement increases, fewer resolutions are passed, lending support to Hypothesis 1. In years when the preferences of the permanent members are more similar, more resolutions are passed. In many ways, these results come as no surprise, but empirically testing this idea and finding that it holds is an important way to verify an untested, underlying assumption of our spatial model.

To compare the relative importance of these factors, we looked at their substantive impact. First, we generated the predicted number of resolutions that would be passed in a year with the highest variation or most disagreement (holding all the other variables at their means).[17] In such a year, our model expects that roughly eighteen resolutions would pass. In contrast, in a year with the lowest variation in preferences or most agreement (again holding the other variables at their means), we expect that sixty-three resolutions would pass. In terms of historical activity, between 1946 and 2018, the Council passed an average of thirty-three resolutions, so the difference between high and low disagreement years is very meaningful. In contrast, going from the minimum number of agenda items to the maximum, only decreases the number of resolutions by seven.

[15] We have also experimented with estimating pair-wise S-score averages for all the P5 countries, but opted to use the ideal points with the anchoring to the UN because the analysis is annual and not issue specific, which makes the coefficient of variation of P5 ideal points a more appropriate and interpretable measure of preferences.

[16] Regression output in Table B.8 in the Appendix B.

[17] These quantities of interest were generated using the margins command in Stata.

4.3 A Closer Look: Security Council Decision Making and Peacekeeping in Sierra Leone

In the quantitative analysis, we focus on the way that plenary time is allocated and the number of resolutions that pass. To complement that analysis, we now do a deeper dive into what happens in these meetings. Simply holding meetings does not guarantee action. The diplomacy and compromise during those meetings—on all topics—are essential.

To further explore the decision-making process of the UN Security Council, we briefly consider the bargaining that preceded the decision to increase the UN's commitment to keeping peace in Sierra Leone in late 1999 and through 2000. During 2000, the Council held seventy-five private consultations regarding Sierra Leone, suggesting that while members believed that action in Sierra Leone was important, there was a great deal of disagreement among the member nations about what that action should look like. Thirteen public meetings were held, and the mission's mandate evolved and expanded, but even in the verbatim records of these meetings, national representatives refer to the extensive consultation process needed to hammer out compromise.

Looking back on peacekeeping missions in the first decade of the twenty-first century, the United Nations Mission in Sierra Leone (UNAMSIL) is now regarded as a success and seen as a potential model for future missions. In early 2000, however, the prospects for the mission were anything but rosy (Berdal and Ucko, 2015). The Security Council took action on Sierra Leone prior to the creation of UNAMSIL, authorizing economic sanctions in 1997 and a small observer mission (UN Observer Mission in Sierra Leone) in 1998, but much of the heavy lifting on peacekeeping in Sierra Leone was left to the Economic Community of West Africa States Monitoring Group (ECOMOG). When UNAMSIL was initially created, it was expected to work alongside ECOMOG. The situation changed in late 1999 when the Nigerian government, which had been the largest funder and troop-contributor for ECOMOG, decided that it could no longer afford to foot the bill and would pull its troops out. Nigerian leaders were feeling pressure from the public, which had become fed up with their government spending money on regional peacekeeping missions when clean water and electricity were not easily available in all areas of Nigeria (Olonisakin, 2008).

Deciding what to do in Sierra Leone following the Nigerian decision to cease funding ECOMOG was a challenge for the Security Council. Within the Secretariat, some individuals hoped that a Western nation like the UK or Canada or perhaps the US might offer to fill the funding gap to allow Nigerian troops to stay (Olonisakin, 2008). The Nigerian government formally requested that the UN take on funding ECOMOG, but there was no enthusiasm for either of these plans in late 1999, in part because the domestic political environment in the US was not favorable to increasing spending at the UN or on peacekeeping.

The Council authorized a larger mission in October 1999 under the new name: United Nations Mission in Sierra Leone (UNAMSIL), which was tasked with overseeing the implementation of the Lome Peace Agreement and to assist ECOMOG with disarmament and demobilization (un.org). The Security Council authorized 6,000 troops, the maximum that the US (as the primary funder) was likely to approve (Olonisakin, 2008). At that time, members of the Council believed that the Lome Agreement would pacify the Revolutionary United Front (RUF) and decrease tensions in the country. Whether or not advisors in the Department of Peacekeeping Operations (DPKO) agreed with this assessment is unclear, but their recommendations about troops and the nature of the mandate were shaped by what they believed the Council would be willing to agree to (Olonisakin, 2008).

Among the Council members, there was little enthusiasm for action in Sierra Leone. Most of the major powers were more focused on Kosovo. In addition to resistance from funder states like the US, troop-contributing countries were also signaling that while they thought that doing something in Sierra Leone was important, they wanted to keep costs low (Olonisakin, 2008). The lone exception was the UK, which was the penholder nation for issues on Sierra Leone.[18] The UK was a primary sponsor of the Lome Agreement and was invested in creating lasting peace in Sierra Leone (Ucko, 2016).

With the withdrawal of Nigerian troops in early 2000, the Council was now pressed to expand the mandate of UNAMSIL. Many feared that the UNs credibility in the region would be damaged if they did not fill in the gap (Olonisakin, 2008). The mission, however, had become more complicated. Rather than working beside ECOMOG, UNAMSIL would be taking over the peacekeeping effort.

Determining the shape of this expanded mandate was complex. On February 7, 2000, Jeremey Greenstock, the UK representative noted that his vision of

> UNAMSIL is not a Chapter VII peace enforcement operation, but we all recognized in formulating the mandate for the force, as set out in the draft

[18] The UK did not hold the presidency at all during 2000. Their role as penholder was their most important power in this process.

> resolution before us, that this task will require a robust and serious stance against possible threats. "UNAMSIL must act with the determination and the flexibility to see this through. ... Without our continued determination and support, even an expanded UNAMSIL force cannot keep Sierra Leone on its current positive path".
>
> (S/PV.4098)

His enthusiasm for expanding the mandate of UNAMSIL is much stronger than that of the US. In that same meeting, the Chinese ambassador noted, "After several rounds of consultations, the draft resolution to be voted upon now basically reflects the views of all sides in a comprehensive and balanced manner. Therefore, we support this draft resolution" (S/PV.4098). A great deal of private diplomacy was necessary to take this action.

In the early days, some members of the Security Council were still optimistic that the Lome Agreement offered a real opportunity for the creation of a stable peace, and if the UN were there to preside over that new peace all the better. They were quickly disabused of this notion. In May 2000, the Revolutionary United Front (RUF) in Sierra Leone kidnapped five hundred UN peacekeepers and reneged on the peace accord that the peacekeepers were invested in implementing. These actions nearly derailed peacekeeping efforts there and perhaps in Africa more broadly (Berdal and Ucko, 2015).

Eventually, the British took a key leadership position in response to the deteriorating situation in Sierra Leone - both on the ground and in the Council. Given the extreme insecurity in the capital of Freetown, the British opted to send their own troops. In response to uncertainty about UNAMSIL's mission, the British advocated for a robust mandate. Although the British sent only about 800 troops, their willingness to do so signaled resolve to actors on the ground in Sierra Leone and to members of the UN community in New York (Adebajo, 2012).

Now seen as a prime example of robustness, the path to creating a clear mandate and effective enforcement force for UNAMSIL required a great deal of effort for the Security Council and the Secretariat (Adebajo, 2012). In addition to the challenges discussed previously, the Council continued to struggle with the nature of UNAMSIL's mandate. In August 2000, the Council passed Resolution 1313 (S/RES/1313) condemning violence against UNAMSIL, but the member states were only able to agree to a one month extension of the mandate, suggesting a desire for continued discussion and greater oversight (Allen and Yuen, 2014). When the mandate was discussed again in early September, only a three-week extension was granted in Resolution 1317

(S/RES/1317). Finally, in late September, the Council was able to pass Resolution 1321 (S/RES/1321) that extended the mandate for three months, but they also decided to "review the situation no later than October 31, 2000."

During this period, UNAMSIL was also struggling with tensions relating to Indian commander Vijay Kumar Jetley who was overseeing the whole mission. Nigerian troops and officials who were formerly part of the ECOMOG force challenged his authority. The situation worsened when documents Jetley sent to UN headquarters complaining about Nigerian officers and accusing them of inappropriate conduct surfaced (Van Rooyen, 2010). Eventually the Department of Peacekeeping Operations decided to pull all of the Indian contingent from the mission.

At the end of the year, the Council met on December 22 and unanimously voted to approve Resolution 1334 (S/RES/1334) extending UNAMSILs mandate for three months without additional public discussion on the matter. At this point, the worst of the rough spots had passed for the mission. The command and control issues were resolved, and the Indian forces replaced. Despite the challenges, UNAMSIL's mandate would be considered fulfilled by 2002.

The path to success in Sierra Leone was a winding one. Looking at the record of the Security Council's consultations and meetings, it is clear that the member states were uncertain and divided about the best course of action. Once the UK decided to take a leadership role within the Security Council, it was still necessary for them to draft and re-draft resolutions and hold consultations in order to build consensus. Looking at the history of UNAMSIL on the ground or the resolutions passed on Sierra Leone during this period tells part of the story of Council action on Sierra Leone but fails to capture the full diplomatic process. Extensive bargaining among the Council members was needed to create a mandate for UNAMSIL that members would support and that would be effective for keeping peace on the ground.

4.3.1 Discussion

In this chapter, we have explored how both the make–up of the Council and the agenda-setting process influence the way members conduct business and make decisions. International response to threats to peace and security are driven by the agenda-setting process as well as the preferences of the permanent members.

Permanent members clearly play a big role in the issues discussed by the Council and the resolutions passed. Permanent members have served as the penholders on key issues. The threat of the veto power hangs over every decision made in the Council. The Cold War illustrated how disagreement among the permanent members could prevent the Council from playing a major role in international affairs. While disagreement has diminished among the members, it has not disappeared. When agreement is higher between these members—both overall and on specific issues—more work can be done in the Council.

The Council makes strategic choices about how to use their scarce time for discussion and debate. As the Council has taken on a fuller docket of peacekeeping missions and a broader view of international security to include issues like human security as well as terrorism and piracy, Council members have tried to use scarce plenary time to discuss the matters that are most likely to lead to cooperative action. As the legislative bargaining literature suggests, similarity of preferences matters a great deal. Council members are unlikely to sacrifice scarce time to issues where the preferences of the permanent members are deadlocked. The quantitative analysis indicates that the Council schedules more meetings when more bargaining is necessary, a point that is more clearly illustrated by the bargaining surrounding the creation of the mandate of UNAMSIL.

This chapter also illustrates the importance of agenda-setting in the Council. To fully understand the decision-making of the Council, we must look beyond just the resolutions passed and explore the bargaining process that leads to those voted upon compromises. In addition to considering the bargaining between the permanent members, we have also demonstrated the influence that Council presidents have over the agenda. Not all presidents use those powers in the same ways, highlighting key differences between elected members and permanent members.

Elected members have some institutional disadvantages on the Council, but they are finding ways to claim space for themselves and assert influence. Two key ways we can see this are in the distinct ways they use their agenda-setting power in the presidency and in their efforts to expand the agenda with thematic issues.

5

Working Through the Council: A Test of Outside Options on UN Security Council Actions

In early 2003, the UN Security Council heard testimony from US Secretary of State Colin Powell. In an impassioned presentation, Powell presented information he believed proved that the Iraqi regime under Saddam Hussein had acquired weapons of mass destruction and was working to gain nuclear weapons. From Powell's speech, it was clear that the US was planning to take military action against Iraq in the near future.

The US and the UK brought the matter to the Security Council because they hoped at a minimum that the Council would condone the 2003 invasion of Iraq, conferring legitimacy on the endeavor. The information coming from the UN Monitoring, Verification, and Inspection Commission that the Council set up after the 1991 Persian Gulf War contradicted US intelligence on Iraq's weapons program. Given these conflicting reports, other members of the Security Council faced a difficult choice—should they vote for a Council resolution approving of the action in hope of influencing the shape of the US military intervention or should they threaten to veto any draft resolutions because they believed the action was unjustified? They likely understood that the US would take action even without the resolution. How did the US threat to act outside the Council influence behavior inside the Council?

In the case of the 2003 invasion of Iraq, no compromise resolution could be reached. Other members were unable to use the Security Council to influence American behavior on Iraq. This has not always been the case. In nearly every other case post-Cold War, the US has worked multilaterally, seeking support and legitimacy from the Council.

In Chapter 3, we revisited Voeten's (2001) spatial model in which he showed how Council members with the ability to take unilateral action (or use an 'outside option') can influence bargaining inside the Council. His insight is that an

Bargaining in the UN Security Council. Susan Hannah Allen and Amy Yuen, Oxford University Press.
 DOI: 10.1093/oso/9780192849755.003.0005

outside option can fundamentally change the range of possible bargains under consideration. When is the threat of unilateral action credible? To test Voeten's logic, we focus on the likelihood that a member state will pursue an outside option. As that likelihood increases, other members may be more inclined to act *inside* the Council in order to influence the actions of the state with a clear *outside* option.

In Chapter 4, we examined why contentious issues might not get placed on the agenda, focusing on bargaining dynamics inside the Council. States are not limited to action through the Council, however. A credible threat of unilateral action can increase the likelihood that the Council will take up a contentious issue if members believe that compromise within the Council is the only way to ensure an action that is less extreme than the potential unilateral intervention (Hypothesis 2).

The credibility of that outside option is important—the more likely a state is to exercise an outside option, the more likely the Council will be to meet to try and prevent action outside of the Council, reflected in Hypothesis 3. Our focus turns to actions taken inside the Council. Our hypotheses focus on whether a credible outside option increases the likelihood that a meeting will occur. We also explore whether the Council authorizes action. Extending the credibility theory, when the outside option is more likely, we should expect Council action to also be more likely, attempting to avoid unilateral action by one of its members.

5.1 Powerful States and Multilateral Action

To begin, we must consider why powerful states would opt to work through an international organization on security issues. The desire for a force multiplier is a clear incentive for weak states to use these organizations, but why do strong states use them? If a state is able to bear the costs of action alone, it is less clear why they would willingly sacrifice autonomy and flexibility in the high politics arena of international security. Obvious arguments can be made in favor of unilateral action for these states. Neack (1995) suggests that P5 countries are more likely to act unilaterally or take action through regional organizations if civil conflict occurs in a country that the great power believes is strategically important.

The benefits and drawbacks of working multilaterally are well-studied in the literature on international institutions. More recently, these ideas have given way to understanding the conditions under which states will work inside or outside of an institution. Venue-shopping occurs when states choose the institutions where they want to discuss a particular issue—actively avoiding some discussions and actively initiating others in more friendly institutions. Venue-shopping also happens in domestic politics. For example, there are multiple venues where domestic constituents can pursue a change in policy—such as a subnational legislature, national legislature, subnational or national court system. For international institutions, a similar variety of options may exist, depending on the issue. In all of these, the decision on where to have an issue heard depends on the costs to bring it to the institution and the expected outcome (given the decision rules and preferences inside the institution) compared to the value of doing nothing. Acting outside the framework of the UN allows powerful states to limit the influence of other (perhaps powerful) states but at much higher cost (De Jonge Oudraat, 1996; Diehl, 1994; Durch, 1993).

Since 9/11, the US has appeared to view UN Security Council authorization as desirable but not essential. This has increased tension among the Western Three as France and the UK are the most active of the permanent members of the Council (Mahbubani, 2004; Tardy and Zaum, 2015). Disagreement among the Western Three has also complicated relations with the other two permanent members of the Council who have been less enthusiastic about the expanded role of the Security Council in the post-Cold War period. On the other hand, since the 1991 Gulf War, the US has at least approached the Council for support and approval before using force in nearly every instance.

A primary motivation for powerful states choosing to work through international organizations appears to be a desire for action to be perceived by the international community as legitimate. Stone (2011), however, notes that the UN Security Council does not have legitimacy because it faithfully adheres to legal precedents or because it has clear and democratic procedures. The Council has neither of those things, nor is it the most representative body. The legitimacy granted by international institutions varies greatly due to organization features like the breadth of the membership and decision rules. Legitimacy also can also vary across issues and observers (Chapman, 2011). Voeten (2005) explore the political factors behind perceptions of the UN Security Council, arguing that it is treated as legitimate because it acts as an elite pact. UN Security Council authorization is a signal that powerful states in the international system do not view a proposed policy as overly expansive. Because member states and particularly the most powerful states participate voluntarily, the Council achieves a great deal of legitimacy (Voeten, 2005). The decisions made by the Council are binding for member states, and the policies discussed in the Council often have distributional consequences for other states in the international system (Voeten, 2001). Fang (2008) characterizes international institutions as receiving higher quality information about the state of the world; therefore, consulting an institution provides better information about a leader's intentions to a naive domestic audience.

Without approval from an international organization, the international community is less likely to respond favorably to the use of coercive military force. Thompson (2006*a*) suggests that the Security Council plays a uniquely powerful role as a "legitimizer" of state policies involving the use of force. Wallensteen and Johansson (2004) posits that members might use the Council as a forum for sorting out the disagreements among themselves, which in itself confers legitimacy. At this point "intervention without some effort to gain approval is now virtually obsolete, a remarkable feature of contemporary international relations that merits both theoretical and policy attention," (Thompson, 2006*a*). This is not only true for the US, but other permanent members as well. The British also wanted UN Security Council support for 2003 Iraq War—probably more than the Americans (despite choosing to act without it in the end). Russia and France have sought UN or regional cover for interventions in the near abroad or francophone Africa (Thompson, 2006*a*).[1]

Thompson (2009) focuses on the informational function of the Council as the primary mechanism for bestowing legitimacy. Acknowledging that uncertainty is a central cause of conflict, the ways in which leaders can credibly transmit information in crisis situations have implications for avoiding and ending conflict. Thompson emphasizes the fact that international institutions like the UN Security Council can convey information not only about policies but also intentions. The symbolic importance of the UN Security Council makes signals from this body more significant (Hurd, 2002).

The information provided by the UN Security Council is also useful for domestic publics as well as other states (Chapman, 2007, 2011; Chapman and Reiter, 2004). Authorization from the Security Council signals to domestic actors that the use of force is justified and that the threat faced is real (Chapman and Reiter, 2004). Chapman (2007) argues that states' decision to bring an issue to the Security Council is a critical element of leader's efforts to signal information about foreign policy choices. Public statements made in the UN Security Council create a focal point for discussion of the relevant issues

[1] A clear exception has been recent Russian action both in Georgia and in Crimea. Following the end of the observer mission in Georgia and renewed violence, the Council has held frequent discussions concerning Georgia, but has not passed any resolutions (Wallensteen and Johansson, 2014), while the Russians have limited discussion on Crimea.

and give states the opportunity to engage in talk that is less cheap, as public statements increase the political costs of backing down.

While the US clearly does not see the Security Council as the final arbiter on the legitimacy of the use of force (Stedman, 2015), it has demonstrated a willingness to work through the Council, and a desire for action to be perceived as legitimate. When states opt to utilize multilateral action, they are making a clear choice in favor of legitimacy over flexibility and autonomy (Thompson, 2006*a*). In addition, working through the Council is often slow, which is something that can be frustrating for powerful states like the US (Bosco, 2009). As a result, the motives and decision-making of the US has garnered a great deal of attention, when considering the choice to take multilateral action.

For the threat of an outside option to make multilateral action more likely, the US must be willing and able to act alone or with close allies. This is not a given in every situation and cannot be taken as such. A president who is hesitant to engage troops can profoundly shape the opportunities for multilateral action (Voeten, 2001). For a democracy like the US, presidents need public support in order to use force in support of broad foreign policy goals (Chapman and Reiter, 2004). Political will is often just as important as military might.

Despite the desire for approval and legitimacy, the US has chosen to marginalize the Council in certain situations where no consensus could be reached in the Council, for example, using the North Atlantic Treaty Organization (NATO) to respond to the crisis in Kosovo and the Iraq War's Coalition of the Willing.[2] The outside option is most important when there is sharp disagreement between states with the ability to block a multilateral agreement (Voeten, 2001). A heterogeneous group of states places much greater constraints on what actions can and cannot be taken militarily (Thompson, 2006*b*).

Voeten's (2001) model considers some basic factors that would influence the policies that could emerge from the Security Council, based on its very peculiar five veto player voting structure. When a crisis arises, the permanent members must consider whether or not they would like to take action in response. If the intensity of this preference is sufficiently great, the next step is to determine what form that action will take. When considering whether to act within the Council, each of the P5 countries has to look at the status quo (SQ) policy and determine whether or not efforts to adjust that policy within the

[2] See Chapter 7 for a case study of Council discussion involving Kosovo.

constraints of the Council will lead to a policy that will be more preferable. In the end, the two most extreme veto players are the critical factors that decide the range of possible policies. As we showed in Chapter 3, when the status quo lies between the two extreme P5 members' preferences, action is unlikely unless the US has a credible outside option. Voeten shows us that when the outside option is credible, there exists a set of negotiated agreements that rational states would prefer to the outside option. This is the underlying logic for Hypotheses 2 and 3, which we test in the following empirical analysis.

Hypotheses 2 and 3 together suggest that when the two extreme members are farther apart, nothing will happen unless one of the P5 members has a credible outside option. Thus, we must account for the condition that a situation is contentious—meaning the status quo lies between the two extreme P5 members. This is more likely the farther apart the P5 members are spread in their preferences. We must also account for the credibility (or likelihood) of a P5 member intervening in a situation unilaterally.

Even Voeten's simple specification requires the players to compare different possible outcomes. In cases where there is no outside option, the players compare the status quo policy to a proposed alternative and its associated costs. Voeten's spatial model shows that when the status quo falls between the two most extreme P5 members, neither will allow the policy to move in any direction because no matter which way it moves, one of the veto player's is worse off with a change in policy. Not every situation that arises in the Council is one in which the status quo resides between the two extremes. In fact, cases in which no credible outside option exists suggest that action from the Security Council happens because everyone agrees that something needs to happen to address the issue. For example, the conflict over East Timor did not generate any threats of outside intervention from any of the permanent members. In fact, the nearest P5 member is China, and in the late 1990s, China's behavior on the Council followed a pattern of caution and abstention, much like its foreign policy more generally. Thus, how would we explain the peacekeeping mission in East Timor? The permanent members agreed with regional nations, like Australia, that something needed to occur to stop the violence, but no one had enough at stake to mount a unilateral intervention. Thus, the UN sent a peacekeeping mission because the permanent members cared enough to work multilaterally, but not enough to take it on unilaterally. Despite the costs of peacekeeping, the members viewed peacekeeping as a more favorable option than ignoring the violence in East Timor.

Situations in which the status quo lies between the most extreme permanent members are unlikely to change without the outside option. Pursuing an outside option means a nation (or coalition) will act to impose its most preferred outcome on a situation without the input of the other Council members. Thus, the comparison is altered in the shadow of an outside option. Instead of weighing a multilateral policy against the status quo, the permanent members weigh the multilateral policy against the policy that would result from unilateral (or alternative venue) action. Voeten's primary result is that a multilateral policy will move toward the preference of the P5 member with the outside option. The multilateral policy, however, will not be the exact policy of the member with the outside option because pursuing unilateral action is quite costly. Thus, some multilateral policies are better than unilateral action even though they are not the most preferred policy of the member with the outside option because they are close enough to justify foregoing the unilateral intervention costs.

In our empirical analysis, we attempt to capture these expected relationships with a model of US intervention to assess the credibility of the outside option for the US. One of the biggest challenges to analyzing the formal predictions is measurement. We do not have a valid measure of policy alternatives—only preferences of the members based on other observable behaviors (alliance patterns, voting behavior in the UN General Assembly, etc.). We also do not have measures for expected costs of unilateral action. Thus, instead of mapping outcomes to policies, we map them to observable behaviors in the Council, specifically meetings and authorized action. In Hypotheses 2 and 3, we expect the Council to meet and discuss under these conditions. Voeten collapses the negotiating and voting process by focusing only on the resolution vote in his model. But it is possible that negotiations do not go as planned, so the Council may not reach agreement to take action, leading to the occasional unilateral action.[3] We expect, however, that if the US is more likely to intervene, the Council will find a way to reach agreement to avoid defaulting to US unilateral action, since the US has an incentive to avoid paying the costs of unilateral action if the multilateral option is better than taking on the unilateral burden (labeled Hypothesis 3a as a case-specific corollary hypothesis to Hypothesis 3).

Hypothesis 3a *As the likelihood of US intervention increases, the likelihood of UN authorized action also increases.*

[3] Voeten does incorporate uncertainty about the credibility of the outside option, which is what we capitalize on in the analysis.

5.2 Effects of the Outside Option Inside the Council

To test the impact of an outside option, we first need an estimate of the credibility of that outside option. When might the threat of unilateral action by the US make other Council members more willing to agree to policy options closer to the US' preference in order to facilitate multilateral action? After we have an idea of how credible the outside option threat is, we then need to assess whether more credible threats affect decision-making in the Council.

During its first thirty-five years, the UN Security Council passed fewer than twenty-five Chapter VII resolutions. Chapter VII of the UN Charter empowers to Council to take action in response to threats to international peace and security. These resolutions are also notable because they are binding on all members of the broader UN community, not just the Security Council. Since 1990, more than 600 resolutions have been passed under Chapter VII (Wallensteen and Johansson, 2015). Chapter VII resolutions are used to enforce decisions of the Council—either using military or non-military means.

Since the end of the Cold War, the Council has greatly increased the attention given to internal conflicts. Because the Council has become more involved militarily in more civil conflicts in the past 25 years, we focus in this chapter on military action authorized by the Council in response to civil conflicts (both via peacekeeping and military action authorized under Article 42 of the UN Charter).

As a first step, we look at all internal conflicts that have occurred from 1990-2012 according to the Uppsala Conflict Data Project (UCDP) (Gleditsch et al., 2002). UCDP defines a conflict as "a contested incompatibility that concerns government and/or territory where the use of armed force between two parties, of which at least one is the government of a state, results in at least twenty-five battle-related deaths in a calendar year" (Petterson and Eck, 2018). Civil conflicts are internal armed conflicts occurring between a national government and one or more rebel group within the state. We also include internationalized internal armed conflicts, which have the same characteristics as civil conflicts, but they also include military intervention from other states on one or both sides (Petterson and Eck, 2018). Among these conflicts, we estimate the chances that the US would intervene in each civil conflict in a given year.

As a next step, we collected information on interventions into those wars.[4] We drew these data from the International Military Intervention (IMI) dataset

[4] We also looked into using the external support data from the UCDP project Högbladh, Pettersson and Themnér (2011), but their definitions were less precise for military intervention than we were looking for. Their project has a broader view of external support, thus for our purposes, it was a less useful source of intervention data.

Pickering and Kisangani (2009), which builds on previous data collection by Pearson and Baumann (1993). They define intervention as "the movement of regular troops or forces (airborne, seaborne, shelling, etc) of one country inside another, in the context of some political issue or dispute," (Pearson and Baumann, 1993, p. 1). Combining the available data from these two sources, the time frame from this analysis is 1990–2012.[5]

We estimate the probability that the US will be willing to intervene in the conflict based on a variety of factors. First, we consider the capabilities of the US, assuming that intervention will be more likely when the US is investing more in its military (Singer, Bremer, and Stuckey, 1972). To do so, we include a measure of US military spending in a given year as collected in the National Material Capabilities data set by the Correlates of War project. This variable is measured in thousands of current year US Dollars, as reported by the International Monetary Fund (Grieg and Enterline, 2017).[6] As spending increases, we expect the likelihood of US intervention to increase.

The domestic political environment should also affect the likelihood that the US will intervene in a civil war. Domestic politics will have an effect. We know that there are partisan differences regarding foreign policy (McCormick and Wittkopf, 1990, 1992). Historically, Democratic presidents have been less likely to use force (Fordham, 1998). On the other hand, scholars have found Democrats more likely to intervene for humanitarian reasons (Hildebrandt et al., 2013)—an often cited motivation for international action during this period, so we consider the party of the president in power. In addition, electoral timing will likely have an impact. Intervention should be less likely in an election year.

In addition, we take the relationship between the US and the conflict state into account by including capital distance (measured in miles and logged), alliance partnership (according to the Correlates of War project), and trade flows (*Correlates of War Project Trade Data Set Codebook, Verson 4.0*, N.d.). Additionally, we include an indicator for whether or not the conflict state is a former colony of a P5 country, assuming that the US might be less likely to intervene in a state where another permanent member has a clear interest (*Issue Correlates of War (ICOW) Historical State Names Data Set, version 1.3.*, N.d.). Finally, we also include two variables regarding the conflict state itself. We include regime type from Polity IV (*Polity IV Project: Political regime characteristics and transitions, 1800–2007*, 2009) and battle death data from UCDP (Erik Melander, 2016).

[5] We drew these data from the International Military Intervention (IMI) dataset (Pickering and Kisangani 2009), which builds on previous data collection by Pearson and Baumann (1993).

[6] Because of the scale of this variable, we take the natural log of the spending value.

Together, we believe these variables allow us to generate best-guess probabilities of US intervention. Using this information, we can determine if the likelihood affects the decisions of other members on potential Security Council action. Statistically, we use our model of intervention to generate predicted probabilities of US action in each civil conflict. Then we plug these probabilities into the second stage of the analysis as an additional variable.[7]

The second stage of the analysis considers additional factors that influence the decision to take action in the Council. Again, we start with the list of civil conflicts from UCDP, but now the outcome we are interested in is not whether or not the US intervenes, but whether or not the Council authorizes Chapter VII action. The factors that influence multilateral action will differ from those that influence US decision-making on unilateral action. Other members, however, are likely aware of whether or not the US is considering unilateral action, which can influence their decisions about multilateral action. China and Russia may be more willing to engage the Council on issues they care about if they fear there's a good chance that the US might take unilateral action and leave them out of the decision making.

As we did in Chapter 4, we consider the preference variation among the permanent members. We construct our measure using the foreign policy similarity of each permanent member and the conflict nation. To measure affinity, we use S-scores based on common voting in the General Assembly following Signorino and Ritter (1999) to calculate our average affinity and variance measures. The rates of common voting in the UN General Assembly between each P5 country and the conflict nation are summed and divided by five for an average rate of voting together. This tells us the average affinity, but we are interested in the variability in those preferences, so we again calculate the coefficient of variation by finding the standard deviation and dividing that by the mean.[8] We also include the number of vetoes cast in a given year in order to capture a sense of willingness to work together by the permanent members.

Because the Council is interested in decreasing threats to international peace and security, we also include the number of battle deaths in the conflict as a measure of conflict intensity. Previous research has demonstrated that peacekeepers go to the deadliest, most difficult conflicts to resolve (Gilligan and Stedman, 2003). In addition, whether or not a ceasefire has been reached has an impact on the decision to send peacekeepers (Fortna, 2004). As we did in the first stage, we also include an indicator of whether or not the conflict

[7] Because of the noisy nature of these estimates, we bootstrap the errors in the second stage.

[8] This measure of preference variability among the P5 has been used by Allen and Yuen (2014); Copelovitch (2010).

country is a former colony of one of the permanent members. Former colonial masters may maintain influence in these countries.

Over time, the Council has been more willing to authorize peacekeeping missions and to invoke Chapter VII in its resolutions. For that reason, we also control for time.[9] Finally, we explore whether or not the number of existing peacekeeping missions acts as a constraint on the decision to establish additional peacekeeping missions. Assuming that troops and funding are limited, we expect more existing missions to decrease the likelihood that new missions will be created, especially Chapter VII enforcement missions.

5.3 The United States and the Outside Option

Turning to the results presented in the coefficient plot (Figure 5.1[10]), we see the factors that affect the likelihood that the US will intervene in a civil conflict. The US intervenes in just under 9 percent of the years included in the UCDP dataset. Our analysis shows that the US is more likely to intervene in severe conflicts that have high casualty counts. Military and economic ties influence

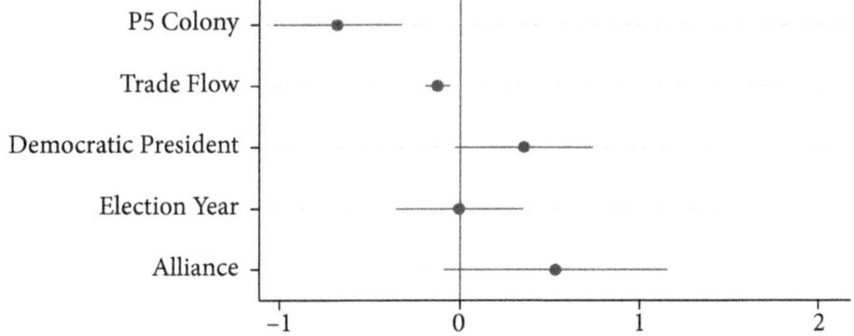

Fig. 5.1 Estimated coefficients and confidence intervals from a logit model of the likelihood that the US will intervene in a given conflict in a given year, 1990–2012

[9] We do so using time, time squared, and time cubed following Carter and Signorino (2010) in order to capture potential nonlinear temporal effects.

[10] Regression output in Table C.1 in the Appendix C.

US intervention, but they work in opposite directions. The US is slightly more likely to intervene where they have an alliance, but they are less likely to intervene as trade flows increase. Interestingly, the domestic political variables like election timing and party of the president are less influential during this time period.

US intervention is less likely in states that used to be colonies of the P5 countries. Because the US was not a major colonial power, it does not have a broad post-colonial foreign policy based on prior ties. France and Britain have a great incentive to take military action based on colonial ties and based on this result the US seems willing to defer to them. The US is neither more nor less likely to take action in faraway places or contingent on regime type.

Taken together, these variables allow us to estimate the likelihood that the US is likely to intervene in a given conflict. For each internal conflict in the UCDP dataset, we generate a predicted probability for the chance that the US will intervene in a particular conflict. We include these estimates in our second stage, which allows us to assess whether or not the increased likelihood of US military intervention increases the chances of UN action in a civil conflict state. The results for the second stage are presented in Figure 5.2[11] These results provide support for Hypotheses 2 and 3. First, we see that as the variability in preferences among the P5 increases, UN-led action in civil conflict is less likely. In addition, these results also provide empirical support for Voeten's (2001) idea that as the likelihood of US intervention increases, those within the Council are more likely to be interested in acting within the UN framework in order to maintain their influence. The credibility of the US outside option is an important predictor of UN action.

Given our interest in the preferences of Security Council members, we find support for the idea that as the variability in Security Council affinity increases, the likelihood of UN action decreases. With the ever present threat of a veto, which in the post-Cold War era is often considered as important or perhaps more important than the actual veto, the Council tends to take action in locations where the permanent members are more similar in their preferences.

Surprisingly none of the characteristics of the conflict—number of battle deaths or the presence of a ceasefire—meaningfully impact whether or not the UN will take action in a given civil conflict year. The only other variable that has an influence is the number of ongoing peacekeeping missions. Rather than acting as a resource constraint, when there are more ongoing missions the Council appears more willing to take on additional actions. This may

[11] Regression output in Table C.2 in the Appendix C.

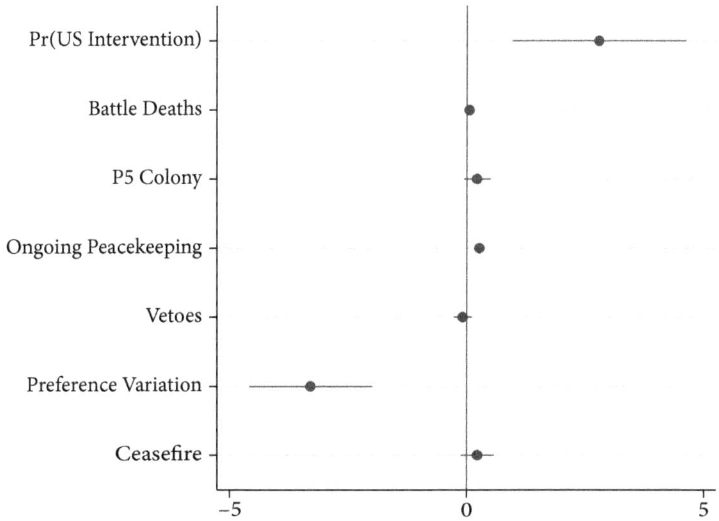

Fig. 5.2 Estimated coefficients and confidence intervals from a logit model of the likelihood that the Security Council will take Chapter VII action in a given conflict in a given year, 1990–2012

reflect the cyclical nature of support for peacekeeping over time. In the early years, support for peacekeeping was high. After the notable failures in Somalia and Rwanda, support for peacekeeping went down and fewer new missions were initiated. There was another period of enthusiasm early in the twenty-first century.

These results provide empirical support for the outside options logic put forth by Voeten (2001), an idea that had not been quantitatively tested. Voeten focused on the role of the US as the most powerful actor in the international system and the most influential member of the Council. What are the political implications of the US outside option influencing the decision-making of other members of the Council?

5.4 Discussion

After the Cold War, more topics have been handled within the Security Council and a great deal more action has been taken. The most prominent explanation for why more action has been occurred in the Security Council is that the preferences of permanent members are more similar. During the Cold War, deadlock occurred because of dissimilar preferences, and after the

Cold War, more cooperation occurred because preferences were more similar. We presented evidence in Chapter 4 that this argument does have some merit. In this chapter, however, we offer a slightly different potential explanation for why the Council has been a more popular forum—the increased influence of the US.

Following the collapse of the Soviet Union, there was no obvious check on US power, creating an opportunity for US to potentially act unilaterally with impunity. One consequence of this increased freedom, however, might be surprising. Counterintuitively, we suggest that the unipolar moment led to more compromise toward the US position in the Council, which resulted in more multilateral activity. This argument suggests that there has not been more cooperation because of shared interests but because the US is relatively stronger and can more credibly threaten unilateral action. Why is this important?

If we shift our vantage point slightly, we see that these findings further bolster our idea that institutions and the rules they embody matter. The increased action in the Council reflects the increased influence of the US, but those actions are occurring within the constraints of the institution. The other permanent members have demonstrated a willingness to concede some ground to the US, but in doing so, they are reining in American influence. For its part, while the US may have to make some concessions to other Council members, as the most powerful actor, it is guiding the general direction of international policy when it works through the Council. The US also benefits from increased perceived legitimacy by acting multilaterally and is able to share the cost burden with other states.

Political factors influence action in the Council both within and beyond the Council chamber. Powerful states like the US have a choice—they can work within the UN system, or they can act beyond its constraints. Other Council members recognize the existence of this choice and take the US threat to exclude them from action seriously. The permanent members are likely assessing whether or not accepting an inside action that is not their most preferred option is preferable to allowing the US to take unilateral action. China and Russia recognize that when they are excluded, the policy selected by the US might be even less preferable than what was proposed within the Security Council.

Members' own preferences and their perceptions of the preferences of other members will interact to influence the choice to work within the UN system. Fears that another member may use an outside option if the UN route is closed to them could lead members to be more willing to make concessions or compromise within the Council to maintain influence over the actions taken. On the other hand, the permanent members have been highly effective over the past 60 years at keeping issues that they did not want discussed off of the Council agenda.

These findings might also have implications for the rise of China. Historically, China has chosen not taken an active role in guiding the agenda, especially compared to the Western Three. If China chooses to become more engaged in the Council, its increased power may diminish the US' ability to credibly threaten outside action. Paradoxically, this could decrease action within the Council, because China may be less willing to make concessions that would allow agreement within the Council, similar to the dynamics in the North Korean case, which we explore in detail in Chapter 6.

6

North Korean Nuclear Proliferation: A Dilemma in the Council

Nuclear non-proliferation is one of the most unifying subjects in the UN Security Council. This is a rare issue of confluence in which the normative standards of each permanent member align such that they share strong preferences to prevent and prohibit nuclear proliferation to other states. Likewise, most non-nuclear and non-permanent member states share the objective to limit (or even roll back) the number of nuclear states in the world.[1]

North Korea's nuclear program is a perennial subject in the Security Council. Since 1993 when North Korea first entered the Council's agenda, activity regarding the small, insular state has increased in both frequency and intensity. In fact, as of this writing, the activity has spanned 25 years in the Council, a surprising amount of time given how unified the member states are against proliferation. A closer look, however, shows that agreement in the Council was bounded, and involved much more compromise than a review of resolutions would suggest. Looking beyond the meeting and resolution counts, we examine the bargaining and compromise that preceded votes in the Council to demonstrate how public costs, incurred after a Council member reveals its preferences to external audiences, influences both the method in which the Council bargains and the outcomes of that bargaining process—the terms set in the resolution text.

Our analysis includes details on US preferences during this period, but our primary focus is on China as the Council member with significant public costs to consider in the North Korean case. The historical record suggests several reasons why China should be the primary focus on this issue. Its proximity

[1] The connection between thematic issues and national ones is worth noting here. Resolutions on thematic issues, like non-proliferation, have direct consequences for national issues, which are often cases of nations that violate some standard set in resolutions on thematic issues. Thus, resolutions on thematic issues may derive from preferences more purely, while resolutions on national issues may be influenced more by other considerations, like outside options and public costs.

Bargaining in the UN Security Council. Susan Hannah Allen and Amy Yuen, Oxford University Press.
 DOI: 10.1093/oso/9780192849755.003.0006

and historical ties to the North Korean regime ensure it has a vested interest in policy toward North Korea, and while the US can project significant military power great distances, China also carries the military advantage that proximity imposes. We explain, however, that China also stands to lose a great deal if international action to manage proliferation leads to the collapse of the North Korean regime. Scholars of modern Chinese UN policy offer several competing explanations for why China does or does not cooperate in the Council, but none consider the public costs logic we present in Chapter 3. We examine the evidence for these explanations from 1993 to the more recent events in 2020. Access to primary sources from the Chinese government and the North Korean regime is quite restricted, but where possible, we examine official statements and records from each to support our analysis.

6.1 Explaining Cooperation in the Council

Much of this book is dedicated to explaining why cooperation succeeds or fails inside the Security Council with an argument that public costs influence strategic choices about the process, which affects policy outcomes. To understand why the Council has acted on the North Korean case as it has, we focus on the decision calculus of the US and China, the two primary P5 members in the debate over North Korea's nuclear program.

We know that the US has been active in the Council since the beginning, but China has increasingly taken substantive action in the Council (voting in favor of resolutions or vetoing, not just abstaining) since it assumed the permanent seat in 1971.[2] Recent studies of China's behavior in the Council highlight three primary political dynamics: the availability and attractiveness of outside options, the concessions Council members can obtain in negotiations, and the political pressures they exert on each other (Wuthnow, 2010, 2013).[3] Further studies also consider the domestic factors that influence international

[2] Originally, the Republic of China was a founding member of the UN, but during the civil war, Chiang Kai-shek and his forces lost control of the mainland. The People's Republic of China (PRC) assumed the seat in place of the Republic of China (Taiwan) since the PRC won control of the large landmass and resources of the territory traditionally considered to be China in 1949. Slowly, the Western delegations began to recognize the reality on the ground and shifted their stance on Chinese membership in the Council in 1971.

[3] Wuthnow offers a broader framework for Chinese behavior in the Security Council, but the propositions he offers can be summarized as Chinese considerations for alternative options like bilateral diplomacy and reaction to the behaviors of other permanent members, specifically the US and Russia. While these are important ideas, our model offers explanations for what makes members more or less flexible around an issue and incorporates features of the institution itself to explain what comes out of it.

policy in China (Oertel, 2014). These explanations do not examine how issues move through the Council, and as we showed in Chapter 3, the process can significantly alter the observed outcomes.

Our own analysis accounts for each of these factors, but we also consider how the public costs of different actions in the Council influenced the substance of the resolutions that resulted from cycles of negotiation and defiance from North Korea. Public costs are costs associated with taking a public position and then having to defend that position during public negotiations inside the Council that end with a vote on a resolution. We identify two types of public costs, those that would follow a veto and those that would follow a resolution passed in the Council. The most natural groups that impose costs on states are domestic groups that stand to benefit or gain from action in the Council. China has domestic groups that fit these roles, but the one-party system limits the power of domestic groups to challenge the party line without taking more extreme measures. For the North Korea case, we argue there are more pressing external public costs that China has considered in all of its negotiations regarding North Korea, specifically what China's public position and actions in the Council suggest for the North Korean regime's survival, the political relationships in the region, and the possibility of US military action. These factors have driven discussion of the North Korean case behind tightly closed doors and have resulted in slow, incremental actions conducted with the consent of all members of the Council. Our argument suggests that when public costs narrow the bargaining range, states looking to pass a resolution through the Council will negotiate privately so as to avoid paying public costs; further, states facing those public costs can use them as bargaining leverage. We trace the negotiations surrounding North Korea's nuclear program to show how action in the Council occurred primarily through private consultations. We further show how China continually tempered resolutions to minimize the likelihood of regime collapse while still accommodating unanimous desire in the Council to do something about North Korea. Finally, we examine how China has adapted to the potential public costs associated with regime collapse, which coincides with major shifts in policy within the UN more recently.

The relationships among North Korea, the US, and China emerged out of the Korean War and, until recently, the alignments remained relatively stable. The US has maintained a military presence in South Korea since the Korean War with troop levels on the peninsula around 25,000. In fact, the US presence in South Korea has continued the antipathy with North Korea and is one reason the North Koreans give for pursuing a nuclear capability. China aligned with North Korea in the war and took over as primary patron when the Soviet Union collapsed. Thus, managing the nuclear issue has involved primarily North and South Korea, the US and China as great power interlocutors, and regional powers Japan and Russia.

While South Korea is most directly threatened by North Korean military actions and in a second Korean War would sustain the most damage, North Korea has repeatedly implicated the US as a main source of grievances. North Korea has issued threats against the US in public statements, usually in response to joint military training exercises with South Korean forces. The war ended in an armistice only, not a formal peace treaty, and so the de facto settlement is roughly the 38th parallel with a demilitarized zone between. The US has maintained military forces in South Korea as a deterrent for any aggressive actions from North Korea. Periodically, the two Koreas have exchanged live fire or endured limited attacks, prompting the US to remain to defend its ally. These conditions also prevent China from abandoning North Korea, though relations between China and North Korea have evolved significantly over time due to China's rise as a global power and as a result of North Korea's entry on the nuclear stage.

6.1.1 Consensus on Nuclear Non-proliferation

Few issues in the Council generate as much agreement among the permanent members as preventing nuclear proliferation. The Nuclear Non-proliferation Treaty (NPT), signed in 1968, included the permanent members of the Security Council, all of whom were nuclear powers then and continue to maintain nuclear arsenals today. These weapons have enormous destructive power, creating a dilemma for states that do not have a nuclear capability—pursue one for protection, or prevent others from gaining the capability to minimize the chances of nuclear war. Cold War dynamics spurred efforts to control the spread of nuclear weapons on the logic that keeping the number of nuclear states small reduced the chances of nuclear exchange that escalated to levels that threaten human annihilation.

The desire to avoid nuclear war became entrenched as a global norm that since 1968 has only been violated fully (via nuclear testing) by four states. In fact, some previously nuclear or nuclear-aspiring states (e.g., Brazil, South Africa, and Ukraine) have given up domestic or inherited nuclear arsenals for various reasons including the expense to maintain them, the negative political effects for possessing a nuclear arsenal, domestic political pressure, and lack of need (lower security threat) (Long and Grillot, 2000).

Established nuclear states also have incentives to prevent proliferation. From a strategic point of view, a nuclear arsenal is a coercive advantage vis-à-vis non-nuclear states and a balancing force against other nuclear states. Proliferation allows new nuclear states to take advantage of that balancing force to credibly resist coercion. Beyond the military advantages, however, established nuclear states also benefit from limiting the number of nuclear states because it lowers the risk of nuclear war. Thus, the permanent members have strategic and normative incentives to prevent the spread of nuclear weapons.

The permanent members' behavior in the Council regarding nuclear (and other Weapons of Mass Destruction (WMD)) proliferation shows that they all share the goal of preventing proliferation quite strongly. Between the NPT and North Korea's first attempt to withdraw from the treaty in 1993, only two states (India and Pakistan[4]) entered the nuclear stage, and they never signed on to the NPT.[5] North Korea was the first signatory to invoke the withdrawal clause, but they stalled the withdrawal process in 1993 and did not return to it until 2003. When North Korea officially withdrew in 2003 and in light of other potential nuclear proliferation in the Middle East,[6] the Council took unified action to institutionalize efforts to prevent nuclear proliferation with Resolution 1540 in 2004.

Discussions leading up to Resolution 1540 illustrate that UN member nations were very concerned about non-state actors gaining access to WMDs. While existing treaties cover details of state-to-state transfers, there were perceived gaps in the coverage of those treaties, which were signed in an international political climate that did not anticipate transnational terrorism. The front matter in the resolution text illustrates this concern:

> *Gravely concerned* by the threat of terrorism and the risk that non-State actors...may acquire, develop, traffic in or use nuclear, chemical and biological weapons and their means of delivery,
> *Gravely concerned* by the threat of illicit trafficking in nuclear, chemical, or biological weapons and their means of delivery, which adds a new dimension to the issue of proliferation of such weapons and also poses a threat to international peace and security ... .
>
> (S/RES/1540)

[4] Pakistan had enough enriched material for a weapon in 1986 but conducted its first test in 1998.
[5] Israel also has a nuclear capability that it has kept secret. They also did not sign on to the NPT.
[6] Specifically, the IAEA investigated Iran's clandestine program, and the US had suspicions that Iraq had also restarted its program which was later found to be untrue.

Thus, in the wake of numerous transnational terrorist attacks, suspicions that terrorist organizations were attempting to obtain WMDs and suspicions and evidence that some states were pursuing clandestine programs, the Council pursued a resolution to reaffirm commitment to non-proliferation and classify potential proliferation to non-state actors as under its purview. The delegations that sponsored Resolution 1540 took unusual steps to garner support from as many UN member nations as possible. Beyond consultations in the Council, sponsoring delegations sought bilateral consultations as they wrote provisions into the resolution. Reference to these consultations appears in the formal meeting record when the vote on 1540 took place.

Resolution 1540 was controversial, not for its stated concerns and goals but for its method of addressing those concerns and reaching those goals. UN member states had numerous concerns broadly summarized in these areas: (1) that the resolution authorized use of force to address potential proliferation because it was approved under Chapter VII, (2) that it constituted overreach because its directives to member states required domestic enforcement[7], and (3) that the Security Council might not be the appropriate forum for these issues and initiatives because it was not an appropriately democratic institution.[8] In fact, the process leading to the final resolution draft was highly unusual, including a public debate in the Council in which all UN member states were invited to attend. Many nations spoke about specific provisions and their implications, but none denied that the risks of WMD proliferation were high and required coordinated effort to contain.

After the sponsors revised the resolution draft in response to feedback, the Council voted unanimously to adopt the resolution. Statements during the meeting showed unusually close unity on the problem of WMD proliferation. For example, the Chinese delegation emphasized that it supported the resolution because the UN has a legitimate role in non-proliferation efforts. It further noted that the stipulations in the resolution were consistent with existing international law.

While Resolution 1540 is not directly about North Korean nuclear proliferation, the resolution is important for the North Korean case for three reasons. First, it establishes that the members of the Council, and most of the wider UN membership, agree that non-proliferation is a primary goal for the maintenance of peace and security. Thus, it establishes a baseline set of preferences

[7] Domestic enforcement meant domestic laws and legal infrastructure were being influence by an international institution—a potential threat to sovereignty.

[8] See the UN press release SC/8070 for a summary of the various comments made at the 4950th meeting or the verbatim meeting record itself.

for issues of non-proliferation. Second, it establishes that countries bear responsibility to join and comply with existing non-proliferation regimes. Third, subsequent resolutions specific to North Korea explicitly reference Resolution 1540 as justification for the actions the Council takes against North Korean nuclear proliferation. In any generic nuclear proliferation case, the permanent members are against it, and further, the members agree that the Council has the authority to act on these cases as a threat to international peace and security.

The patterns and pace of cooperation on North Korea, then, are somewhat slow and fraught, considering the consensus on nuclear proliferation. The US and China approached the problem with very different considerations, despite unified preference on nuclear proliferation. We argue these particular considerations explain the observed behavior in the Council over the last 25 years for all members, but most particularly China.

6.1.2 United States' Preferences

In the 40 years following the armistice that ended the Korean War, the US sought to hold the line in Korea against further communist expansion in Asia. The focus changed abruptly with two developments in the early 1990s. First, the Soviet Union's collapse left only China to fill the void of support for North Korea, since the small regime was highly dependent on patronage from its larger neighbors. Second, North Korea announced its intention to withdraw from the NPT in 1993, which is a very serious step that prompted expectations that it was developing a nuclear weapon.

After the Korean War, the US cemented itself as a firm ally of South Korea, even going so far as to maintain tens of thousands of troops there to demonstrate its commitment to respond to any military action against South Korea. Thus, when the North Koreans announced their intentions in 1993, the Clinton administration considered many options, including military strikes as a response. The decision on what action to take, if any, included several factors, one of which was what it wanted North Korea to do next with regard to its participation in the NPT.

Warren Christopher, who was Secretary of State at the time, characterized the US' desire that North Korea remain a party to the NPT and resume inspections from the International Atomic Energy Agency (IAEA) as required by the treaty (Christopher, 1998). This is the set of actions North Korea had refused before announcing its withdrawal. An obvious result of these preferences is that North Korea abandon any nuclear arsenal ambitions it held. Indeed, the members of the Security Council shared these preferences for North Korean actions regarding its domestic nuclear reactors and its participation in the NPT. Further, the US' preference since 1993 has been that North Korea disarm, open to inspection, and return to the NPT regime, remaining consistent for decades. Variation in preferences has at times included resolving the Korean War with a formal treaty to hopes that opening North Korea up would lead to peaceful regime change.[9]

To get North Korea to change its behavior, however, the US was going to have to act itself. A wide range of options existed, including working through the UN Security Council to generate multilateral action on North Korea. There are no formal enforcement mechanisms codified into the original text of the NPT, so the responsibility to enforce has fallen to the Council, most often in the form of sanctions. Other options included working in bilateral, diplomatic negotiations or pursuing a military solution.

The military solution has always been a complicated option, despite US capability to project enormous power. With several allies so near North Korea, specifically South Korea and Japan, and with China's land access to the peninsula, a military strike has several disadvantages that have consistently made it an unattractive option. Warren Christopher noted how close Seoul is to North Korean artillery and the number of US troops stationed in South Korea at the time (37,000) that would constitute serious losses in a military battle. He further recognized that even though all US military estimates ended with the expectation that the US would triumph, it would come at unacceptably high cost (Christopher, 1998).

The Clinton administration ultimately pursued a diplomatic approach to North Korea's declaration working bilaterally through an opening negotiated by former President Jimmy Carter that led to the *Agreed Framework between the United States of America and the Democratic People's Republic of Korea*, commonly referred to as the "Agreed Framework." This compromise required North Korea to shut down its primary plutonium reactors and the Yongbyon reprocessing plant while the US committed to normalizing diplomatic and economic relationships with North Korea and providing immediate energy

[9] This is particularly evident in former Secretary of State Condoleezza Rice's memoir in which she stated the Bush administration's desires succinctly, "...we pursued the denuclearization of North Korea with three goals in mind: increasing the transparency of Kim Jong-il's nuclear program by 'getting our people on the ground'; reducing the ability of North Korea to make, sell, or use nuclear weapons by retarding Kim's capacity to produce plutonium; and, if Kim was willing to give up his weapons, ending the Korean conflict. And perhaps through diplomacy—not just confrontation—we could end the loathsome regime itself." (Rice, 2011: p. 526)

Fig. 6.1 A Map of the Korean Peninsula

Map reproduced with the permission of CartoGIS Services, Scholarly Information Services, The Australian National University

assistance needs, including building light-water reactors for domestic power production (*Agreed Framework Between the United States and the Democratic People's Republic of Korea*, 1994; Albright and Woodward, 2003). Throughout the Clinton administration's time in office, they worked with North Korea under this framework, but relations over North Korea's missile tests created serious challenges to the longevity of the agreement. What followed was a tumultuous period of sanctions and negotiations that carried over to George W. Bush's administration up to North Korea's formal declaration of withdrawal from the NPT in January of 2003. Consequently, what had been a mostly bilateral process quickly changed to a multilateral one with the opening of the Six-Party Talks.

The Six-Party Talks process included the US, China, Japan, North and South Korea, and Russia. This multilateral process occurred alongside continuing Security Council action as a direct negotiating forum with North Korea. The process similarly ebbed and flowed around nuclear facility declarations, dismantlements, and verification in exchange for energy support and sanctions relief, but progress was halting and ultimately unsuccessful despite several agreements and instances of cooperation in the interim. Security Council action increased substantially following Resolution 1540 alongside and in coordination with the Six-Party Talks, but by the end of 2008, the process seemed stalled indefinitely and in spring of 2009 after another North Korean missile test, North Korea formally withdrew from the Six-Party Talks.[10]

Relations between the US and North Korea deteriorated over the next decade. Some preliminary attempts to restart the Six-Party Talks never came to fruition, and a series of missile tests, satellite launches, and diplomatic crises[11] in the region widened the gulf between the US and North Korea. Despite two high profile summits between Kim Jong Un and Donald Trump and a new Biden administration, no agreement has been struck, and North Korea has resumed missiles tests.

Through the several decades of relations between the US and North Korea, the US position has fluctuated only slightly in what they might be willing to offer in exchange for North Korean cooperation. At the heart of US preferences are North Korean denuclearization in the form of halting all production of

[10] Various non-profit organizations track negotiations around security issues. See the timeline on North Korea from the Ams Control Association (https://www.armscontrol.org/factsheets/dprkchron) and the timeline from the Security Council Report (https://www.securitycouncilreport.org/chronology/dprk-north-korea.php) for more detail on these events.

[11] For example, the South Koreans accused North Korea of sinking a South Korea patrol ship, the *Cheonan*, a charge that North Korea denied. In 2017, the half-brother of Kim Jong Un was assassinated in Malaysia via chemical weapons attack (VX), also denied by the North Koreans.

nuclear material, dismantling nuclear facilities, declaring all nuclear facilities, and giving access to inspectors for verification, as well as complying with its obligations to halt ballistic missile testing and export. The variation primarily involves whether the US would agree to provide or allow others to provide light-water reactors for power generation to North Korea and which sanctions to lift in response to each step of compliance with the obligations set in multiple agreements.

6.1.3 China's Preferences

Given China's proximity, relative size, and historically close relationship with North Korea, all parties to any negotiations around North Korea's nuclear program recognize China's essential role in supporting diplomatic efforts to denuclearize the Korean peninsula. Thus, understanding China's preferences around this issue are crucial to understanding its progress, particularly through the Council, where China carries veto power. This section establishes China's preferences on nuclear proliferation generally and then focuses on the North Korean case specifically. It describes China's relationship with North Korea and identifies the tensions in China's diplomatic calculus in handling North Korea's nuclear evolution.

As the prior section on Resolution 1540 suggested, China joined in the effort to manage nuclear proliferation in the unusual public debate that occurred in the Security Council with the participation of more than a quarter of the UN membership. The sitting Council presented a unified position, acknowledging where concessions were made to address the concerns raised in consultations and public statements. China's own statement in this meeting is illustrative of its commitment to maintaining and enforcing nuclear non-proliferation:

> Preventing the proliferation of weapons of mass destruction (WMD) and their means of delivery is conducive to the maintenance of international peace and security and is in the international community's common interests. For years, United Nations Member States have made important efforts in that regard. In the new international security environment, it is crucial to strengthen international cooperation aimed at developing and improving the existing international non-proliferation regime so that we can respond effectively to the threat of terrorism.
>
> China opposes the proliferation of WMD and of their means of delivery, and we have taken an active part in international non-proliferation efforts. China

has always advocated the complete prohibition and thorough destruction of all kinds of WMD.

(Official Meeting Record S/PV.4950)

These statements are public declarations of their commitment to non-proliferation. Given that this debate occurred after North Korea resumed its declaration and withdrawal from the NPT and concurrently with the negotiations around the Agreed Framework, China most certainly had North Korea in mind. These statements reflect a more general, positive turn toward acting through the UN, a foreign policy change that some China experts date to 2001, when Jiang Zemin served as General Secretary (Oertel, 2014). China's willingness to view the UN as a legitimate institution and the Security Council as the appropriate place to manage international peace and security also meant that it would be able to wield its veto more effectively to ensure Council actions took into account Chinese concerns.

China's Relationship with North Korea

In the North Korean case, the issue of nuclear non-proliferation is less straightforward for China given their historical relationship. The current North Korean regime was born of liberation from Japanese rule following World War II. Just as in every other theater of the war, the issue of occupation had to be determined, and while the allies agreed on a free and independent Korea, the same issues arose in the Eastern theater that arose in others about who would ultimately rule.[12] Thus, as a temporary step, the Americans devised a partition plan to split Korea into occupation zones. Colonel Dean Rusk, who would go on to serve as Secretary of State for President Kennedy, and Colonel Charles Bonesteel were tasked with developing zones of occupation for Korea despite not being experts on Korea. They chose the 38th parallel and were somewhat surprised when the Soviets accepted the plan (Rusk, 1990).[13] This decision determined the boundary for North and South Korea that persists today, but it also shaped the political fates of these countries under divided occupation.

The connection to China was not immediate, however, even after Chinese intervention in the Korean War on behalf of the communist North. The zone of occupation primarily became the responsibility of the Soviet Union, which

[12] See Wolford (2017) for a study of how military coalitions fare after victory.

[13] The story is fascinating. Rusk and Bonesteel used a *National Geographic* map and selected the 38th parallel because the US didn't want an extensive area of occupation and the line put Seoul in the American zone (p. 124). What they did not realize was that the partition gave the North the largest population and much of the industrial development that the Japanese had installed in the colony (Olsen, 2005).

developed its own plan to shape and administer North Korea, even so far as to choose its leadership—bringing the Kim family to power. Descriptions of the political relationships among the North Koreans, Soviets, and Chinese until 1989 vary. Some suggest that North Korea was surprisingly independent of either Communist regime due primarily to the competition that arose between the Soviet Union and China. The argument is that North Korea saw opportunities to play one power against the other to extract as much as possible from the two patrons (Olsen, 2005). Other scholars point to a closer relationship between North Korea and China in the long run because the Soviets removed occupation troops and reduced their engagements in North Korea to focus on their foothold in central Europe. This perspective emphasizes the Chinese role in the Korean War as solidifying the political connection between the regimes (Cumings, 1995). Nonetheless, the collapse of the Soviet Union reinforced the Chinese-North Korea connection. Not long after this critical shift in geopolitics, North Korea issued its withdrawal declaration from the NPT, which is when action in the Council on North Korea first appeared.

When China became the only viable communist patron, the relationship was established but, according to many accounts, the potential for diverging preferences was already apparent. China had begun shifting its economy and governance from a strict communist model in the 1960s, industrializing and positioning itself to open more to international trade. North Korea turned inward. Further, the regimes organized quite differently, such that North Korea consolidated power early in a more loyalist, hereditary regime that sought to capture elites inside the regime, whereas China developed a more traditional, non-hereditary, single-party system (Cumings, 1995).[14]

None of the sources consulted portray the Sino-North Korean relationship as proceeding in lock step. Instead, the relationship has been fraught for decades, particularly because China's leadership pursued more cooperative opportunities with regional neighbors, particularly South Korea, while North Korea maintained a more antagonistic posture. China's regional considerations are contradictory, however, creating a conundrum for whom to engage with and how to handle North Korean provocations. The Chinese government under Hu Jintao pursued a strategic plan that was more open and cooperative regionally, but South Korea's security relationship with the US was a complication that had direct implications for North Korea. Part of longstanding Chinese strategic goals was to maintain North Korea as a strategic

[14] According to You (2001), Mao did not support hereditary succession in communist regimes. Even though Kim Jong-Il assumed leadership after Mao's death and with the (reluctant) approval of Deng Xiaoping, Kim resented that position, which may have reinforced a sense of independence from China.

buffer against the South and indirectly the US (Zhu, 2009). Softening relations between South Korea and China did not alleviate the concerns of US reach on the Korean peninsula, but China did make a more cooperative turn toward the US, which continued to maintain commitments to Taiwan and Japan, the former a particularly thorny issue. Thus, the question seems to have been how far do the Chinese push back against North Korean provocations? To answer this question for each provocation, the Chinese government had to weigh several considerations, which we detail broadly next and incorporate specifically in the following analysis of behavior in the Security Council.

China's Considerations for North Korean Policy

The agenda-setting model in Chapter 3 allows states to incur public accountability costs for policy outcomes in a public setting, thus a first step to explaining China's behavior in the Council is to establish whether and to what extent these costs exist. A natural question for this kind of analysis is also: which costs are most important for China? We focus our analysis here on the period between 2003 and 2008, which encompasses North Korea's resumption of withdrawal from the NPT, a series of missile tests, its first nuclear test, and the suspension of the Six-Party Talks.

Domestic costs

There are many candidates for costs that might influence China's response to North Korea's actions. Looking domestically first, what are the potential domestic costs of policy changes toward North Korea? Given the ideological, historical relationship between the two, it might seem that an iron-clad commitment to supporting North Korea as a kindred communist regime in the "neighborhood" defines Chinese policy. The history given previously, however, challenges this regime-level connection. The histories we consulted each emphasize significant differences between the two regimes, suggesting that an ideological connection was not pure and even sometimes generated conflict (e.g., the succession question in North Korea, economic strategies for development, etc.).[15] There is evidence of a split within the foreign policy establishment of the Chinese Communist Party on North Korea. The International Department of the Chinese Communist Party's Central Committee (CCPCC) sought to maintain and enhance relations with North Korea while the Ministry of Foreign Affairs adopted a position to cooperate more with regional members, subordinating the relationship with North Korea. The overall

[15] See also You (2001).

foreign policy trajectory shows that the Ministry of Foreign Affairs grew in influence at the expense of the CCPCC (Zhu, 2009).[16]

The reasons given for supporting the North Korean regime have focused much more on regional dynamics, specifically as a buffer against South Korea, but the relationship with South Korea has changed as well, creating more space for potential agreements there, particularly during Hu Jintao's leadership. While China still holds the position that North Korea is a necessary buffer, recent policy from Chinese scholars suggests that the need for that buffer is waning. Instead China does not see North Korea's antagonistic relationship with the US as defining its own relationship with the US and thus harbors less commitment to supporting and maintaining North Korea's anti-US position (Zhu, 2009). In fact, China has sought to open more toward its neighbors with whom relations have traditionally been poor to pursue a reduction in tensions and possible economic connections. These developments make North Korea less critical to Chinese regional foreign policy than it has been in the past.

Another potential area of domestic costs might come economically. The economic relationship between China and North Korea, though, is highly imbalanced.[17] North Korea is critically dependent on China to continue the flow of goods (and aid) because regional neighbors and states that could reach North Korea refuse to trade with a regime they view as dangerous and insular. Thus, North Korea's effect on the Chinese economy is small and would primarily be felt along the border with North Korea, suggesting that a purely economic cost is not a critical consideration (Nanto and Manyin, 2010).[18]

International costs

Because China is unlikely to pay large domestic political or economic costs, we look to the potential international costs that might accompany changes in policy toward North Korea. We argue that this is where the bulk of concern rests. China's public statements on foreign policy and the statements of its accredited scholars all suggest that the primary interest is to maintain a stable North Korean regime. This statement encompasses many facets of stability. Consistent with concerns about outside options, China must consider the likelihood that if the status quo remains, another nation may exercise a

[16] Zhu (2009) also cites a public opinion poll suggesting that Chinese citizens carried strong dislike of the North Korean regime, second only to dislike of Japan. Our attempts to confirm this poll, however, were thwarted by limited access to *China Daily*, the news source that published the poll results.

[17] See also Kim and Lee (2002) for a list of the significant power asymmetry across political and military factors as well.

[18] Next, we consider the economic costs of catastrophic regime collapse in North Korea.

potential outside option. In the context of North Korea, the nation with the greatest capacity to make a move outside the UN system is the US. Further, the status quo position in this period is to do nothing about North Korea's withdrawal from the NPT and later nuclear tests. While there is a great deal of uncertainty around whether the US would actually undertake military action against North Korea given China's significant regional advantage, the Chinese must consider this possibility in its decision-making. Thus, we will show in the analysis of actual behavior below whether and how these considerations played a role in China's actions in the Council.

A second factor also affects the likelihood of regime collapse in North Korea—sanctions. Very few states maintain trade with the North Korean regime, and at times, China has had to bail out the regime when its poorly structured economy could not produce essential goods or maintain electricity production to support North Korean industry (You, 2001). North Korea's economy is small and heavily reliant on China as a market and as a source of essential goods like petroleum. Thus, a less violent form of intervention could threaten the survival of the Kim regime in the form of economic sanctions, and it is the primary alternative to the status quo option to do nothing. The Council has focused its resolutions on sanctions for non-compliance, thus China stands in a difficult spot because it holds the lever of control on the North Korean sanctions regime. The veto on the Council allows it to have a direct say in any UN sanctions regime, but as the primary trade partner and aid source for North Korea, China also carries the actual means to enforce sanctions and affect the stability of the North Korean regime. Allowing a full, devastating sanctions regime would do little to the Chinese market, but the collapse of the North Korea regime would be imminent and create much more difficult problems for the Chinese in this period—specifically how to deal with the refugee population and the rapid political change on the Korean peninsula.[19]

From the sources we consulted, China's primary goal is to maintain the stability of the North Korean regime. Both insider sources and external government reports all emphasize this, and each makes reference to the potential refugee problem that China must consider with each policy change (Nanto and Manyin, 2010; You, 2001; Zhu, 2009). We argue that a potential refugee crisis from North Korea represents a significant public cost for the Chinese

[19] As North Korea builds its nuclear arsenal, the problem of regime collapse becomes even more difficult to manage. We consider this issue in the following analysis.

government because of the cascade of consequences that might result if a surge of refugees fleeing North Korea were to occur. Why are North Korean refugees of such concern to China? A 2004 study of North Korean refugee crises argues that if a large exodus of North Koreans to China (or South Korea) were to occur, there is a risk of the North Korean regime collapsing in the way the East German state collapsed in 1989. Whether the causal relationship between defections and state collapse is correct or not, China has expressed concerns that mass defections would lead to collapse and so behaves as though it is a possibility. The study further argues that the primary motivation for North Korean defections and illegal border crossings is economic hardship not political dissidence. North Korea experienced a surge in defections following historic flooding in the mid-1990s that caused widespread famine. While North Korea and China have cooperated to manage illegal crossings, the harshness in response has fluctuated. For decades, the Chinese authorities merely deported North Koreans that held no legal status in China, nor were they willing to grant legal status, and based on these policies, many North Koreans were likely deterred from attempting to cross. In recent years, however, enforcement became looser for several reasons. First, a significant ethnic Korean population lives in the border towns and maintains ties to family in North Korea. Thus many refugees fled to China and found support in these communities despite bearing no legal status. The Chinese government provided no services and the undocumented population provided very cheap, unskilled labor. Thus, the primary concerns about refugees is less about their effects in China than about the effects mass defection would have on the stability of the North Korean regime (Lankov, 2004).[20] Further, the political situation in North Korea has always been quite restricted, so much so that foreign visitors to the nation have been few and the people get almost no contact with the outside world except through communications tightly controlled by the regime.[21] Given the history of North Korean economic crisis migration to China, it is reasonable to connect the effect of economic sanctions to the likelihood of increased migration, and depending on the severity and immediacy of the sanctions regime, the likelihood of a refugee crisis may increase as well.

[20] The reason the Chinese bear little cost for a normal refugee flow is because they refuse to call them refugees and therefore are not obligated to offer assistance. Instead, they consider undocumented North Koreans to be illegal immigrants with no legal status who must survive on their own. Thus, the system in non-crisis periods is a net gain for China, according to Lankov.

[21] Lankov describes how radios in North Korea must be preset and that defectors who have been returned have increasingly smuggled in unregulated radios that are opening the regime up to the outside world in an unregulated way. He notes that younger generations are more politically skeptical because of this exposure and illicit access to South Korean internet.

In prior sections, we recounted China's political relationship with North Korea, which shows a slow but steadily widening gulf between them based on diverging political and economic structures. This divergence also changed the nature of regional relationships as China sought to engage more with South Korea and Japan, while North Korea refused Chinese-style economic reforms and remained closed off from trade in the region. The traditional role for North Korea in Chinese foreign policy was to act as a buffer between capitalist nations who also were allied with the US. China was protected from the possibility of US troops from South Korea at its border during the most contentious periods of the Cold War, and even as tensions relaxed and trade opened up significantly, China maintained a commitment to the buffer role North Korea serves. What would happen if the North Korean regime collapsed? The most consistent consequence scholars and policymakers consider is that the Chinese border would touch South Korea and therefore be in direct contact with a nation where US troops were stationed. This expectation, however, skips over the question of who would be responsible for the political status of North Korea's territory and what role, if any, the US would play. Predictions of this sort are difficult because expectations depend on whether China, South Korea, and the US can develop a plan to manage a North Korean collapse. Public evidence of coordination on this front is scant, and in fact, only recently have there been public calls for China to make contingency plans for regime collapse in North Korea from their own foreign policy establishment.[22] Improving relations between China and the US are reflected in the actions agreed to in the Security Council; however, that relationship is quite fragile and is less cooperative since the Trump Administration's escalation of tariffs. A second issue has become much more relevant, adding a degree of difficulty that did not exist before 2006—North Korea's functioning nuclear arsenal. Since the first successful nuclear test in 2006, North Korea has continued to develop both its fission arsenal and a possible thermonuclear device. Alongside the nuclear developments are missile designs and tests that suggest North Korea may soon be capable of hitting portions of the continental US.[23] Thus, collapse no longer means only mass crisis migration and political upheaval on the peninsula, it also means the possibility of nuclear launch that puts multiple US allies and the US itself at risk, critically raising the stakes of regime failure. Our following analysis of

[22] See for example an article in the East Asia Forum in 2017 in which Jia Quinggua, Dean of the School of International Studies at Peking University, offers specific, modern recommendations to the Chinese government, https://www.eastasiaforum.org/2017/09/11/time-to-prepare-for-the-worst-in-north-korea/. Accessed May 2, 2019.

[23] See estimates of North Korean missile ranges from the Center for Strategic and International Studies, https://missilethreat.csis.org/country/dprk/.

behavior in the Security Council focuses on the early and mid-2000s period, but we briefly explore the more recent developments and Council behavior in a later section.

We have provided evidence that China has consistently been concerned with maintaining North Korean stability as a backstop against significant political and security changes in the region. We have also shown that China believes that economic disaster and refugee migration is the most serious concern in maintaining the North Korean regime. We argue that behavior in the Council, including any public positions China adopts, could potentially destabilize the regime as the expectation of severe sanctions could touch off the collapse China fears. We demonstrate how those concerns have dominated China's behavior in the Council, but we also consider how developments in China's domestic preparations and regional relations have altered those stances moderately, with a corresponding change in behavior in the Council.

6.2 Discussing North Korea in the Council

In this section, we trace the evolving discussion in the Security Council around issues relating to both North Korean nuclear development and their missile tests, which are two related but separate issues on the Council's agenda. As a baseline, we start with reactions when North Korea's nuclear status first appeared on the Council's agenda in 1993. We describe the discussions and attitudes at the time to explain why so little action was taken to deal with North Korea's withdrawal from the NPT. We then proceed to the early 2000s when significant action inside the Council occurred. We describe and explain evolving actions in the Council during this period.

1993 and the NPT

North Korea has maintained an arms-length relationship with the rest of the world for much of its existence. The experience of the Korean War and its economic and political structure isolated the regime from all but its nearest communist neighbors. The regime even conducted numerous state-sponsored acts of terrorism against its southern neighbors, including hijacked airliners, and various bombings against civilians and political figures during the 1960s, 70s, and 80s. The relationship with South Korea was highly antagonistic as was the relationship with South Korea's security alliance partner, the US. Further, North Korea carried a very strong resentment for its former colonizers, Japan, and so had no regional or global connections beyond China and the

Soviet Union. This historical pattern thus renders North Korea's decision to join the NPT in 1985 somewhat puzzling given that this seemingly cooperative move occurred between provocative attacks against its more globally-engaged neighbor. During the 1970s, North Korea sought to build and maintain its own research reactors supplied by the Soviet Union. As part of the technology deal, however, the Soviets insisted that North Korea accede to the NPT (Carrel-Billiard and Wing, 2010).[24]

North Korea's participation in the nuclear treaty regime depended on how the US and its allies in the region addressed North Korea's perceived threats. Thus, the IAEA safeguard agreement came shortly after the US unilaterally removed all nuclear forces from South Korea in 1991 while South Korea declared a prohibition on nuclear facilities that could be used to weaponize nuclear technology. North Korea then allowed a series of inspections in 1992; however, in September the IAEA noted some inconsistencies in North Korea's declared stockpiles, leading to a request for further inspections in February of 1993. North Korea refused and announced its intention to withdraw from the NPT on March 12, touching off the first flurry of activity in the Security Council.[25] The official records show a rapid exchange of letters to the Council from non-nuclear states, North Korea, and some of the permanent members. A joint statement (S/25515) from the US, UK, and Russian Federation questioning the validity of North Korea's security justifications and a call to comply with its obligations reveals a fairly unified stance from three of the five veto powers. From the official records, there was a consultation convened on the withdrawal declaration according to the Council president's statement (S/25562) on the issue. Thus, the discussions around the resolution took place in private, owing to the fact that there was one holdout permanent member—China. We don't have any records from the consultation, but the statements in the public meeting demonstrated near unity among the US, UK, France, and Russia that North Korea did not have a legitimate claim to withdraw and that it was obliged to comply with the safeguard agreements and inspections. The Chinese statement is short and noncommittal, indicating both that China was opposed to nuclear proliferation but also did not believe the Security Council was the appropriate venue for resolving the dispute. Instead, they called for North Korea, the IAEA,

[24] The Soviets wanted North Korea to submit to safeguarding, so North Korea joined the IAEA in 1974. It did not, however, reach a safeguard agreement with the IAEA until 1992.

[25] The Arms Control Association maintains a helpful chronology here: https://www.armscontrol.org/factsheets/dprkchron. The actual order to withdraw from the NPT was transmitted to the Security Council and is enshrined in their official records (S/25386). The order claims the withdrawal is in response to the US and South Korea continuing to hold the Team Spirit training exercises, which were joint military exercises that had taken place every year since 1976.

and the US to negotiate a solution outside of the UN system. They abstained on the resolution vote, offering no positive support but also refusing to halt the process in the Council.

During this diplomatic crisis, China walked a fine line between refusing to abandon North Korea but also refusing to condemn them. The other permanent members tread carefully to avoid alienating China—the only nation with any viable leverage over North Korea. According to the recollections of American negotiators, Joel Wit, Daniel Poneman, and Robert Gallucci, the Chinese had a line they would not cross—any policy that might risk the collapse of the North Korea regime, including harsh sanctions.[26] Here again is a direct reference to China's fear that economic dislocation would create a wave of refugees into northern China and collapse the North Korean regime. They claim China threatened a veto in the Council to leverage weaker language in any statements and push for a slower process; the Chinese even requested that no formal meeting be held to avoid the publicity that would come with an on-the-record discussion.[27]

These motivations and actions are consistent with what our model would predict when a veto member has high public costs, but everyone prefers to take some sort of action on an issue, and there is some small possibility of outside action. The Chinese wanted to avoid encouraging economic refugee flows of people trying to avoid the economic hardships that crippling sanctions would create. They opted to discuss the issue in private and negotiated meaningful but weaker sanctions on the North Korean regime. This decision represents a balancing act between China's desire to manage nuclear proliferation and appease regional members and to avoid triggering the political collapse that might follow mass economic refugee exodus. The public costs come not from domestic groups or even other political regimes but from the population of refugees that might cause political collapse in North Korea and a realignment of the regional relationships.

The American negotiators also picked up on the strained relationship between China and North Korea, however, remarking that North Korea's withdrawal declaration came as a surprise to China, illustrating how the two

[26] The American negotiators also suggested that the Chinese did not think North Korea would be capable of producing a nuclear weapon, which reduced the urgency in forcefully dealing with the withdrawal declaration as well, though China did take precautionary export restrictions just in case.

[27] It's worth noting that Pakistan held the Council presidency in April 1993 and was the only other Council member to abstain on Resolution 825 the following month. It seems reasonable that China's request for private meetings only was granted because of this similarity, though it may have also been in the interest of any other Council member who might have held the presidency to honor that request as part of the developing gradual escalation policy.

nations were not coordinating policy. North Korea chose a risky route testing China's commitment to protect the regime (Wit, Poneman, and Gallucci, 2004). Weighing the possible costs and benefits of a gradual process versus a more direct, aggressive one, the permanent members chose a gradual escalation of diplomatic pressure that also seemed to fit the preferences of South Korea and Japan as well. The first indication of this strategy was the presidential statement in April 1993, requesting North Korea to return to its IAEA obligations.[28]

The pressure built even more in the process of negotiating the resolution that would pass a month later. Ongoing discussions opened the possibility of direct negotiations with the US, which became the negotiating environment for the Agreed Framework. This was China's most preferred option, a negotiated settlement to solve the issue. To reach the stage of formal negotiations, the US waited to see if North Korea would comply with inspections in early May 1993. The negotiators describe the Chinese delegation as more cooperative during discussions of the resolution because of the impending negotiations. The resolution called for North Korea's compliance with the safeguards agreement and explicitly left the door open for further action in the Council. While the resolution text did not create any sanctions, it formalized the expectations of the international community and signaled that more action may be pending without compliance. Perhaps most important, though, is that China did not employ a veto to prevent this action, signaling to North Korea that they were willing to allow coordinated action in the Council and that North Korea should cooperate with the impending talks. One month following, North Korea suspended its withdrawal from the NPT, and eighteen months later, the US and North Korea signed the Agreed Framework.

2003–2007, Withdrawal and the Nuclear Tests

The next resolutions on North Korea did not happen until more than a decade later in 2006, following the collapse of the Agreed Framework and North Korea's formal withdrawal from the NPT in 2003. Between 1994 and 2001, North Korean-US relations improved as both sides adhered, for the most part, to their obligations under the Agreed Framework. North Korea shut down its nuclear plants, cooperating with both IAEA inspections and US inspections during this period, while the US held back new sanctions, allowed heavy fuel shipments, and prepared for construction of the light-water reactors promised to North Korea for domestic energy production. Negotiations during this period turned to ballistic missile testing, an area of technological development that

[28] Presidential Statements are approved by consensus but are not legally binding the way resolutions are.

continued despite the freeze on North Korea's nuclear program. North Korea eventually agreed to a self-imposed moratorium on testing. Several rounds of meetings over this period made halting progress, so much so that by the end of President Bill Clinton's second term, preparations were in the works for a visit to North Korea by the US president before he left office. The visit never materialized, however, because, according to Clinton, there was not enough time to finish the negotiations, which he would hand off to the next president.[29]

Relations between the US and North Korea began to turn in early 2001. Condoleezza Rice, serving as National Security Advisor to President George W. Bush at the time, reflected on the Agreed Framework and the skepticism that reigned to varying degrees within the new administration. The Bush administration was concerned that the terms of the agreement were not strong enough to ensure North Korea was not developing a nuclear capability. Early offers to open negotiations with the new administration were always predicated on strong verifications as part of the process. While some discussion occurred among lower-level staff from both states, negotiations with North Korea reached a standstill, until January 2002 when President Bush gave the State of the Union address in which he characterized North Korea as part of an "Axis of Evil." The administration had dealt with the September 11, 2001 attacks, and foreign policy concern shifted abruptly toward terrorism and heightening concerns about WMD proliferation to non-state actors (Rice, 2011). The bilateral, diplomatic interactions between the US and North Korea languished throughout 2002, though support for the light-water reactors continued while North Korea maintained its missile testing moratorium. In October of that year, however, the US accused North Korea of pursuing a clandestine uranium enrichment program, and from that point relations unraveled quickly—North Korea restarted its reactors, threatened to resume missile testing and expelled IAEA inspectors. The final step was to declare its withdrawal from the NPT, which it had begun a decade earlier and suspended the day before it was to take legal effect. Thus, North Korea announced its withdrawal on January 10, effective January 11, claiming they had met the three-months' notice requirement because of the 1993 declaration. From this point, the negotiations widened to include China and eventually Russia, Japan, and South Korea to try to manage North Korea's nuclear program.

[29] The 2000 American election was also fraught and undecided for a full month after the election took place, which displaced any final objectives the Clinton administration was pursuing. Wit, Poneman and Gallucci (2004) characterize this non-event as a potential missed opportunity to get a sealed deal on a ballistic missile treaty, but they also report North Korean back-tracking at the last minute that threatened the agreement process.

The Six-Party Talks began in August of 2003 and represented the primary negotiating forum to reach agreement with North Korea over its weapons program.[30] Why didn't action occur in the Security Council? Rice contends that the Six-Party Talks would help unify regional powers who had the most at stake with a North Korean nuclear program and would serve to coordinate those actions. Because the Council does not permanently include North and South Korea or Japan, a separate negotiating forum was more practical, though the Council served as the de facto enforcement mechanism for the broad terms of the Joint Statement, issued in September of 2005 in which North Korea "committed to abandoning all nuclear weapons and existing nuclear programs and returning at an early date to the treaty on the nonproliferation of nuclear weapons (NPT) and to IAEA (International Atomic Energy Agency) safeguards."[31] The US reaffirmed it had no nuclear weapons in the theater and had no intention to invade North Korea. Further promises of normalizing relations and continuing discussions were also a part of the agreement.

Though the detailed negotiations happened in the Six-Party Talks, the process was not completely separate from the Security Council. In July of 2006, North Korea conducted several ballistic missile tests, including a long-range type. The test was a failure, but the international community reacted strongly and swiftly. Ten days after the tests, the Security Council issued its first resolution on North Korea since Resolution 825 in 1993. Resolution 1695 strongly condemned the launches, pressed North Korea to return to the NPT and the Six-Party Talks and imposed sanctions on North Korea's sources for missile technology and parts. The resolution passed unanimously. Why did China vote in favor of the resolution? Recall that we described China's primary goal for North Korea was to maintain the stability of the regime, but they also wanted to prevent nuclear proliferation. They also wanted to preserve improving economic relationships with South Korea, Japan, and the US. The resolution text offers a clue to how the Chinese were able to signal their position on North Korea developing a deliverable nuclear arsenal and the value China placed on maintaining good relations with its more recent trading partners. It puts sanctions on missile-related technology and does not impose more painful restrictions on durable goods and fuel supplies. Thus, the sanctions were designed to prevent acquisition of critical missile technology without seriously

[30] According to Condoleezza Rice, President Bush was convinced the only way to carry leverage over North Korea was to bring China into the discussion. The US proposed the Six-Party Talks and intentionally wanted China to take the lead. She recalls President Bush raising the possibility of military action otherwise (Rice, 2011: p. 248).

[31] US Department of State, https://2009-2017.state.gov/p/eap/regional/c15455.htm.

threatening North Korea's economic survival. Statements in the public record from the vote on Resolution 1695 suggest that the Council came together with competing proposals on what to do after the missile test and hammered out an agreement that satisfied all members enough for a unanimous vote. For example, according to Rice, the US agreed to remove authorization under Chapter VII to get the Chinese on board (Rice, 2011). Unanimity is an important signal in this case, because North Korea counts heavily on China as provider of vital goods and support. China might have opted to abstain as it did with Resolution 825, but it did not, sending a clear message to North Korea that it could not count on China to curtail all backlash from its regional partners. The statements from each of the permanent members highlights the unity of the Council on the issue and the course of action (S/RES/1695).

North Korea followed Resolution 1695 with its first nuclear test on October 9, 2006.[32] Five days later, the Security Council passed Resolution 1718, its toughest sanctions on North Korea yet. Since the Joint Statement, progress in the Six-Party Talks had stalled because a bank in Macau, Banco Delta Asia, had been flagged by the US Treasury Department for potential money-laundering activities. The North Korean regime had funds at the bank, which it could not access given the designation.[33] They refused any further negotiations until those funds were released. But their decision to conduct missile tests and a nuclear test in the meantime brought on much greater pressure, not just from the US but all other parties at the Six-Party Talks as well—unifying them in ways not seen before.

North Korea had announced its intention to conduct a test "in the future" on October 3. The Security Council followed that announcement with a Presidential Statement outlining the violations such a test would be and, importantly, threatening to carry out its duty under the UN Charter because a test would represent a "clear threat to international peace and security" (S/PRST/2006/41). China's agreement with this statement shows it expected any nuclear test to be handled in the Security Council. Following the nuclear test, Secretary of State Condoleezza Rice[34] engaged in intensive discussions with the Chinese about how to get North Korea back to the negotiating table. Recollections of American negotiators portray the nuclear test as North

[32] The estimates of the yield varied with most estimates of less than a kiloton, but the seismic readings did resemble a nuclear test—one that American estimates suggest was unsuccessful in creating a chain reaction.

[33] Chris Hill, lead American negotiator at this time, suggested that this designation was intentionally timed to derail the talks—reflecting the disagreements within the Bush Administration on how to handle North Korea (Hill, 2015).

[34] She had moved to this position from National Security Advisor in January of 2005.

Korean defiance in the face of Chinese pressure. Rice reports that the Chinese were only given one hour's warning of the test, prompting them to reach out to President Bush directly to form a response (Rice, 2011). The matter went to the Council immediately, resulting in intense negotiations behind closed doors for how to respond (S/PV.5551). The nuclear test put China in a difficult spot. They were certainly shocked and upset about the nuclear test, issuing very strong language in a statement[35] from the Foreign Ministry:

> On 9 October, the Democratic People's Republic of Korea flagrantly conducted a nuclear test in disregard of the common opposition of the international community. The Chinese Government is firmly opposed to this act.
>
> To bring about denuclearization of the Korean Peninsula and oppose nuclear proliferation is the firm and consistent stand of the Chinese Government. China strongly urges the DPRK to honor its commitment to denuclearization, stop all moves that may further worsen the situation and return to the Six-Party Talks.
>
> To safeguard peace and stability in Northeast Asia serves the interests of all parties involved. The Chinese Government calls on all parties concerned to be cool-headed in response and persist in seeking a peaceful solution through consultation and dialogue. China will continue to make every effort towards this goal.

But, their prepared statement in the Council meeting also shows that they sought to reassure North Korea than sanctions would be suspended or lifted if they complied. Familiar reference to "maintain[ing] peace and stability on the Korean peninsula and in North-East Asia" and strong opposition to the use of force also appear in their statement (S/PV.5551). Resolution 1718 imposed serious sanctions on both military technology and luxury goods that targeted the North Korean regime pointedly and would not lead to large-scale economic collapse. The resolution also created a sanctions committee with the job of monitoring sanctions compliance, issuing periodic reports to the Council. Secretary Rice also noted that the Chinese traveled to North Korea and refused any further spare parts for their military. Despite great public bluster from North Korea, these sanctions brought them back to the negotiating table (Rice, 2011).

[35] Sourced from the Chinese Foreign Ministry's official site: https://www.fmprc.gov.cn/ce/cena/eng/fyrth/t275508.htm . Accessed October 17, 2020.

This process once again reflects how China's preferences and public costs strongly influenced what reactions from the Council looked like following the missile and nuclear tests. Each resolution avoided imposing sanctions on the more critical sources of goods for the North Korean regime (heavy fuel oil, for example) but they were designed to hurt the regime's comfort and its ability to produce new missiles. The differences between the resolutions (namely, that 1718 invoked Chapter VII) also reflect the disparity between the offenses—the first nuclear test is a direct abrogation of all of the non-proliferation efforts that preceded it. In negotiating 1718, though, it's worth pointing out that the resolution references a specific article, Article 41, which precludes military force (Wuthnow, 2013). This was another US concession to help China balance its two major concerns that might cause regime collapse in North Korea, US military action, and economic hardship. All of these discussions happened in private as the Council members worked out how to keep China onboard while trying to toughen reaction to North Korea's infractions. Public discussion would have revealed China's position, both with highly undesirable consequences. If China revealed an unwillingness to punish North Korea severely, then Kim Jong-il might have refused to stop proliferating and increased the risk of military action. If China revealed a desire to stop North Korea at all costs, it might have ignited a refugee crisis that collapsed the Kim regime. Both forms of public costs meant China needed to negotiate in private to try and maintain stability while doing something to respond to the tests.

Unraveling Again, 2008–present

Negotiations through 2008 made progress in reaching agreements, nuclear declarations, and allowing inspections. In return, the US released the Banco Delta Asia funds, allowed shipments of heavy fuel oil and began the process of removing North Korea from its list of state sponsors of terrorism. In the spring of 2009, however, North Korea resumed ballistic missile testing, followed shortly by a second nuclear test on May 25. These acts ushered in a wave of poor relations between North Korea and the other members of the Six-Party Talks, particularly the US, Japan, and South Korea,[36] continuing through the end of 2016 when North Korea carried out its fifth nuclear test. With every test, the Council reacted, but there is variation in the reaction, depending on the type of test.

[36] In fact, relations become hostile and violent in 2010 when North Korea sank the *Cheonan*, a South Korean patrol ship, and fired missiles at a South Korean island, killing soldiers. North Korea also reveal a long-suspected, secret uranium enrichment site that November.

The 2009 missile test prompted a Presidential Statement from the Council that promised an expanded list of individuals and companies subject to sanctions, but the Council did not expand the type of sanctions further. News reports during the time suggest Japan wanted a resolution, but Russia and China would not support it—thus the compromise was a strongly-worded Presidential Statement.[37] It was not until North Korea conducted its second nuclear test on May 25, 2009, that the Council issued a new resolution, Resolution 1874, condemning the test and expanding sanctions to include an arms embargo and financial restrictions. In fact, in the decade following 2009, a pattern of missile tests, sometimes many missile tests, followed by a nuclear test mirrored this pattern of action in the Council. Missile tests generated stern Presidential Statements, while nuclear tests elicited further resolutions. A single exception in this period, Resolution 2087, in January 2013 passed following a significant missile test in December 2012 in which North Korea successfully launched a satellite into space, demonstrating successful ballistic missile capability (most other ballistic missile tests to this point had failed). Resolution 2094 passed following a nuclear test in February 2013 imposing significant financial transaction restrictions, and in March 2016, Resolution 2270 passed denying jet fuel and minerals to North Korea and introduced mandatory inspections of all cargo going to or leaving North Korea. All of these resolutions passed unanimously, but the marks of Chinese concern for North Korean stability persist in the discussions,

> Currently, the situation on the Korean peninsula is highly complex and sensitive, which makes it all the more necessary for us to keep calm and use diplomatic wisdom. China hopes that the parties concerned will meet China half-way, always keeping in mind the overall need to maintain the peace and stability of the Korean peninsula and North-East Asia ....
>
> from the meeting record in which Resolution 2270 passed (S/PV.7638).[38]

North Korea conducted another nuclear test in September 2016, but the Council did not take action until August 2017 with a response to North Korea's Intercontinental Ballistic Missile (ICBM) test in July.[39] The range for that missile is projected to cover large portions of the continental US. Resolution

[37] Associated Press, April 13, 2009, *The Guardian*, https://www.theguardian.com/world/2009/apr/13/un-north-korea-rocket-launch, accessed May 31, 2019.

[38] The meetings in which Resolutions 2087 and 2094 passed did not make time for statements; the members voted unanimously, and the Council president adjourned the meeting.

[39] This is the Hwasong-14 test, range of about 10,000+ km, according to the Center for Strategic & International Studies (CSIS) Missile Defense Project, https://missilethreat.csis.org/missile/hwasong-14/.

2371 restricted coal and seafood exports. Additional activity occurred in late November of 2017 when North Korea conducted another ICBM test,[40] resulting in Resolution 2397, which severely restricts refined and crude oil imports to North Korea. These more recent developments harm the North Korean economy more than prior sanctions because they limit critical exports and imports that sustain the regime.

These sanctions appear to increase the risk of regime collapse in North Korea, so why did China vote in favor of them? It's too soon to consult memoirs of diplomats, but foreign media and foreign policy think tanks report multiple prominent Chinese scholars and advisors recommending China plan for the inevitable collapse or the North Korean regime (Wu, 2017). There are also recent reports in the Western media and foreign policy circles that China is making preparations for possible refugee influx by building refugee camps along the northern border and possibly coordinating a military plan with the US for finding and securing North Korea's nuclear arsenal (Zhao, 2017; Sanger, 2017; Mastro, 2018). If these plans indeed exist, it may explain why China was willing to push more dire sanctions on the North Korean regime. Preparation for North Korea's collapse removes some of the hesitancy in China's policy toward proliferation because they are more prepared for the consequences and potentially may be somewhat reassured that they will have influence on the Korean peninsula as they coordinate with the regional powers, including the US. If these developments are true, then the change in sanctions on North Korea directly track with waning Chinese fears about the regime's collapse, illustrating the importance of those factors in determining behavior in the Council. These conclusions, though, rely on what has been reported in the press, and it is not clear whether the recent and ongoing trade war between the US and China have changed the cooperation on North Korea.

Resolution 2397 was the last Council resolution to impose harsh sanctions on North Korea. Starting in 2018, activity around North Korea's nuclear program stalled despite intense bilateral activity between the US and North Korea and between North and South Korea. Since Resolution 2397, the only resolutions that have passed the Council are those renewing the Panel of Experts, even though North Korea halted testing and dismantled a nuclear testing site in 2018 and then resumed ballistic missile tests in 2019. Why has the Council taken action that represents a holding pattern on North Korea? From the Council meeting records, it appears a rift formed between the US and

[40] The Hwasong-15, an ICBM that could reach all of the US when fully developed and deployed (https://missilethreat.csis.org/country/dprk/).

Russia over sanctions compliance. The US ambassador to the UN, Nikki Haley, pointedly accused Russia of cheating on North Korean sanctions in a public meeting. Russia and China argued that the Security Council should reciprocate the positive developments that the Panel of Experts reported to the Council in 2018. They argued further that the lack of reciprocal action from the Council motivated North Korea's behavior in 2019, following no progress after independent summits between Kim Jong Un and President Trump and between Kim and Moon Jae-in, President of South Korea.

Curiously, the tone of interaction between the US and China on North Korea during this period was steady and cautious, despite the trade war that began in July 2018 between the nations and despite negative, public accusations around the coronavirus pandemic that temporarily shut down China in late 2019 and the US in March of 2020. There is little direct, contentious evidence in the official record that these events have soured the US-China cooperation on North Korea; however, the fact that they have only been able to renew the Panel of Experts may be clear evidence since no new sanctions or diplomatic activity has taken place. The lack of activity on North Korea may also be a result of the pandemic's effect on North Korea itself. Very little information about infection rates in North Korea have escaped, but in his closing speech to the Workers' Party of Korea on April 9, 2021, Kim called on his people to prepare for another "arduous march," a reference to the 1994 famine that seriously threatened the stability of North Korea.[41] World media speculated that the pandemic created a dire economic situation in North Korea, possibly including famine, which is a likely reason for the pause in all testing activity in the small nation in 2020 and possibly further. With the uncertainties of the pandemic, the lack of action in the Council and in North Korea, and with a new American presidential administration, the future of North Korea's nuclear program is difficult to predict.

6.3 Conclusion

Throughout the history of nuclear development in North Korea, the behavior in the Council evolved slowly but very consistently with China's evolving relationship with North Korea. North Korea did not push the envelope until

[41] Quite extraordinary is that this information came through the Korean Central News Agency, North Korea's state media. Speech text accessed directly from the Korean Central News Agency (KCNA) website, April 26, 2021. Article title: Respected Comrade Kim Jong Un Makes Closing Address at Sixth Conference of Cell Secretaries of Workers' Part of Korea.

its relationship with China had taken a firm backseat to the other regional relationships emerging in the post-Cold War era. Initial events at the announcement of North Korea's nuclear ambition in 1993 show China behaving more protectively of North Korea. Chinese preferences precluded actions against the regime until absolutely necessary going so far as to abstain from a resolution vote in 1993 that condemned North Korea's withdrawal from the NPT. In the decades since, China's frustration with North Korea's actions and defiance grew because China truly does not want North Korea to be a nuclear state. But China's behavior also suggests restraint against any aggressive action that might initiate regime collapse.

We have argued that Council members take into account significant public costs that will influence both whether discussion happens publicly or privately and will shape the content of resolutions. The public costs for China in the North Korean case are large—refugee influx and the collapse of the North Korean regime would cause substantial disruption to the regional political dynamics and alter China's national security. These events would impose significant costs for how to manage a sudden influx of millions of North Koreans. China has had to balance these concerns with pressure from regional actors and the US, the only other nation with the capability to pursue a military solution, even if highly unlikely. In the Council and in the Six-Party Talks, China has had to pursue a very cautious line, lest they reveal support for sanctions that would collapse the North Korean economy or signal a military solution that would bring on the refugee influx before any action or collapse actually occurred creating a self-fulfilling crisis. Far from trivial, these public costs are significant, and we and others have argued, they drive China's behavior in the Council with regard to North Korea even to this day. Thus, what should appear to be a simple issue of preventing nuclear proliferation in an otherwise poor and desperate nation has generated more than a generation's worth of activity in the Security Council; activity that continues to churn in the Council to this day.

7

Agenda-Setting in Action: The Cases of Kosovo and the Responsibility to Protect

The agenda-setting model in Chapter 3 provides further insights about strategic agenda-setting, grandstanding behavior, and the effect public costs may have on bargaining inside the institution. Chapter 6 explored several of these dynamics in great detail for the perennial case of North Korea in the Council. This chapter offers two additional cases—the actions around Kosovo in 1998 and 1999 and the process to pass the Responsibility to Protect (R2P) doctrine—as evidence of the influence agenda-setting has on the outcomes in the Council.

The Kosovo case in particular shows instances of Council presidents using the agenda-setting power of the position to try to influence negotiations around what the UN should do in Kosovo. Those members (including elected members) who sought more concerted efforts to coerce Milošević's cooperation held meetings while those who sought to stall the process pointedly ignored the situation, even as crises were unfolding on the ground. We argue that public costs drove much of Russia's concern around Kosovo—despite evidence that shows they knew Milošević would only respond to force. The influence of North Atlantic Treaty Organization (NATO) action is also paramount to the bargaining process in the Council. Kosovo also offers us a case in which we observe grandstanding, which we argue was in the interests of Russia and China, explaining the reason for and timing of the vetoed resolution condemning the NATO bombings.

The case surrounding R2P (Resolution 1674) illustrates how elected members might use the Council presidency to forward their own agenda items—even if it is a long, slow process. Canada devoted a great deal of time and resources to building support for the understandings reflected in Resolution 1674, suggesting that elected members can use public costs and agenda-setting opportunities to forward issues that the permanent members consistently avoid and further, they can do so in ways that bring the veto-wielding members into agreement.

Bargaining in the UN Security Council. Susan Hannah Allen and Amy Yuen, Oxford University Press.
 DOI: 10.1093/oso/9780192849755.003.0007

7.1 Kosovo in the Council

We look at the Council's behavior during the Kosovo crisis starting with the internal violence in 1998 through 1999 when the NATO conducted airstrikes that forced Serbian withdrawal and led to the establishment of the United Nations Mission in Kosovo (UNMIK) and the Kosovo Force (KFOR). We illustrate two primary claims from the model: (1) there is evidence of strategic agenda-setting, (2) public costs affect bargaining inside the Council such that Russia privately approves of NATO bombing without Council approval and then leverages the bombing into a grandstanding opportunity to reinforce its public position on Kosovo. The Kosovo case is a difficult one for our argument because many discussions occurred outside the Security Council until after the NATO bombings, and they appear to be driven by four of the five veto powers in the Council.[1] The pace of action (and inaction) in the Council varies as events unfold on the ground and as delegations cycle through the Council presidency. Further, the catalyst to Serbian withdrawal (NATO bombing) was an outside option that shows Russia attempting to balance its base preferences for Kosovo against public costs and the pressure of possible NATO action.

Kosovo is a landlocked, autonomous region in Serbia, where its political status continues to be in dispute. The events in this case are related most proximally to the breakup of Yugoslavia, a socialist state formed after World War II that included five principal territories (Slovenia, Croatia, Bosnia and Herzegovina, Serbia and Montenegro, and Macedonia). Many historians attribute the source of early political instability in Yugoslavia to the death of Josip Broz Tito, who served as President from 1953 to his death in 1980, as well as several other prominent ministerial positions during that period. The end of the Cold War hastened the breakup of Yugoslavia as four of the five principal territories began to move toward independence against the wishes of Serbia, the dominant province.

Kosovo's push for independence followed years of eroded autonomy, which had been granted in 1974. Slobodan Milošević, President of Serbia, rescinded that autonomy in 1989, which intensified calls for independence. Kosovo was one of the last to attempt full independence during the breakup of Yugoslavia, maintaining pressure against the Serbian government until a pivotal crackdown in 1998. The Council monitored conditions in Kosovo well before the violence began in 1998, but they did so informally through the

[1] The outcomes are the result of venue shopping, but the Council was still heavily active in this period. Indeed, our argument, and others, treat inside and outside options as interdependent, dynamic processes (Thompson, 2009; Voeten, 2001).

Contact Group,[2] the UN Preventive Deployment Mission (UNPREDEP), and the Organization for Security and Cooperation in Europe (OSCE). Following the February violence in 1998, the UK and the US brought the issue to the Council for direct discussion in a formal meeting held on March 31.

That first public meeting set by the Council president was actually the culmination of several prior meetings that happened both inside and outside the Security Council. All of these prior meetings happened in private, and the most substantial ones occurred within the Contact Group. Given the private nature of the Council's consultations, we have no record of informal discussions in the Council—we do know two facts about Kosovo in the Council, however. First, Kosovo did not get its own consultation in the Council before the Council imposed the arms embargo in the public meeting. We also know, however, that the Council discussed Kosovo in private consultations (possibly devoted to other issues, like Bosnia) based on allusions to prior consultations in the summary record of the Repertoire of the Practice of the Security Council and based on statements in the public meeting record. While we have no transcript to confirm this, it seems likely that the Council members eventually decided that discussing Kosovo within the Contact Group would be more productive since it shared similar issues and some actors with the Bosnia case, relied on the same information streams as Bosnia, and included the primary P5 members (except China) and additional European states with resources to bring to the discussion.[3]

Secretary of State Madeleine Albright notes in her memoirs that the US and Russia agreed that civil war in Kosovo would be "disastrous," but they held very different understandings of the cause and potential solutions (Albright and Woodward, 2003). While the Contact Group planted the seed for outside action that would occur the following year, it is notable that Russia was a participating member in this group despite holding different preferences for how to reach a solution. In comparing the professed goals in the empirical record, they negotiated to a near compromise, reflected in a letter submitted to the Security Council from the UK delegation on behalf of the Contact Group.[4] The statement condemned both the Serbian government's crackdown

[2] This was an informal coalition of states negotiating actions and agreements during the Balkan wars, including France, Germany, Italy, Russia, the UK, and the US.

[3] We do have evidence that China did not support action in the Security Council, adopting a narrower view of the Council's purview, and said so in prior consultations. This may have also encouraged negotiation outside of the Council, but the Chinese delegation did not exercise its veto in the vote (*United Nations Security Council 3868th Meeting*, 1998).

[4] Letter from the Deputy Permanent Member Representative of the United Kingdom of Great Britain and Northern Ireland to the United Nations Addressed to the Security Council, S/1998/223.

on civilians and the terrorist activities of the Kosovo Liberation Army (KLA). The European nations and the US were most concerned by the Serbian government's actions, while the Russians were concerned about the KLA. The compromise was to condemn both groups. Further, everyone supported an arms embargo to both sides in Kosovo, but the Western allies could not get the Russians to accept travel and finance restrictions, a difference explicitly included in the letter. Ultimately, the terms in this statement became the terms of Resolution 1160, passed on March 31.[5] The Western powers and Russia agreed that they needed to prevent a civil war in Kosovo, but they differed on how to keep the two sides from all-out battle.

Deliberations over Kosovo provide evidence for our claim that Council presidents have agency enough to set meetings strategically, even though the role does not grant them (or the P5 in particular) complete policy control over any issue. For example, the violence increased significantly in June and July of 1998 with a KLA offensive that drew intense retaliation from the Serbian military and started a surge in internal displacements and refugees across international borders. If Council presidents set meetings non-strategically and only based on what violence is occurring or increasing in volatile situations, then we should expect there to be a meeting about Kosovo during this period, particularly in light of Resolution 1160 passed in March. That July, however, Russia held the Council presidency, but no public meeting or private consultation occurred to address the new violence in the Council.[6] Further, P5 representatives forwarded calls from the European Union to "encourage international security organizations… to consider all options, including those that would require authorization by the Security Council under Chapter VII of the Charter of the United Nations" (European Union, 1998). Instead, Russia worked unilaterally with Serbia and issued a joint statement on Kosovo affirming several principles of withdrawal, free movement, and political settlement. Russia did not choose to enshrine these promises in a Security Council resolution, however. Contrast that to the following month of August when Slovenia held the Council presidency. There are three informal consultations that list Resolution 1160 and a formal meeting with a presidential statement, which represents significant

[5] The Russians were not keen on attending the March 9 meeting that resulted in the compromise, sending a deputy rather than the Foreign Minister, Yevgeny Primakov. He attended the second meeting on March 25, but there was no change to the original statement agreed to on March 9 (Albright and Woodward, 2003).

[6] Records of consultations in the *UN Daily Journal* show no informal consultations related to Kosovo directly. On the agenda, Kosovo meetings were listed as "Report of the Secretary General pursuant to Resolution 1160". There were several meetings around Bosnia and Herzegovina and UNPREDEP, but none directly referencing any action on Kosovo.

activity in the Council on the Kosovo issue. Further, the Council passed Resolution 1199, which included the terms of withdrawal and free movement in the joint statement, when Sweden held the presidency in September. Russia used the seat of Council president to stall just as Proposition 2 predicts, but it could not keep further action from occurring in the following months and could not afford to veto resolutions that contained the terms it had negotiated with Serbia. It became clear, though, that the early attempts to encourage political settlement through arms embargoes had failed, and the veto members held increasingly disparate views of which steps to take next to motivate a political settlement, setting the stage for the outside option and the strategic behavior inside the Council that followed.[7] The divide among the Council was not over the political outcome; the disagreement was over how to get Milošević to cooperate.

Second, developments that led to the NATO bombing show how public costs influence action inside the Council. The US, and eventually, the other Western powers decided to pursue NATO air bombing to compel Milošević to negotiate a political solution with the moderate Kosovar Albanians.[8] In fact, Secretary Albright wanted to discuss it as early as March 1998, when the Serbian military began to push back against KLA attacks. In October, as evidence mounted that the Serbs were not following through with Resolutions 1160 and 1199, NATO issued an activation order to prepare a bombing plan.[9] This development coincides with five consultations in the Security Council and one meeting of the principal ministers of the Contact Group in Heathrow Airport. These consultations led to some subtle but crucial developments in each delegation's willingness to compromise. Albright characterizes the Heathrow meeting as convincing the Europeans that Russia would never allow an authorization of force in the Security Council. Strobe Talbott corroborates this, but adds that Russia's new foreign minister, Igor Ivanov, signaled that Russia would not insist that the Council weigh in on NATO's decision and instead would support NATO presenting an ultimatum to Milošević (Talbott, 2002). The result was to solidify the NATO leadership around authorizing the use of force without the

[7] For example, the Russian delegation made explicit reference to the absence of any authorization to use force or impose sanctions in the draft resolution, in its public statement just before the vote (*United Nations Security Council 3930th Meeting*, 1998).

[8] Within the alliance, there was general agreement that air power would be the next step if diplomacy failed to coerce Milošević, but according to British documents, there was little clarity as to what such an option would entail (Ritchie, 2001).

[9] Albright's memoirs suggest that the flurry of negotiations with Milošević happening at this time were not making progress because he doubted NATO's threats to take more decisive action. The uncertainty about an outside option is an important aspect of what happened inside the Council, as Voeten (2001) argues with specific reference to the Kosovo case.

Council, but it also allowed progress on the issue without invoking public costs in Russia, which led them to privately support an attempt to force Milošević's hand.

Undoubtedly, each nation involved in the decision process considered potential public costs of various actions in Kosovo. For example, the Western nations may have been responding to criticism about prior investment (or lack thereof) in the Bosnian war but demonstrating the public costs effect of this is difficult to untangle from utilitarian or humanitarian motivation for their actions in the Kosovo case because both logics predict more involvement.

Russia is likely the clearest example of how public costs influenced its behavior in Kosovo. If public costs did not matter, Russia might have authorized the use of force through the Security Council to try and end the conflict with more direct influence than NATO action would allow. As Strobe Talbott points out, however, acting through the Council created difficulties for the broader Russian narrative of sovereignty in dealing with separatist movements (e.g., Chechnya). NATO action, however, also creates potential difficulties for our claim that public costs swayed Russian decision-making. Russia was trying to maintain an image of carrying great international influence. NATO action cut Russia out and challenged that image.[10] It also exacerbated concerns about NATO expansion if NATO were successful in Kosovo (Talbott, 2002). We argue, though, that Russia countered the threat NATO action posed to its image by adopting a grandstanding strategy in the Council in an attempt to delegitimize the airstrikes. Thus, we see three developments in October 1998, NATO authorization of force, a Security Council resolution short of authorizing force but passed nonetheless, and an accelerated, interim agreement struck with Milošević that they hoped would be settled at the Rambouillet conference in the early part of 1999. Those talks ultimately collapsed, however, under a Serbian offensive that began March 20, and with a final attempt, the US could not secure Milošević's agreement to the terms at Rambouillet, so NATO airstrikes began on March 24.

The evidence suggests that the permanent members broadly shared similar goals to avoid civil war, massacres, and to maintain the territorial integrity of the former Yugoslavia while restoring the autonomy of Kosovo. The biggest differences were in how to convince Milošević. These conditions fit those that would lead to private discussions in the Council as they honed agreements that all would accept. Further, there is evidence that Russia wanted to avoid invoking domestic accountability costs with its quiet agreement in October

[10] Russia publicly touted its international influence (see Voeten (2001), footnote 35).

1998 that Milošević would only respond to threats of force. While they did not publicly announce agreement with the Western powers, they promised not to insist that the threat of force pass through the Council, which is tacit acceptance of the outside option. Publicly, they were actually proclaiming their influence, but privately, they accepted NATO action as the only effective solution with Milošević because any authorization of force inside the Council risked Russia's reputation domestically. To reinforce its position publicly, Russia took a grandstanding strategy when NATO bombing started, forcing the Western members to veto a resolution condemning the air bombing. China held the presidency, and Russia and China were the only two votes in favor of condemnation.[11] Yet none of these developments precluded the Council from agreeing to establish the United Nations Mission in Kosovo (UNMIK) and authorize NATO-led peacekeeping in 1999, suggesting that the real compromise came behind closed doors, where Russia conceded to using NATO to move a stubborn Milošević, while the Western powers cast vetoes in the Council against condemning the use of force, allowing Russia to bolster its story of unauthorized use of force with its domestic population.

7.2 Canada and the Responsibility to Protect

The R2P doctrine developed from an effort to address the plight of civilians in armed conflict, recognizing the importance of individual citizens and the responsibility nations carry to protect them. It is a controversial approach to understanding sovereignty in the modern international system. The term revises the understanding of sovereignty with three "pillars," or principles, that support the concept. Pillar I establishes that sovereign states have a responsibility to protect civilians from severe violence (e.g., genocide). Pillar II confers a duty on the international community to assist states that ask for help. Pillar III further confers responsibility to the international community to act in accordance with the UN Charter if any nation is unwilling or unable to meet its responsibilities to its population. Skeptical nations argue that some portions of R2P, specifically Pillar III, are in direct tension with the established, working definition of sovereignty as Westphalian sovereignty, which is nearly absolute, excepting cases of self-defense as codified in the UN Charter (Ziegler, 2016*a*). Yet in 2006, the Security Council passed Resolution 1674, enshrining elements of R2P into official UN policy. This case illustrates the role of

[11] The process occurred over the course of two public meetings, one on March 24 (S/PV.3988) and one on March 26 (S/PV.3989) in which the vote took place.

several non-permanent member states, most particularly Canada, in bringing about an important shift in UN policy despite early, staunch opposition from veto-wielding members in the Council.

The discussion of R2P happened in the context of several civil wars, including Bosnia, Rwanda, and Kosovo, where the fighting victimized thousands of civilians. The desire among some policymakers and activists was to bring humanitarian intervention into the forefront of UN policy, resulting in the formal statement in 1996 (Deng et al., 1996). The process to formalizing R2P in the UN, however, required a delegation in a position to bring the discussion forward to act—Canada, an active proponent of protecting civilians in combat zones, seized the opportunity when it sat on the Security Council in 1999.

The process to reach agreement in the UN and more specifically in the Security Council took years of consultation inside and outside the UN structures, but ultimately ended in success. Along with other issues, world leaders at the 2005 World Summit approved R2P as a guiding principle for the UN, and on April 28, 2006, the Council passed Resolution 1674 unanimously, which "*reaffirms* the provisions of paragraphs 138 and 139 of the 2005 World Summit Outcome Document regarding the responsibility to protect populations from genocide, war crimes, ethnic cleansing and crimes against humanity ..." (S/RES/1674).

Paragraph 138.
Each individual State has the responsibility to protect its populations from genocide, war crimes, ethnic cleansing and crimes against humanity. This responsibility entails the prevention of such crimes, including their incitement, through appropriate and necessary means. We accept that responsibility and will act in accordance with it. The international community should, as appropriate, encourage and help States to exercise this responsibility and support the United Nations in establishing an early warning capability.

Paragraph 139.
The international community, through the United Nations, also has the responsibility to use appropriate diplomatic, humanitarian and other peaceful means, in accordance with Chapters VI and VIII of the Charter, to help protect populations from genocide, war crimes, ethnic cleansing and crimes against humanity. In this context, we are prepared to take collective action, in a timely and decisive manner, through the Security Council, in accordance with the Charter, including Chapter VII, on a case-by-case basis and in cooperation with relevant regional organizations as appropriate, should peaceful

> means be inadequate and national authorities manifestly fail to protect their populations from genocide, war crimes, ethnic cleansing and crimes against humanity. We stress the need for the General Assembly to continue consideration of the responsibility to protect populations from genocide, war crimes, ethnic cleansing and crimes against humanity and its implications, bearing in mind the principles of the Charter and international law. We also intend to commit ourselves, as necessary and appropriate, to helping States build capacity to protect their populations from genocide, war crimes, ethnic cleansing and crimes against humanity and to assisting those which are under stress before crises and conflicts break out.
>
> (United Nations General Assembly, 2005)

7.2.1 The Seeds of Opposition to R2P

If we take this understanding of sovereignty to include these responsibilities toward one's own people as the modern guiding principles for the UN, then Resolution 1674 is a rather extraordinary feat given the starting positions of some of the permanent members on the Council. Russia and China were strongly opposed to revising the understanding of sovereignty in any way that would open the door to more intervention. Several UN members who are not permanent members on the Council (e.g., Brazil, India, and Egypt) shared these reservations. The path to reaching a resolution was a long and difficult one. Various descriptions of the negotiations identify several related concerns regarding R2P language—fears that the focus was on intervention, that it would give the US greater power in determining the shape of the international system, and concerns that R2P would be misused for political rather than humanitarian reasons (Ziegler, 2016*a*). China and Russia represented these concerns in their negotiations to develop the language around protecting civilians in armed conflict, but a close reading of their statements show that they were not uniformly opposed to all aspects of R2P.

The Chinese regime, at the time led by Hu Jintao, was opposed to the R2P language and any endorsement of policies that would threaten Westphalian notions of sovereignty. Oertel (2014: p. 172) sums up the concerns in four points, that there exists no legal basis in the UN Charter for intervention beyond self-defense, that intervention justified through these means could be used to pursue the parochial interests of the intervening nation, that this language sets up a confrontation between "Western human rights" and the "collective rights of nations," and finally that it would allow for a "double standard" in applying intervention. In fact, that term appears in formal statements made in the Council early in discussions around protecting civilians in armed conflict, "We call on the international community to discard double standards in the humanitarian sphere and to give equal attention to acts of violence against civilians in armed conflicts around the world, rather than take a selective approach" (S/PV.4046, p. 21).

The Chinese position on R2P evolved during this process, however. Foreign policy elites in the regime began debating the merits of the R2P language, and by 2005, China had endorsed Pillars I and II, focusing their primary objections to what Pillar III implied about intervention against the will of the host state. It declared in a position paper that "Each state shoulders the primary responsibility to protect its own population." They hedge on this notion claiming that internal unrest is complex, so "[p]rudence is called for in judging a government's ability and will to protect its citizens" (*Position Paper of the People's Republic of China on the United Nations Reforms*, 2005: Section III, No. 1). A second point on R2P highlights that China does see the international community as carrying legitimacy to help in cases of massive humanitarian crisis, but they also call for a strictly codified method of response and call on the Security Council specifically as the appropriate venue to determine the response.

Russia, like China, distrusted the motives of the Western nations pushing the revised understanding of sovereignty. Baranovsky and Mateiko (2016) summarize their principal concerns along two dimensions. The Russians also held fast to Westphalian sovereignty as the guiding principle of the UN, though they had shown more flexibility on that front in their own behavior, and certainly more than other states that take an absolutist position (e.g., Venezuela). Like China, Russia also shared concerns about how the use of force would be applied under the R2P language—the double standard concern.

Pillar III conjured a host of related concerns. Who would decide if intervention against an unwilling nation was warranted? Who would be responsible for contributing to those forces?[12] Both Russia and China pushed back against how to define the situations that fall under R2P and argued for clear procedures for who would decide these questions. Russia, in particular, carried strong suspicion of Western motives because the experience of Kosovo was very recent and particularly raw, given NATO's actions (Ziegler, 2016*b*). What was a motivating case for Canada and many other states pushing protection of civilians

[12] Baranovsky and Mateiko (2016) point out that Russian Foreign Minister Sergei Lavrov raised this important question of whether contributing resources was voluntary or compulsory.

was an example of why one should distrust these actions for Russia, since they portrayed NATO bombings as circumventing the Security Council.[13]

7.2.2 Moving R2P Through the Council

In the end, following years of negotiations, the Chinese delegation introduced the draft resolution in April 2006 that would become Resolution 1674 during its month presiding over the Council and voted in favor of it. Russia also voted in favor of the resolution—in fact, it passed unanimously. How did the resolution, enshrining a revised understanding of arguably the most fundamental concept in the UN, pass when there was sustained suspicion and opposition to critical aspects of R2P?

Undoubtedly, the results of the World Summit in 2005 aided the process of moving a resolution in the Council, but this explanation hinges on the momentum behind the R2P language as it came to be specified in many prior conferences that began with Canada's efforts in the role of Council president in 1999 and again in 2000. We argue that Canada, with further assistance from many partner nations, used its position as Council president to bring the issue to the forefront. They leveraged both public and private negotiations extensively inside and outside the Council, which shaped the R2P language into a broadly acceptable form at the World Summit, leading to passage in the Council seven years after it was first introduced.

Efforts to incorporate a *responsibility* dimension to the concept of sovereignty was well under way when Canada won a seat on the Security Council in 1998. The Canadian delegation would go on to hold the presidency twice, once in February 1999 and once in April 2000, before their term on the Council ended. In these two months, Canada devoted enormous plenary time to discussions of growing civilian casualties in civil conflicts and how to protect civilians better. We can also tell from meeting records that Canada took this initiative primarily on its own, working behind the scenes to organize and coordinate members of the Council in preparation for the discussions that would take place publicly and the statements it would issue on behalf of the Council. For example, each speaker in the 3977th meeting of the Security Council thanked the Canadian delegation for their initiative in starting

[13] Though, as we learn in the prior case study, the Russians knew of the bombing plans and agreed to them without passing the policy through the Security Council.

the conversation about civilians in armed conflict (S/PV.3977). We also know that Canada funded and led the International Commission on Intervention and State Sovereignty (ICISS), the main set of conferences that would produce the first attempt to shape and define the responsibility to protect doctrine that would later be refined at the World Summit in 2005.

The annual reports of the Security Council show that during its February term, Canada held five consultations on this issue and three formal meetings. The issues with the most consultations and meetings (eighteen combined) in a single month are Rwanda in 1994 and Sierra Leone in 2000. Most issues average less than one meeting a month, while the average number of meetings and consultations combined each month is thirty-six, according to our data. For an elected member, the meetings devoted to the protection of civilians in armed conflict represent a significant investment of time for a single issue because they are not guaranteed a future seat on the Council to ensure the Council ever discusses a favored issue again.[14]

The delegation started the process with two consultations on February 9 and 11, prior to holding two meetings on February 12, one to allow a briefing from representatives of the International Committee of the Red Cross (ICRC), the United Nations' Children's Fund (UNICEF), and the Special Representative of the Secretary-General for Children and Armed Conflict, and statements from present delegations and a second to release a presidential statement on the issue.

Part of our argument is that Canada sought to use public and private means to gain acceptance for dealing with the issue of protecting civilians in armed conflict. What actions did they use and what effect might they have had on the process? As we have discussed in several prior chapters, information about state motives, resolve, preferences, and even costs, is valuable and may influence the reactions of many different observers, both domestic and international. Opting for private conversations in the form of consultations is a prudent decision to gauge whether Council members will have strong reactions to the topic at hand. While we have no record of the discussions that occurred, it seems clear from the text of the presidential statement issued on February 12 that the consultation included discussion of the content of the presidential statement, which must have unanimous agreement to be issued.

[14] Indeed, Canada has not won election to the Council since the term describe here, despite previously serving once each decade since the UN's inception. They ran for a seat in the 2020 Security Council elections but lost to Ireland.

Using a public forum may have helped activate specific public costs in the process of negotiating around protecting civilians. First, highlighting the human costs of atrocities against civilians created pressure for reluctant regimes to speak up on issues like genocide publicly. Second, and noted with some regularity in the statements given in the public meeting, holding the discussion in an open meeting enhanced the transparency of the proceedings from the start, undoubtedly a nod to other UN members' concerns about how the Council makes decisions (S/PV.3977).[15] In Chapter 3, we listed in Hypothesis 5 that when public costs for veto are larger than public costs for passage of a resolution, a Council president will be more likely to select a public meeting. While Canada was not yet seeking a resolution, they did want to take some measure in the Council to examine the issue and so allowing the public discussion of protecting civilians may have shaped that support as well. In the same meeting when they issued the Presidential Statement, the Council president also requested a report from the Secretary-General on concrete strategies to enhance the protection of civilians (S/PV.3978).[16]

Further, the publicly available content of the discussions at this point did not include any mention of what would become the R2P pillars. Instead, they condemned violence against civilians and intentionally targeting them in civil wars. In fact, part of the public process may also have been to explore the boundaries of the issue—even in the first public meeting, different delegations raised many issues and potential strategies for addressing the shortcomings of efforts to protect civilians, some even claiming that the international body of law to do this correctly already existed and needed to be implemented more effectively (e.g., UK remarks, S/PV.3977). Thus, the effort may not have started as a concerted effort to redefine sovereignty to include responsibility for protecting civilians, but it was a very public process to pressure nations into a declaration of support for protecting civilians in armed conflict. By the end of the ICISS process, it was transparent that the first draft of R2P was meant to define the responsibilities of the host government clearly and provide standards and broad procedures for when the international community was expected to act.

[15] Statements from the UK and Bahrain mention the transparency specifically. During this period, discussions were ongoing about how the Council could be more transparent in its work. In January 2000, the Council agreed to make drafts of resolutions available (UN Press Service, January 4, 2000).

[16] Further, the president gave the Secretary-General seven months to complete the report, coinciding with when the Netherlands would hold the presidency. Perhaps this was strategic, but certainly, they had to consider whether the Netherlands would permit discussion of the report during its time as Council president, which it did.

ICISS and the World Summit 2005

The ICISS was a series of conferences, sponsored and co-supported by the Canadian government,[17] with the purpose of producing a report with recommendations for resolving the tensions between sovereignty and humanitarian action. In the report, the conference attendees sought to define many terms previously used without a common understanding to justify interventions in civil conflicts on behalf of vulnerable civilians. The commission also considered the political dynamics that have affected humanitarian action. The process, according to Ramesh Thakur, one of the principal actors involved, included open discussion and attempts to be inclusive across the wide range of concerns UN member states had around humanitarianism, sovereignty, and intervention (Thakur, 2002). Indeed, the meetings were held in many locations (Canada, Belgium, India, and Mozambique) while consultations were also held in Canada, Switzerland, the UK, the US, Mozambique, Egypt, France, India, China, and Russia (International Commission on Intervention and State Sovereignty, 2001). Most participants were scholars and some lower-level foreign ministers from several nations.[18]

The contents of the ICISS report offered a detailed baseline for discussions that would take place as part of the World Summit in 2005. The transition to this forum is significant because it was a conference at the UN of 170 heads of state—thus the political aspects would influence these discussions much more heavily to produce the World Summit Outcome document (A/RES/60/1), which had to pass the UN General Assembly.

The differences between the two documents highlight the concessions that had to be made to gain broad enough agreement to pass both the UN General Assembly and the Security Council. First, the ICISS report included detailed conditions that warrant intervention (Section 4) and guiding principles that prescribe that the veto members of the Council not issue a veto in cases where they have no vital interests and lists alternative venues in case the Council deadlocks. The World Summit document does not mention intervention criteria and explicitly names the Council as the appropriate venue for cases of intervention, while listing other organizations only as cooperation partners where appropriate. The ICISS report also set a lower standard for when states cede sovereignty to the international community, when states are "unable

[17] Other funders included several American foundations, such as the Carnegie Corporation, the William and Flora Hewlett Foundation, the John D. and Catherine T. MacArthur Foundation, the Rockefeller Foundation, and the Simons Foundation, and funding from the governments of Switzerland and the UK (International Commission on Intervention and State Sovereignty, 2001).

[18] Notably, the listed participants do not include representatives from China.

and unwilling," whereas the World Summit set a higher standard ("manifestly failing"). Finally, the report takes a much stronger stance on the international community's obligations to assist, while the World Summit weakens that obligation (Bellamy, 2008: p. 623). These differences are directly connected to the concerns of skeptical member states, especially Russia and China, who wanted to ensure they did not codify methods of circumventing the Council nor set standards too low for sovereignty or too high for expected assistance. Given the concerns of skeptical states, two of whom sit on the Council, the alternative to making these concessions was likely failure of the entire initiative.

Thus, the public actions of the Canadian government[19] succeeded in generating discussion and extracting commitments from all nations on, at least the understanding that governments are supposed to protect their civilians from crimes against humanity. Opinion on when intervention is justified is quite varied among states, so the costs to vetoing on the basis of intervention was much lower than the possible costs to passing more specific criteria that could potentially put member states in a difficult position in the future. The World Summit outcome represents a moderated position on the issue, allowing all nations to declare respect for protecting vulnerable civilians but maintaining ambiguity (and flexibility) when deciding whether and what to do about it.

7.2.3 A Pivotal Role

How crucial were Canada's efforts to shape and pass an R2P resolution? It is possible that some version of R2P would have come to pass without Canada's efforts. The permanent members were either ambivalent or openly hostile to the concept of R2P, particularly around what the international community was obligated to do if nations could not guarantee the security of civilians. In fact, in many meetings, the Chinese, though invited, refused to participate. Sustained negotiation and attention to the concerns from opposing nations helped shape the consensus through Canada's continuous efforts between 1999 and 2006.

[19] There is one caveat to note about how much influence Canada had on the discussions around R2P and what it means for the ability of a delegation in the Council presidency to bring controversial issues to the Council. Canada had a significant amount of resources to continue supporting the issue once they left the Council. The capacity of a delegation to see the issue through is incredibly important, and delegations with lower capacity may be unlikely to succeed, even if given the chance. The smallest nation ever to sit on the Security Council won election in 2019, St. Vincent and the Grenadines https://news.un.org/en/story/2019/06/1040071.

As we noted previously, the seeds of a discussion around protecting civilians had been planted in earlier actions and statements in the Council, following disastrous civil wars and lackluster peacekeeping performances in the early 1990s. No discussion had taken place in any formal setting within the Security Council, however. Leadership to develop and organize support around these ideas had not risen, even after several episodes of violence against civilians. The first formal action under the heading "Protection of Civilians in Armed Conflict" came with a presidential statement of the Security Council (S/PRST/1999/6) requesting the Secretary-General to present a report to the Security Council on ways to improve protection of civilians in armed conflict during Canada's term in the Council presidency. The statement itself pieces together elements of earlier precedents in various statements and resolutions that form the basic shape of the concern around protection of civilians, particularly referring to violence against and targeting of civilians as well as access to humanitarian aid. In fact, the Canadian delegation campaigned for a seat on the Security Council with issues of human security as one of three issues it hoped to pursue in the Council, and it won the seat with 75 percent of the vote. Because Canada devoted so much time in the Council and so many resources in meetings beyond its term on the Council, it supported the scaffolding for action and negotiation to build wide consensus, bringing in the opposed nations.

Without Canada's sustained efforts inside and beyond the Security Council, it's much less likely that any consensus would have ever been built, much less negotiations to bring the most strongly opposed nations on board. It is important to note that the Chinese delegation held the meeting on Resolution 1674 and even voted in favor of it after starting the process very much opposed to the notion of R2P. Further, the US was not particularly interested in pursuing the discussion. It's also possible that other delegations may have been willing, but little evidence exists to suggest other nations were willing to devote the plenary time and other resources to push the initiative. Canada, as a frequent contributor to peacekeeping missions, had first-hand experience with attempting to protect civilians in dire situations and carried that experience to its foreign policy in the 1990s.

Why did the two most likely objectors, China and Russia, supported the effort in the end? Were these changes due to Canada's ability to persuade them to agree? It seems unlikely that the Russians and Chinese came around to the Canadian position. Instead, the combination of weakened standards for sovereignty and intervention alongside momentum within the international community to address the protection of civilians, may have incentivized the Russians and Chinese to participate. A further benefit might be that

Resolution 1674 identified the "principal organ of the United Nations" as the legitimate bodies for enforcing R2P, which reinforces and emphasizes that other institutions do not carry the same responsibility. Still, Canada's efforts contributed to popular support while compromise resulted in text that was sufficient to earn the assent of China and Russia.

7.3 Conclusions

This analysis illustrates how public costs affect negotiating behavior in two key cases. In Kosovo, public costs forced Russia to maintain a stiff line on UN authorization for bombing Serbia, even though the Russians admitted it was the only way to get Milošević to comply. For Canada, the public costs at first helped encourage discussion of protecting civilians in armed conflict, but as the parameters of the discussion shifted to redefining sovereignty and calling for intervention, the skeptical permanent members protected themselves (and many sympathetic, skeptical nations) from a policy change that might have cemented Western norms of humanitarian intervention into the UN system.

Further, the Kosovo case and to some extent the R2P case, illustrate both the strengths and weaknesses of holding the Council presidency. Kosovo shows us that presidents can delay action, but they cannot preclude it. They can also start discussion even on topics that people have traditionally avoided to jumpstart conversation that might lead to agreement on an otherwise highly controversial topic, such as the R2P process did. There are limits to what the Council president can do, but there are also opportunities that are understudied in the literature on institutions.

8
Conclusion

For seventy five years, the UN Security Council has shaped international response to threats to international peace and security. The Council has not responded to every threat and is unlikely to do so in the future. When the Council takes up an issue, that choice is a strategic one. What are the preferences of the Council members? Is agreement possible? Members must consider the consequences of doing nothing, especially if one of the permanent members has a credible outside option. While the interests of the permanent members matter, bargaining between them as well as the other members of the Council happens within an institution with rules and common procedures. These rules have an effect on what the Council can and cannot agree to do.

Most of the attention on the Council focuses on peacekeeping missions or resolutions. We argue that to understand what shapes those missions and resolutions, we need to understand the process that moves possible issues onto the Council's working agenda, the programme of work. In the formal model, we showed that the Council president can use that position to raise issues strategically. Delegations can anticipate what an agreement (or draft resolution) on a particular issue might look like, and if the anticipated results are better than doing nothing or relying on another state or institution to take action, then the president will want to put this issue on the agenda. On the other hand, the Council president can delay discussion of an issue if the potential agreement is worse than ignoring the issue or allowing another entity to act. Interests are not the only consideration, the costs and the compromises to get everyone on board are important factors that affect whether the Council will discuss an issue.

Second, because elected members get a turn in the presidency, they have an institutionalized mechanism to bring issues to the fore that other members might ignore. Elected members have put several important thematic issues on the agenda and moved their interests ahead on these issues that the permanent members might otherwise have ignored. We present ample evidence of states using the presidency strategically, and we highlight these dynamics in the R2P and Kosovo cases.

Bargaining in the UN Security Council. Susan Hannah Allen and Amy Yuen, Oxford University Press.
 DOI: 10.1093/oso/9780192849755.003.0008

The agenda-setting process and the limited amount of time each delegation serves as the Council president, especially for the elected members, creates pressure to use that time wisely and get things done. Given this efficiency motive, we gave the Council president a small incentive to favor agreement over disagreement. If our model represents a good approximation of the Council's process, then we should never see vetoes. Thus, the occurrence of vetoes is an under-appreciated puzzle, particularly in the modern Council where the likelihood of agreement is much higher than the Cold War era. Why would a Council president choose the inefficiency over ignoring an issue likely to end in veto? Relaxing an assumption about the costs of messaging, we show that vetoes can serve a grandstanding purpose, highlighting splits in the Council that generate public benefits rather than public costs. Thus, a veto member will issue the veto when it expects some gain from that process—and when the Council president also expects some gain from an otherwise inefficient process. While it is possible that uncertainty means a veto is unexpected, in our research we found only one instance in which the other delegations expressed surprise at a veto, when the Chinese abruptly ended United Nations Preventive Deployment Force (UNPREDEP) with a veto of the mandate extension.

Too often, scholars have been content to collapse the institutional politics and bargaining that occurs in the Security Council as merely a reflection of the permanent members' preferences. As a consequence, previous analyses of Council action have ignored important factors that nudge the content of a resolution in one direction or another, leaving most with the impression that the only states that matter are the P5. We built our model so that it is tilted toward veto member dominance, particularly in the voting stage where they are the only actors. Yet, we find that the options they vote on are affected by the Council president and the penholder delegation. States in these position directly influence the content of any potential agreement, and they do so to their own benefit. To be clear, permanent member preferences still matter because they define the range of possible outcomes in any bargain, as intended when the institution was designed. The powerful hold the veto, but they do not hold sway over the entire process. As we and others have shown—process matters. The rules of the institution have an impact.

8.1 Findings

Our empirical strategy is multi-pronged, utilizing both large N analysis as well as case studies when detailed description is needed to trace the decision-making process. Using this approach, we are able to provide new insight into both the broad behavioral patterns in the Council and the relevant factors that shape individual decisions in the Council.

8.1.1 Quantitative Tests

In Chapter 4, we introduced new data on the behavior of the Security Council, which allows us to explore the determinants of the Council's agenda. In this chapter, we also consider the influence of elected members. Council activity has increased since the end of the Cold War, but that activity has continued to wax and wane with the degree of common interest among the permanent members. More meetings occur and more resolutions pass when the P5 have more similar preferences.

Elected members and permanent members use their agenda-setting powers as the Council president in similar but not identical ways. In both cases, there is awareness that action is unlikely on issues where large disagreement exists among the permanent members. Elected member presidents, however, look to bring issues to the Council involving states that have preferences similar to their own. They also are much more likely to focus on thematic issues like climate change and human security in comparison to permanent members. For their part, permanent member states are more likely to use their agenda-setting powers to bring issues to the Council that they are interested in but that are occurring outside of their sphere of influence.

The overall picture presented in Chapter 4 is that while the threat of the veto hangs over much of what the Council does (and does not do), it is not the only factor that influences the resolutions that pass and the peacekeeping missions that are created. The rotating presidency has an influence. The preferences of the member states also matter.

In Chapter 5, we considered the effects of an outside option as a possible alternative to action inside the Council. Voeten's (2001) analysis emphasized the uncertainty around the likelihood of intervention, so we modeled the process in two stages, modeling the possibility of intervention by the United States and then generating predicted probabilities to include in a model of Council meetings.[1] Our findings suggest that as the likelihood of intervention increases, the likelihood of a meeting increases as does the chance of UN action.

[1] Voeten (2001) actually predicts a point on the policy space, but we have no measure for that prediction and so rely on observing a meeting instead.

8.1.2 Case Studies

The statistical studies show us that the environment both inside and outside the Council are important factors that motivate discussion within the Council. What they cannot show us are the shifts in policy that happen during negotiations nor the motivations for the decisions policy-makers take for any given issues. For that analysis, we turn to case studies to trace policy changes incrementally as situations within the Council and on the ground alter the decision calculus for the members of the Security Council.

In Chapter 6, we traced the issue of North Korean nuclear proliferation in the Council. The case illustrates the influence of factors that have received less attention on the security side of the literature on international institutions, specifically the role of external public costs. We showed that the interests of the permanent members are unequivocally to prevent nuclear proliferation. In the case of North Korea in particular, no permanent member has close affinity with the regime—not even China, an historic defender in the region. Why then, has the issue persisted for more than twenty-five years?

We know that China has regularly attempted to rein in the efforts of the Council to impose harsh consequences on North Korea, despite only tenuous political affinity with the small nation and the fact that the North Korean economy is not critical to China's economic growth directly. We also find few domestic political reasons that explain a moderate policy toward North Korean nuclear proliferation. In fact, China's public statements make clear that it does not support the program, and private remarks suggest real irritation when North Korea violates a ban on testing or provokes regional players in some way. We found substantial evidence that China's behavior in the Council is driven by two related factors—how severe consequences would affect economic migration from North Korea to China and the stability of the North Korean regime and how those factors affect the stability of the region more generally. The Chinese are careful not to signal that they will support dire sanctions on North Korea for fear of sparking a refugee crisis that might collapse the regime. Thus, negotiations have always happened in private, and resolutions have always been weakened to slowly pressure the Kim regime to change direction, leading to an ebb and flow of discussion and action in the Council ever since North Korea first appeared on the agenda. The potential public costs of revealing a preference to stop North Korean nuclear proliferation using all economic means necessary risks collapse. Further evidence supports this argument in that China has quietly made preparations for the demise of the Kim regime which has coincided with cautious increases in sanctions in the last five years. This case is an illustration of our claims that meetings are chosen strategically, and in this case private consultations provide the widest possibility for agreement and action. It also shows that even though very powerful states have strong preferences, in this case about nuclear proliferation, and military capability they cannot simply pursue that policy—they are often restrained by factors, like international public costs, that might seem insignificant but are in fact crucial to the decision calculus.

We examined two other cases in Chapter 7 that reveal additional evidence showing how the Council president sets the agenda strategically, how public costs influence the decision calculus of the Council members, and how elected members can wield influence in an institution traditionally heralded as a tool for the veto members to get their way. The Kosovo case is one in which the Council could not reach agreement to act in the moment, yet behind the scenes, the holdout, Russia, admitted that aerial bombing was the only way to break the stalemate on Kosovo. The potential loss of credibility in the region and at home, however, meant the Russians could not allow the Council to authorize military action since they had expressly spoken against it. At the same time, NATO's decision to act without Council approval served the Russians well because it created a grandstanding opportunity to save face in the Council and subsequently broke Milošević's intransigence on the ground in Kosovo. The events also show that Russia used its time in the seat of the Council presidency to ignore Kosovo at a critical moment, stalling momentum behind the Council taking action and forcing Russia's hand.

We then turned to the efforts of an elected member, Canada, to raise a sticky issue on the protection of civilians in armed conflict. Elected members frequently use their time in the Council to push thematic issues, but the responsibility to protect doctrine represented particular threats to some of the permanent members. With words and actions, Russia and China consistently refused to relinquish the primacy of Westphalian notions of sovereignty in the UN. Through patience and sustained discussion and negotiations, Canada raised the issue in its two stints in the Council presidency, jumpstarting discussions that led to R2P. Outside the Council, Canada led the effort in a series of conferences that ended in the World Summit outcome in 2005 and Resolution 1674, assisted by other elected members sitting in the presidency in 2006. This case, and our argument, by no means suggest that elected members can overwhelm the veto members—but we do find space and opportunity for elected members to negotiate issues that the veto members are otherwise content to ignore.

8.2 Implications

We began from the premise that to understand when action happens in the Council, we needed to look more closely at the potential inside options. Our analysis of the bargaining process inside the Council built in the institutional structure that legislative bargaining has shown influences outcomes in a domestic setting. Our findings challenge several long-standing notions about security institutions.

First, the rules matter in that they provide a framework for how and when the Council takes up an issue. We've shown that public discussions can generate quite different possibilities for agreement than private ones. Given these differences, a strategic Council president can choose whether the discussion is public or private depending on which format is more likely to end with an agreement closest to her ideal point. Second, a Council president can raise an issue for discussion that others have ignored or, conversely, ignore a pressing issue as a crisis unfolds on the ground to gain a better bargaining position. There is room in security institutions for less powerful states to influence how a powerful organization manages a crisis or security issue.

Second, power and preferences are incredibly important, but they are not the only important factors that shape agreements in the Council. We show with our quantitative analysis that the variation in preferences has a systematic effect on the likelihood of discussion and agreements in the Council but that any single state's preferences do not. This suggests that the negotiating environment is very important, and that there is also a great deal of leeway in many cases that affect bargaining outcomes besides the preferences of a veto member. A further implication is that short-handing the decision making to a comparison of preferences misses some very important factors that can shift outcomes substantially.

These points imply a broader implication—that black-boxing the institution, either because it seems like a pass-through for powerful states or because it seems wholly ineffective, misses the crucial bargaining and cooperation that reflects a shared value for the post-World War II grand bargain that persists today. States have the ability to work outside the institution, just as a domestic interest group can have multiple venues to achieve its policy goals without resorting to organized violence, but there are efficiency gains to working through the central institution, and often the policy compromise is worth making. The Security Council has increased its legitimacy, activity, and effectiveness since the end of the Cold War. While realists might argue that the prospect of nuclear war is what maintained the peace and continues to do so, they have little to say about why the Council is so much more active. We argue that there is benefit to international cooperation, some of which might be that the Council allows for public rebuke of nations that take action outside the institution. Gaining legitimacy through mutual consent can affect public opinion and domestic and international support.

For national policy makers, these results would suggest that a seat on the Council is a valuable asset and investment in one's UN delegation is important. There are opportunities to nudge policy in a favorable direction in the Council. For non-state actors like non-government organizations (NGOs), they should be strategic in how they lobby the Council; recognizing who might raise an issue and when seems crucial for pushing a cause. Likewise, there may be issues which they know the Council will never discuss and so should invest resources elsewhere.

Finally, policy-makers oftentimes have to settle for compromises that are less than their most desired outcome to see action on contentious issues. Since these compromises are common because of the diversity of interests in the Council, assessing the effectiveness of any Council actions requires a consideration of what compromises had to be struck to get all members on board. Increasing the effectiveness of a particular action may involve not just hoping for different preferences but also potentially alleviating whatever additional factors (like risks borne from public costs) may influence a Council member's willingness to agree to a resolution.

Overall, introducing some features of legislative bargaining to international security institutions uncovers where the pressure points and strategic levers exist. Our analysis highlights several new areas that deserve further exploration. First, the penholder in our analysis actually carries a great deal of influence over the draft text that the Council considers when it votes. In what ways might this encourage or discourage cooperation in the Council?

We also note that a delegation's capacity to make the case for its position on an issue may be limited, particularly for elected members. What effect does capacity have on whether less powerful states can move the Council? Relatedly, is it possible for less powerful states to gain some leverage over the veto members with agenda-setting power, similar to Vreeland and Dreher's argument that elected members can extract concessions for their vote in the Council?

Lifting the lid on the Council's bargaining process can help us see who has influence and why. In turn, we can understand how and why the Council chooses to involve itself in some situations and not others.

8.2.1 A Note on Security Council Reforms

We mentioned in Chapter 1 that many studies of the Council try to understand its effectiveness—how well does it address threats to international peace and security—and that some of that research supports calls to make reforms in the Council. There are two broad avenues for reform. The first is reforming the operational aspects of actions the Council takes. The most obvious example is peacekeeping, in which the Department of Peace Operations has grown and become more professionalized with training standards, formal agreements with combatants, and other changes that try to affect on-the-ground operational effectiveness. The second avenue for reform is at a much higher level, and these are calls to make the Council more representative and more transparent. How would these potential reforms affect how the Council functions?

While there are many potential proposals and no consensus on needed reforms, we can give some speculative insight on a few of the more prominent proposals related to changing the make-up of the Council that have been reported among Council observers like the Security Council Report, an independent monitoring agency.[2] We recognize, however, that the most consequential changes (like expanding the veto) are very unlikely to happen because the permanent members will veto any changes to the Council structure and process that they think will reduce their power and influence.

A very common proposal is to increase the number of veto members on the Council. One of the vexing questions for a proposal of this sort has been whom to grant veto power to. Should it be rising nations like India and Brazil? Should it be economic powerhouses like Germany or Japan? Should it be states from underrepresented regions, like Africa, South America, and the Middle East? Reformers calling for more veto members have competing goals, and this prevents them from reaching consensus on a proposal to forward. Further, theoretical research and historical experience has shown that more institutional

[2] The Security Council Report offers summaries and analysis of the Council's actions and is staffed by policy academics. They are supported by several national governments, none of which are P5 members, and various private foundations, very like a domestic policy think tank. See for example their summary of potential Security Council reforms, https://www.securitycouncilreport.org/monthly-forecast/2019-09/in-hindsight-security-council-reform.php.

veto players risks increasing the frequency that the members deadlock over contentious issues (O'Neill, 1999). If one of the ways institutions "die" is from deadlock happening so often that members are forced to seek relief elsewhere most of the time, then more veto players may risk weakening the influence of the Security Council over time. Any reform of this nature also requires the current veto members to approve expanding the veto members, but they are very unlikely to do so.

Another proposal is to increase the elected members to make the overall Council more representative since the UN membership has grown so much since the last expansion of the Council in 1963. This could potentially be a good development in that more states would sit in the Council presidency and set the agenda, so more diverse interests have the opportunity to bring up issues that might otherwise be ignored. It's also worth noting that the elected members can effectively veto a resolution in the current system as long as they can coordinate enough members to either abstain or vote against a resolution. We often forget that at least four elected members *must* vote in favor if all of the permanent members vote for a resolution to pass. There are many combinations of votes (and abstentions) that can stop a resolution, but if we look at the most extreme, where the permanent members are all voting in favor (none abstaining) but the elected members want the resolution to fail, then a larger pool of elected members makes it less likely that the elected members can coordinate a sufficient number of elected members to refrain from voting in favor, assuming the passage rule remains nine votes in favor to pass. If they expand the number of elected members, however, the voting rule is likely to increase for passage as well. Currently, if the Council expands to sixteen members, a nine-votes-in-favor rule is still a majority. Beyond sixteen members, however, the bar for passage must increase, or the Council risks a vote outcome in which a minority voted in favor. Thus, the discussion is not just over whether to expand the elected members but also what the new voting rule might be, depending on how many additional elected members there might be. The larger the voting rule, the easier it is for the elected members, in the extreme case, to stop the permanent members from pursuing an action without the support of the E10 members. A much fuller analysis of how the expansion of the membership and changes to the voting rule affect the likelihood of different outcomes would tell us more, but expansion does not automatically reduce the power imbalance between the elected and permanent members.

Another suggested reform involves rebalancing representation by geographic region. The motivation behind these proposals is to get more voices on the Council. Normatively, this aligns with our notions of (more) equal representation, suggesting that more voices from those regions might increase activity and discussion of those regions. The results of our empirical analysis in Chapter 4, however, challenge this assumption. It shows that geographic closeness is not systematically related to what issues elected members choose to put on the Council's agenda.

One final category of reforms has involved making the Council's deliberations more transparent. Transparency in governing serves the goal of accountability, but as we showed with the model in Chapter 3, and others have argued in other governing contexts, sometimes transparency ends up interfering with the ability to make needed concessions to reach an agreement. Our model suggests that closed-door deliberations can play an important role, and we show in the Kosovo case how they helped break the impasse on what to do with Serbia's intransigence while Russia was caught with public costs that prevented them from outright allowing Council approval of NATO intervention.

This book sheds light on the strategic behavior affecting institutional bargaining in the Security Council. Our model and analysis show avenues for political actors to exert influence over discussions inside the Council and shift them, even if ever so slightly, in ways that are more favorable to their preferences through the institution's structure. Different paths through the institution can produce very different outcomes for a given issue, and even whether the Council decides to take up the issue at all. If we want to understand why the Council takes action for some issues and ignores others, we need to be able to compare the inside and outside alternatives. Further, if the UN members states are ever able to coordinate on proposed changes, we can model how those changes might affect Council behavior compared to today.

APPENDIX A

Chapter 3 Proofs and Extensions

Here, we provide the mathematical analysis to support the logic given in this chapter. Returning to Hypothesis 1, we can show this relationship with a simple expansion of Voeten's (2001) original model. We assume the preferences are given for each veto member, and behavior follows accordingly. Given these preferences and assuming a distribution of possible status quo (SQ) policies, we can calculate the likelihood that the status quo falls outside of the veto member extremes. Here, we assume all the possible status quo policies are distributed uniformly across the unidimensional policy space.[1] To calculate the probability that the status quo falls to one side of all veto members, we need to find the area under the distribution between zero and the nearest veto member and add it to the area between the farthest veto member and one. We use the cumulative distribution function (CDF)[2] for the uniform distribution to derive the formula

$$CDF(x) : \frac{x - a}{b - a}$$

where the distributional range is $[a, b]$ and x marks the range of interest from a to x such that $x \leq b$. Thus, the likelihood that the status quo is outside the range of extremes (i.e., the situation is cooperative) is

$$\text{CDF}(x_{SQoverride}) = \frac{x_l - 0}{1 - 0} + \frac{1 - x_u}{1 - 0} = 1 - x_u + x_l \qquad \text{(A.1)}$$

This equation shows that as the distance between the two most extreme veto members gets smaller, the chances of a status quo override increase because the likelihood that the SQ is outside of the contentious range of policies increases. Figure A.1 shows the increase visually.

The following are the formal solutions to the agenda-setting model presented in Section 3.2.5. We operationalize the utility for different policy outcomes with the quadratic loss function, which we expand in the formal derivations. Our game has complete but imperfect information, so we employ a subgame perfect Nash equilibrium concept to solve it.

[1] We could assume many different possible distributions, but issues on the agenda are put there by a variety of actors beyond the Security Council, so we expect much more variation in items on the agenda. Is there a distribution that seems more plausible than the uniform? We can't make the case that there is. Second, even if we used a more sophisticated distributional assumption, the logic we present still holds, as long as that distribution is continuous.

[2] The CDF of any distribution gives the probability that a quantity of interest falls within a range of that distribution. The CDF is the integral of the probability density function (PDF), which reflects the probability of a given value in the range of possible values. So in a uniform distribution, the probability of any value along the policy space is equal to the probability of any other possible value along the policy space.

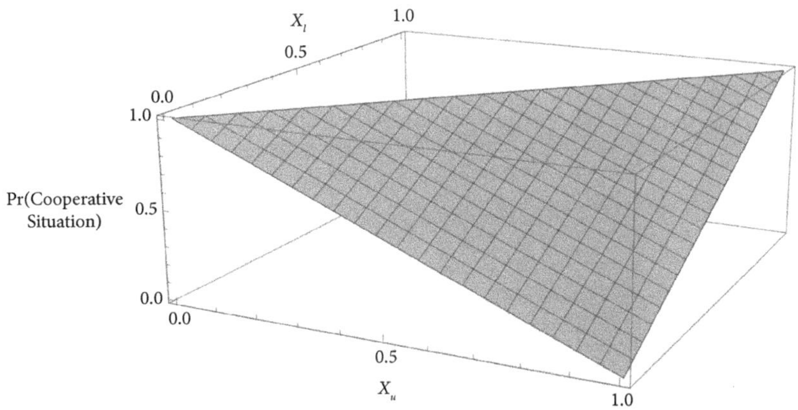

Fig. A.1 Likelihood of a cooperative situation

The Regular Agenda-setting Process (No Outside Option)

The Voting Subgame

We begin at the last subgame, which we call the *voting game*, because it is the simultaneous decision of all five veto members on how to vote on a given resolution text. To solve this stage of the model, we examine the conditions under which a resolution will pass to determine whether a range of acceptable resolutions among five veto players exists. Each player simply weighs the payoff from choosing to vote in favor of a new resolution against the payoff for issuing a veto. The payoffs each player realizes depends on what all the other veto members choose to do. If everyone votes to pass a new resolution, then each player gets a payoff associated with the new resolution. For a private consultation process that is

$$U_i(x_v^*) - g \tag{A.2}$$

and for a public meeting process that is

$$U_i(x_c^*) - g - A_i. \tag{A.3}$$

If anyone votes to veto a resolution, then the payoff for the vetoer is

$$U_i(x_{sq}) - d - n \tag{A.4}$$

in a private consultation process and

$$U_i(x_{sq}) - d - n - z_i \tag{A.5}$$

in a public meeting, reflecting the internal unity cost for vetoing. The payoff to the other members voting to pass a resolution if one member chooses to cast a veto is

$$U_i(x_{sq}) - d \tag{A.6}$$

in a private consultation process and

$$U_i(x_{sq}) - d - z_i \tag{A.7}$$

in a public meeting.

Every veto member chooses to pass a resolution after a private consultation when everyone else votes to pass and

$$U_i(x_v^*) - g > U_i(x_{sq}) - d - n$$

and each will choose to pass after the first veto when

$$U_i(x_{sq}) - d > U_i(x_{sq}) - d - n.$$

Since $n > 0$, there will always be only one veto cast, since delegations who may have wanted to veto can get the outcome at a slightly lower cost if they vote to pass after the first veto is cast.[3] A delegation will choose to veto if everyone else votes to pass and

$$U_i(x_v^*) - g < U_i(x_{sq}) - d - n$$

A similar logic works for the public meeting, where everyone votes to pass when everyone else will pass if

$$U_i(x_c^*) - g - A_i > U_i(x_{sq}) - d - n - z_i \tag{A.8}$$

but veto if everyone else decides to pass and

$$U_i(x_c^*) - g - A_i < U_i(x_{sq}) - d - n - z_i. \tag{A.9}$$

And again, all other members will pass given a single veto if

$$U_i(x_{sq}) - d - z_i > U_i(x_{sq}) - d - z_i - n,$$

which is always true because $n > 0$.

The next step is to identify what choices the penholder and Council president make at their nodes. We assume the penholder is a veto member, so, if the overlapping range exists, then there exists a proposed policy that is better than the status quo for the penholder, by definition. Thus, the realized proposed resolution in this situation is the penholder's ideal point if that preference falls inside the overlapping range, or to the extreme of the overlapping range in the direction of the penholder's preference. If any veto member chooses to veto, we assume the penholder sets the proposed resolution at its ideal point since there is no overlapping range from which to choose a viable, alternative proposal.[4]

Define $[n] = \{1, 2, 3, 4, 5\}$,

[3] By the rules of Nash equilibrium, no two members would veto simultaneously because each would rather vote to pass given that the other is vetoing.

[4] We selected the most *efficient* equilibrium since there are multiple equilibria in this scenario.

$$x_v^l = \max_{i \in [n]} \left\{ x_i - \sqrt{-g + n + d + x_i^2 - 2x_i x_{sq} + x_{sq}^2} \right\} \tag{A.10}$$

$$x_v^u = \min_{i \in [n]} \left\{ x_i + \sqrt{-g + n + d + x_i^2 - 2x_i x_{sq} + x_{sq}^2} \right\}, \tag{A.11}$$

where x_v^l and x_v^u denote the agreement range boundaries. The lower bound is set by the rightmost veto member's lowest acceptable policy, while the upper bound is set by the leftmost veto member's highest acceptable policy.

$$x_v^* = \begin{cases} \underset{x_v \in [x_v^l, x_v^u]}{\operatorname{argmax}} \{x_v | -(x_{ph} - x_v)^2 - g\}, & \text{if } x_v^l < x_v^u \text{ and} \\ & -(x_{ph} - x_v)^2 - g > -(x_{ph} - x_{sq})^2 - d \\ x_{ph}, & \text{otherwise} \end{cases}$$

The penholder's choice in a public meeting scenario is defined by a range that takes external public costs into account.

Define $[n] = \{1, 2, 3, 4, 5\}$,

$$x_c^l = \max_{i \in [n]} \left\{ x_i - \sqrt{d - g + n + z_i - A_i + x_i^2 - 2x_i x_{sq} + x_{sq}^2} \right\} \tag{A.12}$$

$$x_c^u = \min_{i \in [n]} \left\{ x_i + \sqrt{d - g + n + z_i - A_j + x_i^2 - 2x_i x_{sq} + x_{sq}^2} \right\}, \tag{A.13}$$

where x_c^l and x_c^u denote the agreement range boundaries. The lower bound is set by the rightmost veto member's lowest acceptable policy, while the upper bound is set by the leftmost veto member's highest acceptable policy.

$$x_c^* = \begin{cases} \underset{x_c \in [x_c^l, x_c^u]}{\operatorname{argmax}} \{x_c | -(x_{ph} - x_c)^2 - g\}, & \text{if } x_c^l < x_c^u \text{ and} \\ & -(x_{ph} - x_c)^2 - g > -(x_{ph} - x_{sq})^2 - d \\ x_{ph}, & \text{otherwise} \end{cases}$$

In comparing the overlapping ranges between public meetings and consultations, the consultation ranges are primarily determined by the preferences of the veto members, which overlap when g is sufficiently low, and the preferences are close enough together or far enough from the status quo to make wide ranges possible. For the public meetings, the effects of the public costs loom much larger because they are unique to each veto member. Again, comparative statics analysis helps show how these ranges move as the parameters change.

The Council president then compares the proposed resolution that emerges from the penholder's decision to the proposal that would emerge from a public meeting and the status quo situation that would persist with no meeting at all. The UNSC president makes that decision based on the delegation's own preference, and here, it is highly relevant that the elected ten rotate through the presidency.

First, the Council president chooses "No Meeting" over any meeting that ends in veto because $d > 0$ and $z_j > 0$.

$$U_{prez}(x_{sq}) > U_{prez}(x_{sq}) - d$$

$$U_{prez}(x_{sq}) > U_{prez}(x_{sq}) - z_{prez}.$$

To see a consultation occur, the following conditions must hold:

<u>Consultation>No meeting</u>

$$g < d + x_{prez}^2 - 2x_{prez}x_{sq} + x_{sq}^2, \text{ and}$$

$$x_{prez} - \sqrt{-g + x_{prez}^2 - 2x_{prez}x_{sq} + x_{sq}^2} < x_v^* < x_{prez} + \sqrt{-g + x_{prez}^2 - 2x_{prez}x_{sq} + x_{sq}^2}$$

<u>Consultation>Public meeting</u>

$$A_{prez} > -x_{prez}^2 + 2x_{prez}x_{sq} - x_{sq}^2, \text{ and}$$

$$x_{prez} - \sqrt{A_{prez} + x_{prez}^2 - 2x_{prez}x_c^* + x_c^{*2}} < x_v^* < x_{prez} + \sqrt{A_{prez} + x_{prez}^2 - 2x_{prez}x_c^* + x_c^{*2}}$$

If a veto occurs in the public meeting process, the payoff is strictly less than the payoff for no meeting, so the binding constraint is the comparison between a consultation and no meeting.

To see a public meeting occur, the following conditions must hold:

<u>Public meeting>No meeting</u>

$$A_{prez} < x_c^{*2} + 2x_c^* x_{prez} - 2x_{prez}x_v^* - x_v^{*2}$$

For this condition to hold, $x_c^* > x_v^*$, which is possible depending on the penholder's situation in each meeting scenario.

<u>Public meeting>Consultation</u>

$$g < x_{prez}^2 - 2x_{prez}x_{sq} + x_{sq}^2 - A_{prez} \text{ and}$$

$$x_{prez} - \sqrt{x_{prez}^2 - 2x_{prez}x_{sq} + x_{sq}^2 - A_{prez} - g} < x_c^* < x_{prez} + \sqrt{x_{prez}^2 - 2x_{prez}x_{sq} + x_{sq}^2 - A_{prez} - g}$$

If a veto occurs in the consultation process, the payoff is strictly less than the payoff for no meeting, so the binding constraint is the comparison between a public meeting and no meeting.

Equilibrium Behavior

Proposition A.1 (Proposition 3) *The strategy profile (private; x_v^*, x_c^*; all pass, all pass) constitutes a subgame perfect equilibrium.*

Proposition A.2 (Proposition 4) *The strategy profile (private; x_v^*, x_{ph}; all pass, i vetoes while all others pass) constitutes a subgame perfect Nash equilibrium.*

To get a consultation, the cost of multilateral action must be sufficiently low while the net public costs ($A_i - z_i > 0$) for the delegation holding the presidency must be sufficiently high. These requirements ensure that the agreement the penholder chooses in a consultation falls within the range of acceptable agreements for the delegation holding the Council Presidency in that month generating higher utility compared to the status quo, while the agreement chosen in the public process produces lower utility for the president's delegation. In other words, negotiations in private discussions result in resolution text that is better for the Council president than no resolution, and the public costs the Council president would incur from a public negotiating process would result in a less desirable resolution or a vetoed resolution, depending on conditions in the public meeting voting game.[5]

Proposition A.3 (Proposition 5) *The strategy profile (public; x_v^*, x_c^*; all pass, all pass) constitutes a subgame perfect Nash equilibrium.*

Proposition A.4 (Proposition 6) *The strategy profile (public; x_{ph}, x_c^*; i vetoes while all others pass, all pass) constitutes a subgame perfect Nash equilibrium.*

To choose a public meeting, different conditions must hold, specifically that the net public costs are no longer too high to produce a range in which the chosen resolution fits and yields the highest utility compared to a consultation. This equilibrium can swing widely in either direction, generating more flexibility or putting much stricter restraints on the range of agreements depending on each permanent member's public cost. If vetoing generates higher costs, the permanent member will be more tolerant of multilateral action, while higher costs for passage reduces tolerance for multilateral action costs. But these effects only lead the president to choose a public meeting when they generate policy payoffs that are better than a consultation or the status quo. Again, a public meeting is still possible even if a consultation would end in veto, but the utility for the policy from a public meeting must be better for the Council president than ignoring the issue.

Proposition A.5 (Proposition 7) *The strategy profile (no meeting; x_{ph}, x_{ph}; i vetoes while all others pass, i vetoes while all others pass) constitutes a subgame perfect equilibrium.*

When the cost of multilateral action is too high, or there is no range for which all five veto members overlap, then the issue will not be selected for discussion during the month in which that specific delegation holds the UNSC presidency because both meeting processes end in veto which is strictly worse than ignoring the issue.

[5] The difference between Propositions 3 and 4 are what happens in the public meeting voting game, off the path of play.

Grandstanding

To observe the veto, two constraints must be met if $z < 0$: At least one veto member must value vetoing over passing in the public meeting environment, and the Council president must be willing to choose the public meeting knowing it will end in veto.

Member i vetoes in a public meeting when

$$U_i(x_c^*) - g - A_i < U_i(x_{sq}) - d - n - z_i. \tag{A.14}$$

Because we have not altered the value of n in this scenario, we still only observe a single veto since the expected utilities preserve the value of unity within the Council, reflected in the payoffs to the other veto members given one member vetoes,

$$U_i(x_{sq}) - d - z_i > U_i(x_{sq}) - d - z_i - n,$$

which is always true because $n > 0$.

An identical logic for the penholder also holds, that is, the penholder, knowing the veto is imminent will set the policy at his ideal point as the most efficient equilibrium outcome (though technically multiple equilibria are possible).

The most significant change is in the Council president's decision. A veto will only be observed as the final outcome when the Council president's utility for the veto outcome is better than both the private consultation outcome and the no meeting outcome.

<u>Public meeting (veto)>No meeting</u>

$$z_{prez} < -d - n$$

<u>Public meeting (veto)>Consultation (pass)</u>

$$z_{prez} < g - d - n + 2x_p x_{sq} - x_{sq}^2 - 2x_p x_v^* + x_v^{*2}$$

If a veto occurs in the consultation process, the payoff is strictly less than the payoff for no meeting, so the binding constraint is the comparison between a public meeting and no meeting.

Solution to the Agenda-Setting Game with an Outside Option

The following are the formal specification and proofs for the game with an outside option. The subscript "0" denotes payoffs and actions for the intervener.

Following are the formal solutions to the agenda-setting model when an outside option exists. We operationalize the utility for different policy outcomes with the quadratic loss function, which we expand in the formal derivations. Our game has complete but imperfect information, so we employ a subgame perfect Nash equilibrium concept to solve it. We begin at the last subgame, which we call the *voting game*, because it is the simultaneous decision of all five veto members on how to vote on a given resolution text. There are two pure strategy Nash equilibria for the voting subgame, one in which everyone passes the resolution and one in which a single veto member decides to veto, while all others vote to

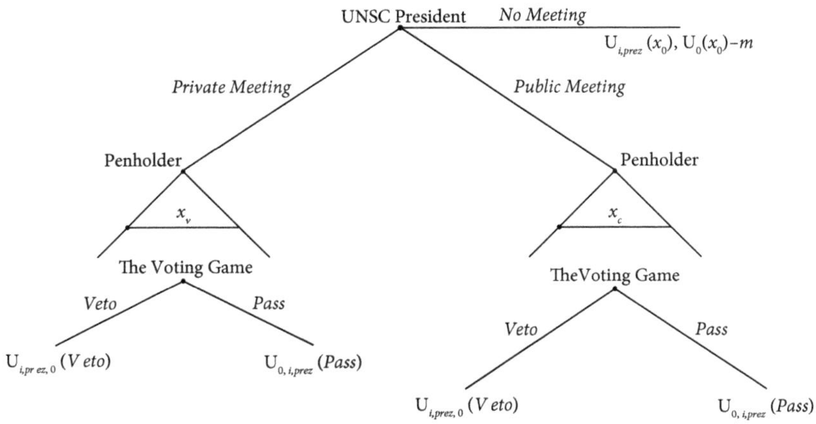

Fig. A.2 An extensive form game of UNSC agenda-setting with an outside option

Table A.1 Payoffs in the consultation voting game

	Veto | All Pass	**Veto | Veto**	**Pass | All Pass**	**Pass | Veto**
Member i	$U_i(x_0) - d - n$	$U_i(x_0) - d - n$	$U_i(x_v^*) - g$	$U_i(x_0) - d$
Council president	$U_{prez}(x_0) - d - n$	$U_{prez}(x_0) - d - n$	$U_{prez}(x_v^*) - g$	$U_{prez}(x_0) - d$
Intervener	$U_0(x_0){-}d{-}n{-}m$	$U_0(x_0){-}d{-}n{-}m$	$U_0(x_v^*) - g$	$U(x_0) - d - m$

Table A.2 Payoffs in the public meeting voting game

	Veto | Veto	**Veto | All Pass**	**Pass | All Pass**	**Pass | Veto**
Member i	$U_i(x_0){-}d{-}n{-}z_i$	$U_i(x_0){-}d{-}n{-}z_i$	$U_i(x_c^*) - g - A_i$	$U_i(x_0) - d - z_i$
Council president	$U_{prez}(x_0) - d - n - z_{prez}$	$U_{prez}(x_0) - d - n - z_{prez}$	$U_{prez}(x_c^*) - g - A_{prez}$	$U_{prez}(x_0) - d - z_{prez}$
Intervener	$U_0(x_0) - d - n - z_0 - m$	$U_0(x_0) - d - n - z_0 - m$	$U_0(x_c^*) - g - A_0$	$U(x_0) - d - z_0 - m$

pass. These results are close to reality, since vetoes are fairly rare, and vetoes from multiple veto members is even rarer. Every veto member chooses to pass a resolution after a private consultation when everyone else votes to pass and

$$U_i(x_v^*) - g > U_i(x_0) - d - n$$

or substituting in the quadratic loss specification

$$-(x_i - x_v^*)^2 - g > -(x_i - x_0) - d - n.$$

For this to hold, g must be sufficiently small

$$g < d + n - x_0^2 - 2x_0x_i + x_i^2$$

and

$$x_i - \sqrt{d - g + n + x_0^2 - 2x_0x_i + x_i^2} < x_v^* < x_i + \sqrt{d - g + n + x_0^2 - 2x_0x_i + x_i^2}. \quad (A.15)$$

The constraint in Equation A.15 is the range of possible policies that the veto member would accept, given the policy if the intervener exercises the outside option, the costs of multilateral action, the veto reputation cost (n) and the opportunity costs paid for holding the meeting.

Next, each veto member will choose to pass after the first veto when

$$U_i(x_0) - d > U_i(x_0) - d - n.$$

Since $n > 0$, there will always be only one veto cast, since delegations who may have wanted to veto can get the outcome at a slightly lower cost if they vote to pass after the first veto is cast.[6] A delegation will choose to veto if everyone else votes to pass and

$$U_i(x_v^*) - g < U_i(x_0) - d - n$$

or substituting in the quadratic loss specification

$$-(x_i - x_v^*)^2 - g < -(x_i - x_0) - d - n.$$

The intervener, who we assume is a veto member as well, passes the resolution when

$$-(x_0 - x_v^*)^2 - g > -(x_0 - x_0)^2 - m - n.$$

The payoff calculation is simpler in this case, because a veto sets the policy to the intervener's most preferred outcome, yielding a zero value to the policy portion of the utility equation and rendering the comparison between pass and veto as one between the costs of intervention (m) and the costs via multilateral action and the policy value tradeoff. Thus, it is quite plausible for an intervener to be willing to accept policy off of its ideal point if the costs are sufficiently low and the policy is close enough to yield greater overall utility. This happens when

$$g < d + m + n$$

and

$$x_0 - \sqrt{m - g + n} < x_v^* < x_0 + \sqrt{m - g + n}. \quad (A.16)$$

If more than one veto player sees a benefit to vetoing a resolution, then there are multiple possible equilibria in which each veto member who would like to veto is the sole member casting the veto. We have no further criteria to distinguish which veto outcome would occur, but the historical record suggests coordination among vetoers, which is not the focus on this model, so we leave that to future, separate analysis. What matters is that a vetoed resolution is the outcome under these conditions, which influences what happens at the next stage.

6 By the rules of Nash equilibrium, no two members would veto simultaneously because each would rather vote to pass given that the other is vetoing.

A similar logic works for the public meeting, where everyone votes to pass when everyone else will pass if

$$U_i(x_c^*) - g - A_i > U_i(x_0) - d - n - z_i$$

or substituting in the quadratic loss specification

$$-(x_i - x_c^*)^2 - g - A_i > -(x_i - x_0)^2 - d - n - z_i.$$

Thus, for a veto member to pass a resolution in a public meeting

$$g < d + n - A_i + x_0^2 - 2x_0x_i + x_i^2 + z_i$$

and

$$x_i - \sqrt{d - g + n - A_i + z_i + x_0^2 - 2x_0x_i + x_i^2} < x_c^* < x_i + \sqrt{d - g + n - A_i + z_i + x_0^2 - 2x_0x_i + x_i^2}. \quad \text{(A.17)}$$

but veto if everyone else decides to pass and

$$U_i(x_c^*) - g - A_i < U_i(x_0) - d - n. \quad \text{(A.18)}$$

And again, all other members will pass given a single veto if

$$U_i(x_0) - d - z_i > U_i(x_0) - d - z_i - n,$$

which is always true because $n > 0$.

Finally, the intervener's calculations are to pass when

$$-(x_0 - x_c^*)^2 - g - A_0 > -d - m - n - z_0,$$

which holds when

$$g < d + m + n \quad \text{(A.19)}$$

and

$$x_0 - \sqrt{d - g + m + n - A_0 + z_0} < x_c^* < x_0 + \sqrt{d - g + m + n - A_0 + z_0}. \quad \text{(A.20)}$$

or pass after the first veto

$$-m - d - z_0 > -m - d - z_0 - n,$$

which is always true since $n > 0$. Veto if all others pass and

$$-(x_0 - x_c^*)^2 - g - A_0 < -d - m - n - z_0.$$

The next stage of the game involves the delegation serving in the penholder role to select the actual resolution policy that is voted on in the last stage. If the conditions for passage hold in the voting game, there exists a range of resolutions that all veto players would accept, bounded on both sides by the veto player with the highest cutpoint for the lower boundary and veto player with the lowest cutpoint for the upper boundary. Within this range, the penholder maximizes their delegation's expected utility within the resolution bounds defined by the cutpoints.

For the consultation scenario:

Define $[n] = \{1, 2, 3, 4\}$,

$$x_v^l = \max_{i \in [n]} \left\{ x_i - \sqrt{-g + n + d + x_i^2 - 2x_i x_0 + x_0^2},\ x_0 - \sqrt{m - g + n} \right\} \tag{A.21}$$

$$x_v^u = \min_{i \in [n]} \left\{ x_i + \sqrt{-g + n + d + x_i^2 - 2x_i x_0 + x_0^2},\ x_0 + \sqrt{m - g + n} \right\}, \tag{A.22}$$

where x_v^l and x_v^u denote the agreement range boundaries.

Set x_v^* such that

$$x_v^* = \begin{cases} \underset{x_v \in [x_v^l, x_v^u]}{\operatorname{argmax}} \{x_v \mid -(x_{ph} - x_v)^2 - g\}, & \text{if } x_v^l < x_v^u \text{ and} \\ & -(x_{ph} - x_v)^2 - g > -(x_{ph} - x_0)^2 - d \\ x_{ph}, & \text{otherwise} \end{cases}$$

if the penholder is not the intervener. Set x_v^* such that

$$x_v^* = \begin{cases} \underset{x_v \in [x_v^l, x_v^u]}{\operatorname{argmax}} \{x_v \mid -(x_{ph} - x_v)^2 - g\}, & \text{if } x_v^l < x_v^u \text{ and} \\ & -(x_{ph} - x_v)^2 - g > -(x_{ph} - x_0)^2 - d - m \\ x_{ph}, & \text{otherwise} \end{cases}$$

if the penholder is the intervener.

When the penholder is a veto member, we know already that there is a range of resolutions that the delegation serving as penholder would accept. The penholder sets the resolution as close to its ideal point as possible where it is still within the range of passable resolutions. A penholder that is not a veto member may still get greater utility from a resolution than an intervention; however, the second constraint may or may not be met even if the first one is, in this case. If it is not met, an elected member can scupper a resolution deliberately by choosing its own ideal point, in theory. But, if an elected member attempted this, it is likely that delegation would be replaced as penholder rather than allow the resolution text to be set outside of an agreement range.

In a public setting, a similar process occurs, but it takes into account the public costs in this process: define $[n] = \{1, 2, 3, 4\}$,

$$x_c^l = \max_{i \in [n]} \left\{ x_i - \sqrt{-g + n + d + z_i - A_i + x_i^2 - 2x_i x_0 + x_0^2},\ x_0 - \sqrt{d - g + m + n - A_0 + z_0} \right\} \tag{A.23}$$

$$x_c^u = \min_{i \in [n]} \left\{ x_i + \sqrt{-g + n + d + z_i - A_i + x_i^2 - 2x_i x_0 + x_0^2},\ x_0 + \sqrt{d - g + m + n - A_0 + z_0} \right\}, \tag{A.24}$$

where x_c^l and x_c^u denote the agreement range boundaries.

Set x_c^* such that

$$x_c^* = \begin{cases} \underset{x_c \in [x_c^l, x_c^u]}{\text{argmax}} \{x_c | -(x_{ph} - x_c)^2 - g\}, & \text{if } x_c^l < x_c^u \text{ and} \\ & -(x_{ph} - x_c)^2 - g > -(x_{ph} - x_0)^2 - d \\ x_{ph}, & \text{otherwise} \end{cases}$$

if the penholder is not the intervener. Set x_c^* such that

$$x_c^* = \begin{cases} \underset{x_c \in [x_c^l, x_c^u]}{\text{argmax}} \{x_c | -(x_{ph} - x_c)^2 - g\}, & \text{if } x_c^l < x_c^u \text{ and} \\ & -(x_{ph} - x_c)^2 - g > -(x_{ph} - x_0)^2 - d - m \\ x_{ph}, & \text{otherwise} \end{cases}$$

if the penholder is the intervener.

At the first stage, the Council president must decide whether to take up an issue and in what meeting format. Anticipating the resolutions that would come from a consultation and a public meeting, the Council president compares these scenarios to the payoff for ignoring the issue in that month, that is, staying with the status quo. Because the Council president is most often not a veto member (by virtue of the alphabetically rotating system each month and the ten elected members compared to the five veto members) the Council president's preferences may be quite different than the permanent members or the penholder.

First, the Council president will not select any meeting that ends in veto over ignoring the issue because the president's payoff for veto is strictly lower than the payoff for ignoring the issue since $d > 0$.

$$-(x_{prez} - x_0)^2 > -(x_{prez} - x_0)^2 - d$$

For the Council president to select a consultation, the utility for a passed resolution from a private consultation process must be greater than both the utility for a resolution from a public process and the utility for the status quo.

Choose consultation over no meeting when

$$-(x_{prez} - x_v^*)^2 - g > -(x_{prez} - x_0)^2$$

g is sufficiently small

$$g < x_0^2 - 2x_0 x_{prez} + x_{prez}^2 \tag{A.25}$$

and x_v^* is in the range

$$x_{prez} - \sqrt{x_0^2 - 2x_0x_{prez} + x_{prez}^2 - g} < x_v^* < x_{prez} + \sqrt{x_0^2 - 2x_0x_{prez} + x_{prez}^2 - g}. \quad \text{(A.26)}$$

Choose consultation over public meeting when

$$-(x_{prez} - x_v^*)^2 - g > -(x_{prez} - x_c^*)^2 - g - A_{prez}$$

A_{prez} is sufficiently large

$$A_{prez} > -x_c^{*2} + 2x_c^*x_{prez} - x_{prez}^2 \quad \text{(A.27)}$$

and x_v^* is in the range

$$x_{prez} - \sqrt{A_{prez} + x_c^{*2} - 2x_c^*x_{prez} + x_{prez}^2} < x_v^* < x_{prez} + \sqrt{A_{prez} + x_c^{*2} - 2x_c^*x_{prez} + x_{prez}^2}. \quad \text{(A.28)}$$

Choose public meeting over no meeting when

$$-(x_{prez} - x_c^*)^2 - g - A_{prez} > -(x_{prez} - x_0)^2$$

g is sufficiently small

$$g < x_0^2 - 2x_0x_{prez} + x_{prez}^2 - A_{prez} \quad \text{(A.29)}$$

and x_c^* falls in the range

$$x_{prez} - \sqrt{x_0^2 - 2x_0x_{prez} + x_{prez}^2 - g - A_{prez}} < x_c^* < x_{prez} + \sqrt{x_0^2 - 2x_0x_{prez} + x_{prez}^2 - g - A_{prez}}. \quad \text{(A.30)}$$

Choose public meeting over consultation when

$$-(x_{prez} - x_c^*)^2 - g - A_{prez} > -(x_{prez} - x_v^*)^2 - g$$

A_{prez} is sufficiently small

$$A_{prez} < x_{prez}^2 - 2x_{prez}x_v^* + x_v^{*2} \quad \text{(A.31)}$$

and x_c^* falls in the range

$$x_{prez} - \sqrt{x_{prez}^2 - 2x_{prez}x_v^* + x_v^{*2} - A_{prez}} < x_c^* < x_{prez} + \sqrt{x_{prez}^2 - 2x_{prez}x_v^* + x_v^{*2} - A_{prez}}. \quad \text{(A.32)}$$

Choose no meeting over consultation when the inequality in Equation A.25 does not hold, or if it does hold, when the policy falls outside of the range defined in Equation A.26. Choose no meeting over public meeting when the inequality in Equation A.29 does not hold, or if it does hold, when the policy falls outside of the range defined in Equation A.30.

APPENDIX B

Chapter 4 Tables

Table B.1 Determinants of agenda for all Council presidents

Variable	**Coefficient** (Std. Err.)
Avg P5 Affinity	1.263**
	(0.214)
P5 Preference Variation	−3.173**
	(0.376)
Time on the Agenda	−0.024**
	(0.001)
Peacekeeping Mission	0.504**
	(0.020)
Total Resolutions	−0.012**
	(0.001)
Affinity with President	0.519**
	(0.051)
Capital Distance	0.035**
	(0.012)
Time	−0.017
	(0.014)
$Time^2$	0.008**
	(0.002)
$Time^3$	0.000**
	(0.000)
N	19891
Log-likelihood	−15669.819
$\chi^2_{(10)}$	2861.933

Significance levels: † : 10% * : 5% ** : 1%
Table corresponds to Figure 4.2 in the text.

Table B.2 Determinants of agenda for P5 presidents

Variable	**Coefficient** (Std. Err.)
Avg P5 Affinity	2.086**
	(0.351)
P5 Preference Variation	−2.669**
	(0.627)
Time on the Agenda	−0.024**
	(0.001)
Peacekeeping Mission	0.472**
	(0.034)
Total Resolutions	−0.011**
	(0.002)
Affinity with President	0.139†
	(0.081)
Capital Distance	0.101**
	(0.025)
Time	−0.031
	(0.023)
$Time^2$	0.009**
	(0.003)
$Time^3$	0.000**
	(0.000)
N	6693
Log-likelihood	−5384.735
$\chi^2_{(10)}$	925.617

Significance levels: † : 10% * : 5% ** : 1%
Table corresponds to Figure 4.3 in the text.

Table B.3 Determinants of agenda for E10 presidents

Variable	**Coefficient** (Std. Err.)
Avg P5 Affinity	0.116
	(0.278)
P5 Preference Variation	−4.250**
	(0.483)
Time on the Agenda	−0.023**
	(0.001)
Peacekeeping Mission	0.538**
	(0.025)
Total Resolutions	−0.012**
	(0.001)
Affinity with President	1.026**
	(0.072)
Capital Distance	0.006
	(0.014)
Time	−0.001
	(0.017)
$Time^2$	0.006**
	(0.002)
$Time^3$	0.000**
	(0.000)
N	13198
Log-likelihood	−10226.353
$\chi^2_{(10)}$	1950.728

Significance levels: † : 10% * : 5% ** : 1%
Table corresponds to Figure 4.4 in the text.

B.1 Multinomial Models

The following tables present the results of the supplementary analysis using multinomial modeling. The reference categories for all of these results are no action on an agenda item in a given month. Time controls were also included in these models as they were in the ordered models, but they were dropped from the tables to make them less visually complex. The results presented in these models lead to very similar insights to those presented in the ordered models in the text. The degree of agreement among the permanent members always matters, regardless of who holds the presidency. While elected members are more likely to hold meetings on countries with similar foreign policy preferences to their own, permanent members care about their respective regional influences.

B.2 Count Models of Council Activity

Table B.4 Multinomial analysis for all presidents

Variable	**Coefficient**	**(Std. Err.)**
	Consultations Only	
Avg P5 Affinity	−0.923	(0.733)
P5 Preference Variation	−5.828**	(1.410)
Time on the Agenda	−0.039**	(0.003)
Peacekeeping Mission	0.182*	(0.079)
Total Resolutions	−0.002	(0.004)
Affinity with President	0.427*	(0.198)
Capital Distance	0.038	(0.048)
Intercept	−1.296	(1.365)
	Public Meetings Only	
Avg P5 Affinity	3.846**	(0.360)
P5 Preference Variation	−6.657**	(0.641)
Time on the Agenda	−0.027**	(0.001)
Peacekeeping Mission	0.299**	(0.034)
Total Resolutions	−0.018**	(0.002)
Affinity with President	0.777**	(0.089)
Capital Distance	0.078**	(0.021)
Intercept	−6.860**	(0.675)
	Consultations and Public Meetings	
Avg P5 Affinity	0.998**	(0.368)
P5 Preference Variation	−3.695**	(0.643)
Time on the Agenda	−0.035**	(0.001)
Peacekeeping Mission	0.915**	(0.036)
Total Resolutions	−0.018**	(0.002)
Affinity with President	0.716**	(0.086)
Capital Distance	0.043*	(0.021)
Intercept	−2.681**	(0.680)
N	19891	
Log-likelihood	−15207.753	
$\chi^2_{(30)}$	3499.418	

Significance levels: † : 10% * : 5% ** : 1%

Table B.5 Multinomial analysis for P5 presidents

Variable	**Coefficient**	**(Std. Err.)**
	Consultations Only	
Avg P5 Affinity	-1.326	(1.126)
P5 Preference Variation	−9.131**	(2.253)
Time on the Agenda	−0.046**	(0.006)
Peacekeeping Mission	0.064	(0.132)
Total Resolutions	−0.001	(0.007)
Affinity with President	0.073	(0.317)
Capital Distance	0.087	(0.082)
Intercept	−0.120	(2.054)
	Public Meetings Only	
Avg P5 Affinity	5.447**	(0.593)
P5 Preference Variation	−5.409**	(1.088)
Time on the Agenda	−0.028**	(0.002)
Peacekeeping Mission	0.271**	(0.058)
Total Resolutions	−0.016**	(0.003)
Affinity with President	0.254†	(0.140)
Capital Distance	0.193**	(0.042)
Intercept	−10.357**	(1.152)
	Both Consultations and Public Meetings	
Avg P5 Affinity	2.096**	(0.588)
P5 Preference Variation	−2.980**	(1.062)
Time on the Agenda	−0.035**	(0.002)
Peacekeeping Mission	0.858**	(0.060)
Total Resolutions	−0.018**	(0.003)
Affinity with President	0.168	(0.136)
Capital Distance	0.126**	(0.042)
Intercept	−4.694**	(1.135)
N	6693	
Log-likelihood	−5200.962	
$\chi^2_{(30)}$	1212.878	

Significance levels: † : 10% * : 5% ** : 1%

Table B.6 Multinomial models for E10 presidents

Variable	Coefficient	(Std. Err.)
	Consultations Only	
Avg P5 Affinity	−1.529	(1.006)
P5 Preference Variation	−4.673*	(1.833)
Time on the Agenda	−0.034**	(0.004)
Peacekeeping Mission	0.284**	(0.100)
Total Resolutions	−0.002	(0.005)
Affinity with President	1.046**	(0.282)
Capital Distance	0.017	(0.059)
Intercept	−0.911	(1.842)
	Public Meeetings Only	
Avg P5 Affinity	2.093**	(0.466)
P5 Preference Variation	−8.418**	(0.814)
Time on the Agenda	−0.025**	(0.001)
Peacekeeping Mission	0.337**	(0.041)
Total Resolutions	−0.019**	(0.002)
Affinity with President	1.474**	(0.127)
Capital Distance	0.029	(0.024)
Intercept	−3.856**	(0.852)
	Both Consultations and Public Meetings	
Avg P5 Affinity	−0.677	(0.492)
P5 Preference Variation	−5.282**	(0.836)
Time on the Agenda	−0.033**	(0.002)
Peacekeeping Mission	0.973**	(0.045)
Total Resolutions	−0.018**	(0.002)
Affinity with President	1.441**	(0.122)
Capital Distance	0.006	(0.024)
Intercept	−0.085	(0.886)
N	13198	
Log-likelihood	−9937.866	
$\chi^2_{(30)}$	2322.487	

Significance levels: † : 10% * : 5% ** : 1%

Table B.7 Count model of thematic issues

Variable	**Coefficient** (Std. Err.)
Total Monthly Activity	0.025**
	(0.003)
Elected President	0.147*
	(0.072)
Time Controls	Yes
Intercept	−1.531**
	(0.326)
Dispersion Parameter	
ln(alpha)	−15.234**
	(1.880)
N	264
Log-likelihood	−456.863
$\chi^2_{(23)}$	240.706

Significance levels: † : 10% * : 5% ** : 1%

Table B.8 Annual aggregate counts of UN Security Council activity

	(1) Consultations		(2) Meetings		(3) Resolutions	
Preference Variation	−1.463***	(0.450)	−2.007***	(0.525)	−2.073***	(0.203)
Vetoes	−0.044	(0.051)	−0.017	(0.060)	−0.081**	(0.036)
Total Agenda Items	0.003	(0.003)	−0.003	(0.002)	0.001	(0.002)
Constant	8.036***	(0.862)	9.956***	(1.043)	8.535***	(0.481)
Dispersion Parameter						
ln(alpha)	−1.043***	(0.349)	−2.107***	(0.318)	−2.493***	(0.273)
Observations	30		30		45	

Robust standard errors in parentheses.
* $p \leq 0.10$ ** $p \leq 0.05$, * * * $p \leq 0.01$
Table corresponds to Figure 4.9 in the text.

APPENDIX C

Chapter 5 Tables

This appendix includes tables for the regression analyses presented in Chapter 5.

Table C.1 Determinants of US intervention

Variable	**Coefficient** (Std. Err.)
Battle Deaths	0.107*
	(0.048)
Regime Type	−0.032†
	(0.018)
US Military Spending	1.468**
	(0.323)
Capital Distance	0.173
	(0.285)
P5 Colony	−0.682**
	(0.180)
Trade Flow	−0.127**
	(0.034)
Democratic President	0.352†
	(0.196)
Election Year	−0.006
	(0.179)
Alliance	0.530†
	(0.318)
Intercept	−31.693**
	(7.459)
N	739
Log-likelihood	−157.216
$\chi^2_{(9)}$	56.897

Significance levels: † : 10% * : 5% ** : 1%
Table corresponds to Figure 5.1 in the text.

Table C.2 Determinants of UN intervention

Variable	**Coefficient** (Bootstrapped Std. Err.)
Pr(US Intervention)	2.777**
	(0.936)
Battle Deaths	0.055
	(0.046)
P5 Colony	0.213
	(0.141)
Ongoing Peacekeeping	0.261**
	(0.054)
Vetoes	−0.084
	(0.094)
Preference Variation	−3.287**
	(0.662)
Ceasefire	0.217
	(0.176)
Time	−1.503**
	(0.273)
$Time^2$	0.173**
	(0.031)
$Time^3$	−0.005**
	(0.001)
Intercept	−2.415**
	(0.825)
N	612
Log-likelihood	−281.071
$\chi^2_{(10)}$	73.178

Significance levels: † : 10% * : 5% ** : 1%
Table corresponds to Figure 5.2 in the text.

Bibliography

Adebajo, Adekeye. 2012. *UN Peacekeeping in Africa: From Suez Crisis to the Sudan Conflict*. Jacana Media. Boulder, CO: Lynne Rienner.

Agreed Framework Between the United States and the Democratic People's Republic of Korea. 1994. Geneva, Switzerland. International Atomic Energy Agency. **URL**: *https://www.iaea.org/sites/default/files/publications/documents/infcircs/1994/infcirc457.pdf*

Albright, Madeleine and Bill Woodward. 2003. *Madeleine Albright: Madam Secretary*. New York, NY: Miramax Books.

Allen, Susan and Amy Yuen. 2014. "The Politics of Peacekeeping: UN Security Council Oversight Across Peacekeeping Missions." *International Studies Quarterly* 58(3): 621–632.

Andersen, Thomas Barnebeck, Henrik Hansen, and Thomas Markussen. 2006. "US Politics and World Bank IDA-lending." *The Journal of Development Studies* 42(5):772–794.

Axelrod, Robert. 1984. *The Evolution of Cooperation*. New York: Basic Books.

Axelrod, Robert and Robert O. Keohane. 1985. "Achieving Cooperation under Anarchy: Strategies and Institutions." *World Politics* 38(1):226–254.

A Year After Iraq War: Mistrust of America in Europe Even Higher, Muslim Anger Persists. 2004. Washington, DC: Pew Research Center. **URL**: *https://www.pewresearch.org/global/2004/03/16/survey-report/*

Bailey, Michael, Strezhnev Anton, and Erik Voeten. 2017. "Estimating Dynamic State Preferences from United Nations Voting Data." *Journal of Conflict Resolution* 61(2):430–456.

Bailey, Sidney and Sam Daws. 1995. *The United Nations: A Concise Political Guide*. Lanham, MD: Barnes and Noble Books.

Bailey, Sidney and Sam Daws. 1998. *The Procedure of the UN Security Council*. New York, NY: Oxford University Press.

Bailey, Sydney. 1969. *Voting in the Security Council*. Bloomington, IN: Indiana University Press.

Bailey, Sydney. 1994. *The UN Security Council and Human Rights*. New York, NY: St. Martin's Press, Inc.

Baranovsky, Vladimir and Anatoly Mateiko. 2016. "Responsibility to Protect: Russia's Approaches." *The International Spectator* 51(2):49–69.

Barbieri, Katherine, Omar M. G. Keshk, and Brian Pollins. 2009. "Trading Data: Evaluating our Assumptions and Coding Rules." *Conflict Management and Peace Science* 26(5):471–491.

Barbieri, Katherine and Omar M. G. Omar Keshk. 2016. *Correlates of War Project Trade Data Set Codebook*, Version 4.0. Online: **URL**: *http://correlatesofwar.org*.

Bellamy, Alex. 2008. "The Responsibility to Protect and the Problem of Military Intervention." *International Affairs* 84(4):615–639.

Bennis, Phylis. 1996. *Calling the Shots: How Washington Dominates Today's U.N.* New York: Olive Branch Press.

Berdal, Mats and David Ucko. 2015. "The Use of Force in UN Peacekeeping Operations: Problems and Prospects." *The RUSI Journal* 160(1):6–12.

Bosco, David L. 2009. *Five to Rule Them All: The UN Security Council and the Making of the Modern World*. New York, NY: Oxford University Press.

Boutros-Ghali, Boutros. 1999. *Unvanquished: A US-UN Saga*. New York: Random House.

Bueno de Mesquita, Bruce and Alastair Smith. 2010. "The Pernicious Consequences of UN Security Council Membership." *Journal of Conflict Resolution* 54(5):667–686.

Carnegie, Allison and Austin Carson. 2020. *Secrets in Global Governance: Disclosure Dilemmas and the Challenge of International Cooperation*. Cambridge, UK: Cambridge University Press.

Carrel-Billiard, François and Christine Wing. 2010. *IPI on the Nuclear Non-Proliferation Treaty*. April 30. International Peace Institute. New York, NY **URL**: *https://www.ipinst.org/2010/04/ipi-on-the-nuclear-non-proliferation-treaty*

Carrubba, Clifford, Matthew Gabel, and Charles Hankla. 2008. "Judicial Behavior under Political Constraints: Evidence from the European Court of Justice." *American Political Science Review* 102(4):435–452.

Carter, David and Curtis Signorino. 2010. "Back to the Future: Modeling Time Dependence in Binary Data." *Political Analysis* 18(3):271–292.

Center for Strategic and International Studies. June 14, 2018. "Missiles of North Korea." the Center for Strategic and International Studies: Washington, DC. **URL**: *https://missilethreat.csis.org/country/dprk/*

Chapman, Terrence. 2007. "International Security Institutions, Domestic Politics, and Institutional Legitimacy." *Journal of Conflict Resolution* 51(1):134–166.

Chapman, Terrence. 2009. "Audience Beliefs and International Organization Legitimacy." *International Organization* 63(4):733–764.

Chapman, Terrence. 2011. *Securing Approval: Domestic Politics and Multilateral Authorization for War*. Chicago, IL: The University of Chicago Press.

Chapman, Terrence and Dan Reiter. 2004. "The UN Security Council and the Rally' Round the Flag Effect." *Journal of Conflict Resolution* 48(6):886–909.

Christopher, Warren. 1998. *In the Stream of History: Shaping Foreign Policy for a New Era*. Palo Alto, CA: Stanford University Press.

Claude, Inis. 1963. *The Changing United Nations*. New York, NY: Random House.

Claude, Inis. 1966. "Collective Legitimization as a Political Function of the United Nations." *International Organization* 20(3):367–379.

Cohen, Bejamin V. 1951. "The Impact of the United Nations on United States Foreign Policy." *International Organization* 5(2):274–281.

Copelovitch, Mark. 2010. "Master or Servant? Common Agency and the Political Economy of IMF Lending." *International Studies Quarterly* 54(1):49–79.

Cortell, Andrew and James Davis. 1996. "How Do International Institutions Matter? The Domestic Impact of International Rules and Norms." *International Studies Quarterly* 40(4):451–478.

Cortright, David and George A. Lopez, eds. 2000. *The Sanctions Decade: Assessing UN Strategies in the 1990s*. Vol. 1. Boulder, CO: Lynne Rienner Publishers.

Corwin, Phillip. 1999. *Dubious Mandate: A Memoir of the UN in Bosnia, Summer 1995*. Durham, NC: Duke University Press.

Crowley, S.P. and J.H. Jackson. 1996. "WTO Dispute Procedures, Standard of Review, and Deference to National Governments." *American Journal of International Law* 90:193.

Cumings, Bruce. 1995. *Divided Korea: United Future?* Headline Ithaca, NY: Foreign Policy Association.

Daws, Sam and Loraine Sievers. 2016. *Arria-Formula Meetings, 1992-2016*. Technical report: Security Council Report.

De Jonge Oudraat, Chantal. 1996. The United Nations and Internal Conflict. In *The International Dimensions of Internal Conflict*, ed. Michael Brown. Cambridge, MA: MIT Press.

Deng, Francis M., Sadikiel Kimaro, Terrence Lyons, Donald Rothchild, and I. William Zartman. 1996. *Sovereignty as Responsibility: Conflict Management in Africa*. Washington, DC: Brookings Institution Press.

Diehl, Paul F. 1994. *International Peacekeeping*. Baltimore, MD: Johns Hopkins University Press.

Doyle, Michael W. and Nicholas Sambanis. 2006. *Making War and Building Peace: United Nations Peace Operations*. Princeton, NJ: Princeton University Press.

Dreher, Axel, Jan-Egbert Sturm, and James Raymond Vreeland. 2009*a*. "Development Aid and International Politics: Does Membership on the UN Security Council Influence World Bank Decisions?" *Journal of Development Economics* 88(1):1–18.

Dreher, Axel, Jan-Egbert Sturm, and James Raymond Vreeland. 2009*b*. "Global Horse Trading: IMF Loans for Votes in the United Nations Security Council." *European Economic Review* 53(7):742–757.

Durch, William J. 1993. *The Evolution of UN Peacekeeping: Case Studies and Comparative Analysis*. Henry L. Stimson Center, New York, NY: St. Martin's Press, Inc.

Erik Melander, Therese Petterson, and Lotta Themner. 2016. "Organized Violence, 1989–2015." *Journal of Peace Research* 53(5):727–742.

European Union. 1998. "Letter Dated 19 June 1998 From the Permanent Representative of United Kingdom of Great Britain and Northern Ireland to the United Nations Addressed to the Secretary-General." S/1998/554.

Fang, Songying. 2008. "The Informational Role of International Institutions and Domestic Politics." *American Journal of Political Science* 52(2):304–321.

Fang, Songying and Randall W. Stone. 2012. "International Organizations and Policy Advisors." *International Organization* 66(4):537–569.

Fearon, James D. 1994*a*. "Domestic Political Audiences and the Escalation of International Disputes." *American Political Science Review* 88(3):577–592.

Fearon, James D. 1994*b*. "Signaling versus the Balance of Power and Interests: An Empirical Test of a Crisis Bargaining Model." *Journal of Conflict Resolution* 38(2):236–269.

Finnemore, Martha. 2003. *The Purpose of Intervention: Changing Beliefs about the Use of Force*. Ithaca, NY: Cornell University Press.

Fordham, Benjamin. 1998. "Partisanship, Macroeconomic Policy, and US Uses of Force, 1949–1994." *Journal of Conflict Resolution* 42(4):418–439.

Fortna, Virginia Page. 2004. "Does Peacekeeping Keep Peace? International Intervention and the Duration of Peace After Civil War." *International Studies Quarterly* 48(2): 269–292.

Fortna, Virginia Page. 2008. *Does Peacekeeping Work? Shaping Belligerents' Choices After Civil War*. Princeton, NJ: Princeton University Press.

Gibbs, David. 1997. "Is Peacekeeping a New Form of Imperialism?" *International Peacekeeping* 4:122–128.

Gilligan, Michael and Stephen John Stedman. 2003. "Where Do the Peacekeepers Go?" *International Studies Review* 5(4):37–54.

Gleditsch, Nils Petter, Peter Wallensteen, Mikael Eriksson, Margareta Sollenberg, and Havard Strand. 2002. "Armed Conflict 1946–2001: A New Dataset." *Journal of Peace Research* 39(5):615–637.

Goodrich, Leland M. 1972. "The United Nations Security Council." In *The United Nations: Past, Present, and Future*, ed. James Barros. New York: Free Press.

Grieg, Michael and Andrew Enterline. 2017. "National Material Capabilities (NMC) Data Documentation Version 5.0." **URL:** *https://correlatesofwar.org/data-sets/national-material-capabilities*

Groseclose, Tim and Nolan McCarty. 2001. "The Politics of Blame: Bargaining Before an Audience." *American Journal of Political Science* 45(1):100–119.

Haftel, Yoram, and Alexander Thompson. 2006. "The Independence of International Organizations: Concept and Applications." *Journal of Conflict Resolution* 50(2): 253–275.

Haveman, Jon and David Hummels. 2004. "Alternative Hypotheses and the Volume of Trade: the Gravity Equation and the Extent of Specialization." *Canadian Journal of Economics/Revue canadienne d'économique* 37(1):199–218.

Highlights of Security Council Practice. 2014. United Nations publication, New York, NY. **URL:** *http://www.un.org/en/sc/repertoire/data/highlights_2014.pdf*

Hildebrand, Robert C. 1990. "Dumbarton Oaks." *The Origins of the United Nations and the Search for Postwar Security.* University of North Carolina Press. Chapel Hill, NC. pp. 237–240.

Hildebrandt, Timothy, Courtney Hillebrecht, Peter M. Holm, and Jon Pevehouse. 2013. "The Domestic Politics of Humanitarian Intervention: Public Opinion, Partisanship, and Ideology." *Foreign Policy Analysis* 9(3):243–266.

Hill, Christopher. 2015. *Outpost: A Diplomat at Work.* New York, NY: Simon & Schuster.

Högbladh, Stina, Therése Pettersson, and Lotta Themnér. 2011. "External Support in Armed Conflict 1975–2009: Presenting New Data." In *52nd Annual International Studies Association Convention, Montreal, Canada.* pp. 16–19.

Hulton, Susan. 2004. "Council Working Methods and Procedure." In *The UN Security Council: From the Cold War to the 21st Century*, ed. David Malone. Boulder, CO: Lynne Reinner Publishing.

Hurd, Ian. 2002. "Legitimacy, Power, and the Symbolic Life of the UN Security Council." *Global Governance* 8:35.

Hurd, Ian. 2008. *After Anarchy: Legitimacy and Authority in the United Nations Security Council.* Princeton, NJ: Princeton University Press.

Hensel, Paul R. "Territory, Contentious Issues, and International Relations." Oxford Research Encyclopedia of Politics. 24. Oxford University Press.

Ikenberry, G. John. 1999. "Institutions, Srategic Restraint, and the Persistence of American Postwar Order." *International Security* 23(3):43–78.

International Commission on Intervention and State Sovereignty. 2001. "The Responsibility to Protect." Ottawa, ON, Canada. International Development Research Centre **URL:** *https://idl-bnc-idrc.dspacedirect.org/bitstream/handle/10625/18432/IDL-18432.pdf?sequence=6&isAllowed=y*

Jebb, Sir Gladwyn. 1952. "The Role of the United Nations." *International Organization* 6(4):509–520.

Jessup, Philip C. 1949. "The U. N. Begins to Show Power Against Power; It has proved that nations can be made responsive to ideas of general welfare. The U. N. Begins to Show Power." *The New York Times Magazine*, p. SM12.

Jia, Quinggua. 2017. "Time to Prepare for the Worst in North Korea." *East Asia Forum.* **URL:** *https://www.eastasiaforum.org/2017/09/11/time-to-prepare-for-the-worst-in-north-korea/*

Johns, Leslie. 2007. "A Servant of Two Masters: Communication and the Selection of International Bureaucrats." *International Organization* 61(2):245–275.

Keating, Colin. 2015. "Power Dynamics Between Permanent and Elected Members." In *The UN Security Council in the 21st Century*, ed. Bruno Stagno, Ugarte Sebastian von Einsiedel, and David M. Malone. Boulder, CO: Lynne Reinner Publishing.

Keohane, Robert O. 1984. *After Hegemony: Collaboration and Discord in the World Political Economy*. Princeton, NJ: Princeton University Press.

Keohane, Robert O. 1998. "International Institutions: Can Interdependence Work?" *Foreign Policy* 110:82–96,194.

Kim, Samuel S. and Tai Hwan Lee. 2002. "Chinese-North Korean Relations: Managing Asymmetrical Interdependence." In *North Korea and Northeast Asia*, ed. Samuel S. Kim and Tai Hwan Lee. Lanham, MD: Rowman and Littlefield Publisher.

Kindleberger, Charles. 1973. *The World in Depression 1929–1939*. London: Penguin.

Krasner, Stephen. 1973. "State Power and the Structure of International Trade." *World Politics* 28(April):317–347.

Krasner, Stephen D. 1982. "Regimes and the Limits of Realism: Regimes as Autonomous Variables." *International Organization* 36(2):497–510.

Krasner, Stephen D. 1983. *International Regimes*. Ithaca, NY: Cornell University Press.

Kurizaki, Shuhei. 2007. "Efficient Secrecy: Public Versus Private Threats in Crisis Diplomacy." *American Political Science Review* 101(3):543–558.

Kuziemko, Ilyana and Eric Werker. 2006. "How Much is a Seat on the Security Council Worth? Foreign Aid and Bribery at the United Nations." *Journal of Political Economy* 114(5):905–930.

Lankov, Andrei. 2004. "North Korean Refugees in Northeast China." *Asian Survey* 44(6):856–873.

Leventoğlu, Bahar and Ahmer Tarar. 2005. "Pre-negotiation Public Committment in Domestic and International Bargaining." *American Political Science Review* 99(3):419–433.

Lipson, Charles. 1984. "International Cooperation in Economic and Security Affairs." *World Politics* 37(1):1–23.

Long, William J. and Suzette R. Grillot. 2000. "Ideas, Beliefs, and Nuclear Policies: The Cases of South Africa and Ukraine." *The Nonproliferation Review* 7(1):24–40.

Lupton, Danielle. 2020. *Reputation for Resolve: How Leaders Signal Determination in International Politics*. Ithaca, NY: Cornell University Press.

Mahbubani, Kishore. 2004. The Permanent and Elected Council Members. In *The UN Security Council From the Cold War to the 21st Century*, ed. David Malone. Boulder, CO: Lynne Rienner.

Malone, David. 2000. "Eyes on the Prize: The Quest for Nonpermanent Seats on the UN Security Council." *Global Governance* 6(1):3–23.

Mastro, Oriana Skylar. 2018. "Why China Won't Rescue North Korea: What to Expect if Things Fall Apart." *Foreign Affairs* 97(1):58–66.

McCormick, James M. and Eugene R. Wittkopf. 1990. "Bipartisanship, Partisanship, and Ideology in Congressional-Executive Foreign Policy Relations, 1947–1988." *The Journal of Politics* 52(4):1077–1100.

McCormick, James M. and Eugene R. Wittkopf. 1992. "At the Water's Edge: The Effects of Party, Ideology, and Issues on Congressional Foreign Policy Voting, 1947–1988." *American Politics Quarterly* 20(1):26–53.

Mearsheimer, John. 1995. "The False Promise of International Institions." *International Security* 19(3):5–49.

Meisler, Stanley. 1995. "Dateline UN: A New Hammarskjöld?" *Foreign Policy* 98(Spring): 180–197.

Mingst, Karen A. and Margaret P. Karns. 1995. *The United Nations in the Post-cold War Era*. Westview Press.
Morgenthau, Hans J. 1967. *Politics Among Nations*. 4th ed. New York: Alfred A. Knopf.
Nanto, Dick and Mark Manyin. 2010. "China-North Korea Relations." Report R41043 (December 28) U.S. Congressional Research Service.
Neack, Laura. 1995. "UN Peace-Keeping: In the Interest of Community or Self?" *Journal of Peace Research* 32(2):181–196.
Nicolson, H.G. 1954. *The Evolution of Diplomatic Method: The Chichele Lectures Delivered at Oxford, November 1953*. Praeger Pub Text. Westport, CT.
Oertel, Janka. 2014. *China and the United Nations: Chinese Policy in the Areas of Peace and Development in the Era of Hu Jintao*. Baden Baden, Germany: Nomos.
Olonisakin, Funmi. 2008. *Peacekeeping in Sierra Leone: The Story of UNAMSIL*. Boulder, CO: Lynne Reinner Publishing.
Olsen, Edward. 2005. *Korea, the Divided Nation*. Westport, CT: Praeger Security International.
O'neill, Barry. 1996. "Power and Satisfaction in the United Nations Security Council." *Journal of Conflict Resolution* 40(2):219–237.
O'Neill, Barry. 1999. *Symbols, Honor, and War*. Ann Arbor, MI: University of Michigan Press.
Pearson, Frederic S. and Robert A. Baumann. 1993. *International Military Intervention, 1946–1988*. Vol. 6035. Ann Arbor, MI: ICPSR.
Petterson, Therése and Kristine Eck. 2018. "Organized violence, 1989–2017." *Journal of Peace Research* 55(4):535–547.
Pickering, Jeffery and Emizet Kisangani. 2009. "The International Military Intervention Data Set: An Updated Resource for Conflict Scholars." *Journal of Peace Research* 46(4):589–600.
Polity IV Project: Political Regime Characteristics and Transtions, 1800–2007. 2009. College Park, MD: University of Maryland.
Position Paper of the People's Republic of China on the United Nations Reforms. 2005. China: Foreign Ministry of the People's Republic of China.
Putnam, Robert. 1988. "Diplomacy and Domestic Politics: The Logic of Two-Level Games." *International Organization* 42(3):427–460.
Rice, Condoleeza. 2011. *No Higher Honor: A Memoir of My Years in Washington*. New York: Crown Publisher.
Ritchie, Sebastian. 2001. "Air Power Victorious? Britain and NATO Strategy During the Kosovo Conflict." In *Air Power History: Turning Points from Kitty Hawk to Kosovo*, ed. Sebastian Cox and Peter Gray. Portland, OR: Frank Cass Publishers.
Ritter, Emily and Scott Wolford. 2012. "Bargaining and the Effectiveness of International Criminal Regimes." *Journal of Theoretical Politics* 24(2):149–171.
Ruggie, John G. 1993. *Multilateralism Matters: The Theory and Praxis of an Institutional Form*. New York, NY: Columbia University Press.
Rusk, Dean. 1990. *As I Saw It*. New York: W.W. Norton & Company.
Sanger, David. 2017. "A Tillerson Slip Offers a Peek Into Secret Planning on North Korea." *New York Times*. **URL**: *https://www.nytimes.com/2017/12/17/us/politics/tillerson-north-korea-china.html*
Sanger, David and Choe Sang-Hun. September 5, 2017. "U.S. is Pressing for Oil Embargo on North Korea." *New York Times*, p. A1.
Sarooshi, Dan. 1999. *The United Nations and the Development of Collective Security: The Delegation by the UN Security Council of its Chapter VII Powers*. Oxford UK: Oxford University Press.

Schachter, Oscar and Christopher C. Joyner. 1995. *United Nations Legal Order*. Cambridge UK: Cambridge University Press.

Schelling, Thomas C. 1966. *Arms and Influence*. New Haven, CT: Yale University Press.

Schlid, Georg. 1995. *Bretton Woods and Dumbarton Oaks: American Economic and Political Postwar Planning in the Summer of 1944*. London: Palgrave Macmillan.

Schultz, Kenneth. 1999. "Do Democratic Institutions Constrain or Inform? Contrasting Two Institutional Perspectives on Democracy and War." *International Organization* 53(2):233–266.

Schultz, Kenneth. 2005. "The Politics of Risking Peace: Do Hawks or Doves Deliver the Olive Branch?" *International Organization* 59(1):1–38.

Shepsle, Kenneth A. 1979. "Institutional Arrangements and Equilibrium in Multidimensional Voting Models." *American Journal of Political Science* 23(1):27–59.

Shepsle, Kenneth A. and Barry Weingast. 1987. "The Institutional Foundations of Committee Power." *American Political Science Review* 81(1):85–104.

Sievers, Lorraine and Sam Daws. 2014. *The Procedure of the UN Security Council*. Fourth ed. New York, NY: Oxford University Press.

Signorino, Curtis S. and Jeffery M. Ritter. 1999. "Tau-b or Not Tau-b: Measuring the Similarity of Foreign Policy Positions." *International Studies Quarterly* 43(1): 115–144.

Singer, J. David, Stuart Bremer, and John Stuckey. 1972. "Correlates of War National Military Capabilities Index Version 3.02: Capability Distribution, Uncertainty, and Major Power War, 1820–1965." In *Peace, War and Numbers*, ed. Bruce Russett. Beverly Hills, CA: Sage.

Smith, Alastair. 1998. "International Crises and Domestic Politics." *American Political Science Review* 92(3):623–638.

Snyder, Glenn and Paul Diesing. 1977. *Conflict Among Nations: Bargaining, Decision-Making and System Structure in International Crises*. Princeton, NJ: Princeton University Press.

Stahn, Carsten. 2003. "The Ambiguities of Security Council Resolution 1422 (2002)." *European Journal of International Law* 14(1):85–104.

Stasavage, David. 2004. "Open-Door or Closed-Door? Transparency in Domestic and International Bargaining." *International Organization* 58(3):667–703.

Stedman, Stephen John. 2015. "The United States in the Security Council." In *The UN Security Council in the 21st Century*, ed. David M. Malone and Sebastian von Einsiedel. Boulder, CO. Lynne Reinner Publishing.

Stiles, Kendall W. 2006. "The Power of Procedure and the Procedures of the Powerful: Anti-Terror Law in the United Nations." *Journal of Peace Research* 43(1):37–54.

Stone, Randall W. 2008. "The Scope of IMF Conditionality." *International Organization* 62(3):589–620.

Stone, Randall W. 2011. *Controlling Institutions: International Organizations and the Global Economy*. Cambridge, UK: Cambridge University Press.

Talbott, Strobe. 2002. *The Russia Hand: A memoir of Presidential Diplomacy*. New York, NY: Random House.

Tardy, Thierry and Dominik Zaum. 2015. "France and the United Kingdom in the Security Council." In *The UN Security Council in the 21st Century*, ed. David M. Malone, Sebastian von Einsiedel, and Bruno Stagno Ugarte. Boulder, CO: Lynne Reinner Publishing.

Thakur, Ramesh. 2002. "Intervention, Sovereignty and the Responsibility to Protect: Experiences from ICISS." *Security Dialogue* 33(3):323–340.

Thompson, Alexander. 2006*a*. "Coercion through IOs: The Security Council and the Logic of Information Transmission." *International Organization* 60(1):1–34.

Thompson, Alexander. 2006*b*. "Screening Power: International Organizations as Informative Agents." In *Delegation and Agency in International Organizations*, ed. Darren Hawkins, David Lake, Daniel Nielson, and Michael Tierney. Cambridge, UK: Cambridge University Press.

Thompson, Alexander. 2009. *Channels of Power: The UN Security Council and U.S. Statecraft in Iraq*. Ithaca, NY: Cornell University Press.

Thorhallsson, Baldur. 2012. "Small States in the UN Security Council: Means of Influence?" *The Hague Journal of Diplomacy* 7(2):135–160.

Trachtenberg, Marc. 2012. "Audience Costs: An Historical Analysis." *Security Studies* 21(1):3–42.

Tsebelis, George. 2002. *Veto Players: How Political Institutions Work*. Princeton, NJ: Princeton University Press.

Ucko, David. 2016. "Can Limited Intervention Work? Lessons from Britain's Success Story in Sierra Leone." *Journal of Strategic Studies* 39(5-6):847–877.

United Nations Development Programme. 1994. "Human Development Report: New Dimensions of Human Security." New York, NY: UN Publications. **URL:** *http://www.hdr.undp.org/en/content/human-development-report-1994*

United Nations General Assembly. 2000. "Report of the Panel on United Nations Peace Operations." A/55/305-S/2000/809.

United Nations General Assembly. 2005. "2005 World Summit Outcome." A/60/L.1.

United Nations Protocol and Liaison Services. 2016. "Permanent Missions to the United Nations No. 306." New York, NY: ST/PLS/SER.A/306.

United Nations Secretary-General. 1992. "An Agenda for Peace: Preventive Diplomacy, Peacemaking and Peace-keeping." A/47/277-S/24111.

United Nations Security Council. 1950. "Security Council." *International Organization* 4(3):434–441.

United Nations Security Council. 2012. *The Security Council: Working Methods Handbook*. New York, NY: United Nations.

United Nations Security Council 3868th Meeting. 1998. New York, NY: S/PV.3868.

United Nations Security Council 3930th Meeting. 1998. New York, NY: S/PV.3930.

United Nations Security Council 8039th Meeting. 2017. New York, NY: S/PV.8039.

Van Rooyen, Frank. 2010. "Blue Helmets for Africa: India's Peacekeeping in Africa". In *Emerging Powers and Global Challenes Programme Occasional Paper 60*. South Africa: South Africa Institute for International Affairs.

Voeten, Erik. 2001. "Outside Options and the Logic of Security Council Action." *American Political Science Review* 95(4):845–858.

Voeten, Erik. 2005. "The Political Origins of the UN Security Council's Ability to Legitimize the Use of Force." *International Organization* 59:527–557.

von Einstiedel, Sebastian, David Malone, and Bruno Stagno Ugarte, eds. 2015. *The UN Security Council in the 21st Century*. Boulder, CO: Lynne Reinner Publishing.

Vreeland, James Ray and Axel Dreher. 2014. *The Political Economy of the United Nations Security Council: Money and Influence*. Cambridge, UK: Cambridge University Press.

Wagner, R. Harrison. 2007. *War and the State*. Ann Arbor, MI: University of Michigan Press.

Wallensteen, Peter and Patrick Johansson. 2004. "Security Council Decision in Perspective". In *The UN Security Council: From the Cold War to the 21st Century*, ed. David Malone. Boulder, CO: Lynne Rienner.

Wallensteen, Peter and Patrik Johansson. 2015. "The UN Security Council: Decisions and Actions." In *The UN Security Council in the 21st Century*, ed. Bruno Stagno Ugarte, Sebastian von Einsiedel, and David M. Malone. Boulder, CO: Lynne Reinner Publishing.

Wilcox, Francis O. 1945. "II. The Yalta Voting Formula." *American Political Science Review* 39(5):943–956.

Wit, Joel S., Daniel B. Poneman, and Robert L. Gallucci. 2004. *Going Critical: The First North Korean Nuclear Crisis*. Washington, DC: Brookings Institution Press.

Wolford, Scott. 2017. "The Problem of Shared Victory: War-Winning Coalitions and Postwar Peace." *The Journal of Politics* 79(2):702–716.

Wu, Wendy. 2017. "'North Korea is a Time Bomb': Government Advisers Urge China to Pepare for War." *South China Morning Post*. **URL**: *https://www.scmp.com/news/china/diplomacy-defence/article/2124613/north-korea-time-bomb-government-advisers-urge-china*

Wuthnow, Joel. 2010. "China and the Processes of Cooperation in UN Security Council Deliberations." *Chinese Journal of International Politics* 3(1):55–77.

Wuthnow, Joel. 2013. *Chinese Diplomacy and the UN Security Council: Beyond the Veto*. New York: Routledge.

You, Ji. 2001. "China and North Korea: A Fragile Relationship of Strategic Convenience." *Journal of Contemporary China* 10(28):387–398.

Zhao, Christina. 2017. "China Preparing for North Korea Crisis, Mass Exodus by Building Refugee Camps on Border." *Newsweek*. **URL**: *https://www.newsweek.com/china-building-refugee-camps-north-korea-boarder-745256*

Zhu, Feng. 2009. "Shifting Tides: China and North Korea." In *The Architecture of Security in the Asia-Pacific*, ed. Ron Huisken. Canberra, ACT, Australia: Australian National University E Press.

Ziegler, Charles. 2016*a*. "Critical Perspectives on the Responsibility to Protect: BRICS and Beyond." *International Relations* 30(3):262–277.

Ziegler, Charles. 2016*b*. "Russia on the Rebound: Using and Misusing the Responsibility to Protect." *International Relations* 30(3):346–361.

Index